T0163560

Religion and Society in
Post-Emancipation Jamaica

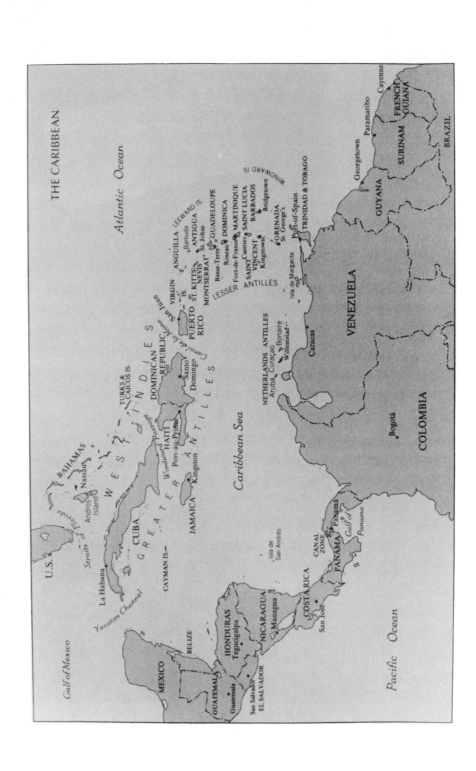

THE CARIBBEAN

Atlantic Ocean

Gulf of Mexico

U.S.A.

Florida

BAHAMAS

Nassau

Andros
Island

Straits of Florida

La Habana

CUBA

Yucatan Channel

CAYMAN IS.

MEXICO

Guatemala

GUATEMALA

San Salvador

EL SALVADOR

BELIZE

HONDURAS

Tegucigalpa

NICARAGUA

Managua

COSTA RICA

San José

PANAMA

CANAL
ZONE

Panamá

Gulf of
Panama

Isla de
San Andres

Caribbean Sea

GREATER

Windward Passage

HAITI

Port-au-Prince

JAMAICA

Kingston

A N T I L L E S

W E S T

I N D I E S

TURKS &
CAICOS IS.

DOMINICAN
REPUBLIC

Santo
Domingo

Mona Passage

Canal de la Mona

PUERTO
RICO

San Juan

VIRGIN
IS.

ANGUILLA

Barbuda

ANTIGUA

LEEWARD IS.

St. Johns

ST. KITTS

NEVIS

MONTSERRAT

GUADELOUPE

Basse-Terre

DOMINICA

Roseau

MARTINIQUE

Fort-de-France

SAINT LUCIA

Castries

SAINT
VINCENT

Kingstown

GRENADA

St. George's

WINDWARD IS.

BARBADOS

Bridgetown

TRINIDAD & TOBAGO

Port-of-Spain

LESSER ANTILLES

NETHERLANDS ANTILLES

Aruba

Bonaire

Curaçao

Willemstad

Isla de Margarita

Caracas

VENEZUELA

COLOMBIA

Bogotá

GUYANA

Georgetown

SURINAM

Paramaribo

FRENCH
GUIANA

Cayenne

BRAZIL

Pacific Ocean

Religion and Society in Post-Emancipation Jamaica

Robert J. Stewart

THE UNIVERSITY OF TENNESSEE PRESS / KNOXVILLE

Frontispiece: The Caribbean, 1990. From *The Caribbean: The Genesis of a Fragmented Nationalism*, by Franklin W. Knight. Copyright © 1990 by Oxford University Press, Inc. Reprinted by permission. Photograph by Irwin Arthur.

The paper in this book meets the minimum requirements of the American National Standard for Permanence of Paper for Printed Library Materials. ∞ The binding materials have been chosen for strength and durability.

Library of Congress Cataloging in Publication Data

Stewart, Robert J., 1944–
    Religion and society in post-emancipation Jamaica / Robert J. Stewart. — 1st ed.
    p.   cm.
    Includes bibliographical references and index.
    ISBN 0-87049-748-0 (cl.: alk. paper)
    ISBN 0-87049-749-9 (pbk.: alk. paper)
    1. Christian sects—Jamaica—History—19th century. 2. Sociology, Christian—Jamaica—History—19th century. 3. Jamaica—Church history— 19th century. I. Title.
BR645.J3S74   1992
277.292'081—dc20   91-41997
                                                        CIP

for Edward Kamau Brathwaite

Contents

Maps

Figures

Foreword

The idea for this study grew from my concerns—when I was working in Jamaica as a Jesuit—with the problems and contradictions of
missionary work in the island, and developed as an attempt to understand the nineteenth-century origins of these problems. It became
a study of religion and religious groups in the formation of Jamaican
creole society, defined in Edward Kamau Brathwaite's terms (in *The
Development of Creole Society in Jamaica*) as one in which a colonial polity reacts, as a whole, simultaneously to metropolitan pressures and
to internal adjustments made necessary by the relationships of class
and color. The study is also intended to amplify Philip Curtin's concept (in *Two Jamaicas: The Role of Ideas in a Tropical Colony*) of the role
of religion in the relationships and conflicts of European and African Jamaica, as well as to continue into the post-emancipation
period Mary Turner's examination of missionary work during slavery (in *Slaves and Missionaries: The Disintegration of Jamaican Slave
Society*), although my concerns do not exactly parallel hers. The
importance of Monica Schuler's work (*"Alas, Alas, Kongo": A Social History of Indentured African Immigration into Jamaica*) is obvious, and my study might be considered a dialogue with her on
the role of religion in nineteenth-century Jamaica. Above all, my
study attempts to support the concept of incomplete creolization
that Brathwaite presents throughout his writings.

Although the book is mainly about Jamaica after emancipation, which was enacted by Parliament in 1833 to be effective in 1834, I have taken 1831 as the significant beginning for the study. In December of that year the biblically inspired Sam Sharpe, Baptist leader or "daddy" in the parish of St. James, led the last great slave rebellion in the history of the island. Eighteen sixty-five would have been a tidy final date; it was in that year that black Baptist deacon Paul Bogle led the next major insurrection, the famous Morant Bay Rebellion. I avoided the temptation to stop triumphantly at that event, however, and decided to proceed untidily into a fifteen-year period after the rebellion in order to examine the consequences of that and earlier developments in the shaping of later nineteenth-century Jamaican history, a subject that remains under-researched.

I wish to thank all those librarians and church and missionary archivists in Jamaica, London, Oxford, Boston, New York, Philadelphia, and Washington, D.C., who assisted me with material for this study. Most essential were the documents in the archives of the English Province of the Society of Jesus, the Baptist Missionary Society, the Church Missionary Society, the Society for the Propagation of the Gospel, the London Missionary Society, the Wesleyan-Methodist Missionary Society, and the Public Record Office in London.

The New England Province of the Society of Jesus provided, when I was a member, the time and funds necessary to begin and carry out the bulk of the research. Dr. Robin Lester, as headmaster of Trinity School in New York City from 1975 to 1986, was most generous with facilities, funds, and moral encouragement.

Monica Schuler's rigorous review of my research helped to keep me on track. Rev. Dr. Horace Russell, former pastor of the historic East Queen Street Baptist Church in Kingston, Jamaica, and now professor of historical theology at the Eastern Baptist Theological Seminary in Philadelphia, provided insights, criticism, and sources from beginning to end. I am most grateful to Professor Edward Kamau Brathwaite of the University of the West Indies and New York University, who guided me meticulously through the writing in person, in correspondence, and in spirit.

Preface

A neglected outpost of the Spanish Empire, Jamaica was easily captured by a Cromwellian expedition in 1655. During the eighteenth century the island thrived and then began to decline as a sugar plantation colony in the British mercantile empire. The population came to consist mainly of a minority of whites, a majority of blacks, and a steadily increasing group of coloreds, offspring of masters and slaves. The whites, mainly plantation owners, attorneys, and personnel, and a small number of colonial administrators, were primarily from England, Scotland, Wales, and Ireland. There was also a small number of Portuguese Jews. Until the abolition of the trade in 1807, the black slaves were imported from shifting West African coastal and hinterland sources between Senegambia and Angola. They were at first the ancestors, then the fellow slaves, of an increasing creole black population. The island government became a planter oligarchy which, through a narrow property and racial franchise, controlled the elective Assembly, the parish vestries, and the law courts. The sociopolitical order began to shift with the granting of civil and political rights to free blacks, coloreds, and Jews in 1830 and the abolition of slavery in 1834.

Full and immediate freedom was not granted to the slaves by the Imperial Abolition Act. The 311,070 emancipated slaves were obligated to a period of apprenticeship which required them to labor without pay for their former owners: forty and one-half hours per week for praedials, or plantation workers, for six years, and unlimited hours for nonpraedials, or house servants, for four years. Apprenticeship became more a form of planter compensation than the transitional period of black tutelage envisioned by abolitionists. The contradictions of the system caused it to be terminated for all apprentices on 1 August 1838.

Although the apprenticeship experiment was intended to shore up a declining sugar industry, it ultimately failed at this task. Planters dealt harshly with freed laborers, who resisted new forms of servitude such as wage and rent slavery. Immigrant laborers were imported as substitutes for Afro-Jamaican workers. First Europeans, then liberated Africans, Cuban *emancipados*, and Asians arrived to work on the plantations. Meanwhile, the 1846 British Sugar Duties Act opened the West Indian sugar industry to the merciless winds of free trade, ensuring that no labor supply scheme could save the industry. Successive floods, droughts, and epidemics exacerbated economic difficulties, causing hardships for planters, retailers, laborers, and small farmers alike.

Most of the ruling class adhered to the established Church of England or to the Scottish Kirk. Refugees from revolution and war in Haiti and the Spanish Caribbean and mainland restored Roman Catholicism to the island. The slaves practiced and adapted forms of African traditional religion. From the later eighteenth century, nonconformist missionary churches attracted increasing numbers of slaves and free blacks and coloreds. The arrival of freed slaves from the North American colonies during the war for independence was the catalyst for a Native or Black Baptist tradition. African arrivants after emancipation brought fresh forms, and reinvigorated older creole ones, of African religion. Asian immigrants, unlike in Trinidad and

Guyana where they were more numerous, had little influence on Jamaican religious culture.

Statistics on institutional religious affiliation in the nineteenth century are scattered and based on varying denominational criteria for membership. At emancipation, only 9 percent of the over 300,000 slaves were recorded by the main nonconformist missions as members. Official Colonial Office ecclesiastical figures, provided by Jamaican Blue Book returns (annual governors' reports), were only of regular church attendance, not membership, and only for the Anglican church until after 1855, when the other major denominations were included. The figures do not in themselves indicate that Jamaica was a society suffused with religion. After 1855 through 1880, the returns show that the regular church-attending percentage of the total population remained fairly steadily at about 40 percent.

Other statistical and nonstatistical observations, however, support the view that Jamaica was a society in which religious affiliation and practice were increasingly important concerns. Restrictions on missionary preaching and punishment of praying slaves prior to emancipation slowed potential growth in mission membership until after 1834. But the five-year trend of membership increase after that in the strongest denomination, the Baptists, was 200 percent, and the number of inquirers, roughly equal annually to the number of baptized members, increased at a similar rate. The other denominations, although not equaling Baptist growth, also claimed rapid increases in membership. And the apparently moderate church-attending percentage recorded in the Blue Books actually indicate a steady increase, as the island's population grew from about 378,000 in 1855 to 506,000 in 1880. Moreover, the non-European sector of the population remained around the 1834 figure of 96 percent (about 80 percent black throughout the period), suggesting that any increase in church attendance would have been overwhelmingly among colored and black Jamaicans.

Church and mission figures were made more tenuous by certain post-emancipation developments. The population shift from older centers of settlement within and among parishes made religious census-taking difficult. The increasing number of native breakaway churches and of so-called "outbreaks" of Afro-creole Myalism (a Jamaican syncretism of African spirit belief and apocalyptic Christianity) caused the rate of increase of congregational membership to peak in the early 1840s. The church allegiances of Jamaican blacks tended to be pragmatically flexible and simultaneous: they would shift their attachments for what European religious ministers saw as secular reasons; or they would belong to one of the Euro-Christian congregations for the access to land, housing, education, and political influence that such membership might provide, while retaining truly affective and cognitive commitment to Afro-creole religious groups and practices. As William James Gardner, the most scholarly of nineteenth-century missionary writers on Jamaica, cautioned in his 1873 *History of Jamaica* (342), "Statistics have a certain value, though not so much in relation to missionary efforts as many good men suppose."

European missionary impact and the creative response of Afro-Jamaican religion resulted in the creolization of Christianity. The process was not one of black acculturation but of interculturation—a conflicting, contradictory, and never quite finished synthesis. What we see in the period under study are Christian ideas and well-formed denominational structures undergoing an alteration of consciousness and organization in black Jamaica.

European Protestant missionaries brought to Jamaica an evangelical Christianity that emphasized preaching, instruction, and observable response in word, moral behavior, and church adherence. Contrary to the moral latitudinarianism of the Anglican clergy in plantation Jamaica, the missionaries preached the inherent depravity of humankind, a disease of heart and soul inherited from Adam's fall, which humanity could do nothing on its own to repair. To believe that any righteous act aside from the acceptance of God's forgiveness could undo that state of sin was itself the sin of pride.

The evangelicals encountered an African religious world, the elements of which they summed up with the words "heathen," "pagan," and "superstitious." That world was, however, derived from a coherent West African cosmology in which the interpenetrating worlds of the physically living and of gods, ancestors, and spirits baffled the rationalistic distinction of sacred and secular that had split Western consciousness. In that world, moral value was not so much derived from an individualistic relationship with a Supreme Being, who was generally regarded by Africans as aloof and remote from human daily concerns, but was rather a function of community. Acts were "good" or "bad" depending on their effect on the equilibrium of the family or village. There was no eschatological tension. Ultimate reality was distinctly worldly and temporal—not mechanistically, but through a primal unity of material and spiritual, represented, for example, in the land as the here-and-now medium of the community of the living and the dead. In the matrix of family, clan, and nation, communication with departed family and ancestors was essential in the maintenance of social well-being, order, and peace.

The powers of the universe, personalized in spirits and deities, were focused through certain natural features, such as rocks, mountains, great trees, lakes, streams, and rivers. The importance of water for washing away uncleanness and receiving power preceded by unreckonable time the Christian introduction of baptism among the slaves. The primary purpose of African ceremony, expertly managed by specialists, was the maintenance of communication with these personalized powers, not in the Christian sense of the focusing of mind and heart on "higher" realities but by making them real (in Yoruba, *she orisha*, "to make the god") in a kinetic and somatic way. Religious specialists and ceremonial participants sought the augmentation of positive force by recognizing and invoking the powers of the spirits and by letting them manifest themselves through the human body.

The adaptations in metropolitan thought and organization that occurred in Jamaica were effected by the denominations to deal better, in their view, with the problems of evangelization in a society formed in the trinity of slavery, the plantation, and colonialism. The adaptations were to a large extent defensive—to preserve the purity of "true religion" against both African heathenism and plantocratic corruption. But to a large extent also they served to catalyze the re-creation of Christianity by the mainly black membership. The complicating factor, the shadow that fell between intent and outcome, was racism. While racism theoretically could have prevailed to the extent of forcing the white-led Christian denominations into being nothing more than plantation churches, that was not the outcome; nor, however, were the churches able to mount a thorough attack on the system of social, political, and economic relationships that grew out of slavery and did not end with emancipation.

The responses of the white-led churches to Jamaica and Jamaicans during the period were conditioned by several intellectual, moral, and social dilemmas. They inherited unresolved ideas from the Western Christian tradition on slavery and freedom. They were caught up in the concern for social control in free society, positing the substitution of religious motivations of duty for the physical constraints of slavery. They were, with the notable exception of the

Baptists, straightjacketed by theoretical distinctions between the religious and the secular. Conflicts over issues of class, color, race, and native leadership affected their decisions. What happened for the most part was that the white-led Christian church assumed a position of ambiguity and compromise.

The situation in which they found themselves, however, was not one of stable equilibrium but of conflict, mostly simmering, sometimes approaching the boiling point, and twice in the period erupting past that point, with Sam Sharpe's "Baptist War" in 1831–32 and Paul Bogle's Morant Bay Rebellion in 1865. The conflict, of course, predates the buildup of Christian evangelization; it was endemic from the initial exploitative relationship of European and African on the plantation.

These are the observations and presumptions behind this study, and this is the question for which it provides some answers. What role did religion, or the agents of religion, both European and Afro-Jamaican, play in the conflicts that characterized the process of creolization in post-emancipation Jamaica?

CHAPTER 1

Church and Mission in Jamaica

ORGANIZATION

An understanding of the organizational infrastructure—lines of authority and command, and apportionment of responsibility—of the church and mission groups in nineteenth-century Jamaica is necessary in order to appreciate the opportunities and the limitations of white ministers of religion in their relationships with their congregations, and the possibilities of black and colored initiatives within these organizations.

Prior to 1799, the Anglican ordinary for the island of Jamaica was the bishop of London. In that year, his jurisdiction was annulled and reconstituted in an island Ecclesiastical Commission consisting of five resident commissaries, the rectors of the parishes of Kingston, St. Andrew, St. James, St. Elizabeth, and St. Catherine.[1] This arrangement lasted until the issuance of letters patent by George IV in July 1824 creating the Bishopric of Jamaica. Christopher Lipscomb was installed as the first bishop in Kingston on 15 February 1825. The Clergy Act of that year—reenacted in 1836, 1847, and 1858—defined the regimen of the Church of England in Jamaica as conforming to the laws and canons currently in force in the Church in England, except that the governor, representing the Crown, retained the authority to present and induct Anglican priests to vacant livings as well as to remove them.[2]

Lipscomb adopted a policy of tight centralization, partially in order to weaken the intimate clergy/planter alliance that had been forged in Jamaica. Immediate opposition to the curtailment of their former independence was voiced by many of the older clergy, of whom G. W. Bridges, rector in St. Ann, was the chief spokesman.[3] The negrophobic pro-planter clergy that Bridges represented had never seriously carried out evangelization among the slaves, and nonconformist missionary groups had begun to get a foothold among them. The imperial mandate behind the establishment of the Jamaican bishopric was that the slaves should be brought into the Anglican church and that "a community of feeling" should be thus created between the planters and their bondsmen.[4] Neither that mandate nor Lipscomb's plans included any policy of indigenization that would encourage a native clergy—black, brown, or white.

Bishop Lipscomb died on 4 April 1843. He was succeeded by Aubrey Spencer, who had been bishop of Newfoundland since 1839. Reginald Courtenay, archdeacon of the county of Middlesex in Jamaica since 1853, was consecrated bishop in April 1856 and appointed coadjutor bishop of Jamaica with the title of bishop of Kingston; Spencer, still bearing the title of bishop of Jamaica, retired in poor health to England, where he died in 1872. Courtenay retired in 1879.[5]

The system of authority and subordination was intricately detailed in the canons of the church and constituted a structure of controls in the legislative, executive, and judicial spheres internally (diocesan, parochial, congregational) and externally (West Indian provincial synod and court and British committee of reference).[6] What is noteworthy about the system is that, while there was lay participation throughout the internal structure, congregational and lay initiative was controlled all along the line by the central authority of the bishop, alone or in synod, which authority in turn was subordinated to the external control of the archbishop of the West Indies and the bishops of the British committee of reference.

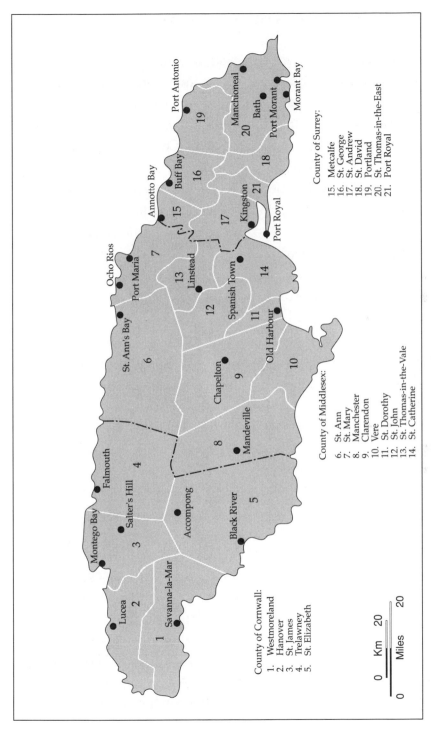

County of Cornwall:
1. Westmoreland
2. Hanover
3. St. James
4. Trelawney
5. St. Elizabeth

County of Middlesex:
6. St. Ann
7. St. Mary
8. Manchester
9. Clarendon
10. Vere
11. St. Dorothy
12. St. John
13. St. Thomas-in-the-Vale
14. St. Catherine

County of Surrey:
15. Metcalfe
16. St. George
17. St. Andrew
18. St. David
19. Portland
20. St. Thomas-in-the-East
21. Port Royal

Jamaica, 1855. Drawing by University of Tennessee Cartographic Services.

Parallel to this structure, however, and not completely under its control, were the Anglican missionary endeavors of the Church Missionary Society and the Society for the Propagation of the Gospel. The C.M.S. was the outgrowth of the British Eclectic Society of 1783, consisting of evangelical clergy and laymen of the Church of England. In 1786 the society first discussed foreign missions. The C.M.S. was probably formed in 1799 at an Eclectic Society meeting at which Rev. John Venn laid down the founding principles. Venn and the C.M.S. were specifically anti–high-church, and consequently relations with the bishops in England were hardly cordial. The first bishop did not join the C.M.S. until 1841. As Anglican clergymen, the missionaries of the C.M.S. had to be ordained by Anglican bishops, but archdiocesan and diocesan control extended little beyond that, as the C.M.S. itself chose its missionaries, selected the foreign stations, paid the passage, and provided the salaries. C.M.S. work was originally intended exclusively for Africa and the Orient, as it was expected that the S.P.G. and its allied Society for the Propagation of Christian Knowledge would serve missionary needs in the Americas.[7] The S.P.G., however, had neglected Jamaica in favor of the eastern Caribbean and did not begin its engagement with the Anglican church in the island until 1834. When the Diocese of Jamaica came into existence in 1824, there were no Anglican missionaries on the scene, and the C.M.S. took the opportunity to send its men in 1825.

The distance between the C.M.S. and the Anglican hierarchy that had existed in England was carried over to Jamaica. While ecclesiastical law required that C.M.S. missionaries as Anglican clergymen had to be licensed by the bishop in Jamaica, there was a conflicting principle of jurisdiction in that the C.M.S. Committee in London set policy and procedure, chose its missionaries, and managed its own finances. Furthermore, the committee, supported by the Colonial Office, defended the principle of itineracy for its missionaries in what was considered a pioneering venture in Jamaica.[8] The idea was that the C.M.S. would set up mission stations and schools that would in time be absorbed into the Jamaican church.

The C.M.S. missionaries also justified their itineracy as giving them more flexibility in counteracting the influence of nonconformist missionaries, especially the Baptists, whose congregational form tended, it was alleged, to preserve rather than wipe out the heathenism of the blacks, and whose activity posed a general threat to the tranquility of the island. In the climate of suspicion that existed on the island, however, the planters were often as wary of the C.M.S. as they were of any other missionary group; the committee of the C.M.S. had in 1823 committed itself to emancipation, and the itineracy of the society's missionaries made them indistinguishable, in the eyes of many of the planters, from Baptists or Methodists.[9]

Sensitive to the opinions of the planters, who "considered the establishment of their bishopric rather as a compliment to themselves than as a boon to their slaves," as Mathieson put it,[10] and reluctant to license missionary clergymen whose organization and finances were not entirely under his control, Bishop Lipscomb was moved to complain that C.M.S. independence was "greatly subversive of the peace and discipline of the Church."[11] He consistently insisted that he determine the districts and plantations where C.M.S. missionaries should work. And, while the importation of new clergymen from England seemed in line with the bishop and the colonial office's desire to weaken the influence of the older clergy, the bishop's attempts to prevent C.M.S. itineracy hindered the implementation of that policy.

Largely because the disagreements between the diocese and the C.M.S. were never resolved, and because the C.M.S. discerned more pressing needs in Africa, the society phased out its work in Jamaica in the late 1840s. The S.P.G. continued its financial support of certain clergy, but this was terminated by 1866, greatly in protest against the failure of the Jamaican church to foster a native clergy.

The Wesleyan-Methodist Missionary Society (M.M.S.) was born in the 1780s under Dr. Thomas Coke's direction. His visit to Jamaica in 1789 can be taken as the commencement of the society's connection with the island. The key terms of organization in the Methodist missionary structure were conference, district, district meeting, district chairman, and circuit. The Jamaican mission belonged to the British Conference, or in other words, to the Wesleyan-Methodist church in England. General policy on missions was set and pursued by the Committee of the M.M.S. in London. The committee, for example, required missionaries to give due submission to civil and ecclesiastical (Anglican) authorities in Jamaica.[12] The committee also reserved final say over whether a missionary in the field would be allowed to marry, and whether his choice of a bride was suitable. Tight control of mission funds was also exercised by the committee.

Jamaica was designated a missionary district within the British Methodist Conference. The basic unit within the district was the circuit. Chapels in one area (e.g., Kingston) were grouped into a circuit under the supervision of a senior missionary. Even though the Committee in England acted as ultimate legislature and court of appeal, local matters were under the governance of the district meeting headed by the district chairman. Decisions on disciplinary matters and on the application of committee policy to Jamaican affairs were taken by the district meeting, consisting of all full-fledged missionaries, excluding candidates and those on disciplinary probation. It appears that the meeting occurred at least annually but was more often than that convened for special business. The chairman was not supreme in meeting and could be overruled, disciplined, or dismissed by majority decision, as happened in the case of Thomas Pennock, who objected to the limits on the missionary's freedom of action imposed from England. Pennock was succeeded as district chairman in 1837 by the more conservative Jonathan Edmondson, whose tenure lasted until 1866 when he was succeeded by John Mearns. Edmondson's long chairmanship ensured administrative stability but did not allow mission policy to adapt to changing times.[13]

The lay class-leader and ticket system, for which the Baptists became notorious in Jamaica, was actually the invention of John Wesley. The ticket system came first. The Wesleyans in England originally called their local congregations "societies," and each society member was issued a ticket which was renewed periodically upon spiritual and moral reexamination. Later, Methodist groups were organized into classes of twelve with a lay leader. The purpose was to strengthen control over membership and to make more efficient the collection of funds. The system was carried over into Jamaica, but in a more limited and tightly controlled way than that employed by the Baptists. Wesley himself had emphasized his personal supervision of each class leader, and the circuit missionaries and district chairman were expected to do the same in Jamaica.[14] The status of local or lay preacher was a cut above that of class leader but was just as controlled and entailed little initiative on the part of the preacher.

Baptist mission organization was similar in some respects to that of the Methodists but differed in important ways. The Baptist Missionary Society (B.M.S.), organized in 1792 as the Particular Baptist Society for Propagating the Gospel among the Heathen,[15] was also administered by a Committee in London that set general policy. Baptist congregational procedure, however, allowed for the independence of individual congregations in the mission territory. The first instance of a mission station resigning all claim on the B.M.S. in Jamaica occurred in 1833, when the Annotto Bay congregation invited Josiah Barlow to be its pastor. The Baptist minister for the area, Whitehorne, handed over the premises to Barlow with the approval of the B.M.S. Barlow assumed his position with the clear understanding that he was not a missionary of the B.M.S.[16]

The rest of the Jamaican mission remained under the administration and financial control of the B.M.S. Committee until 1842, when the Jamaican Baptists became independent, forming the Western and Eastern Unions. This move was not supported unanimously by the Jamaican missionaries, however, and many problems and conflicts, especially over financial support, followed. The two unions were later organized into one Jamaica Baptist Union.[17] Not all Baptist congregations were required to join, as congregational and voluntary principles were upheld. An important difference between the Baptist Union and the Wesleyan District Meeting was that the former was conceived of as purely an agreement among congregations, whereas the latter was an administrative association of ministers.

The Baptist missionaries adopted the ticket–and–class-leader system of the Methodists and used it so extensively that it appeared to be a Baptist innovation. They employed slaves as leaders, and both before and after emancipation did not insist on literacy as a requirement for leadership. Often headmen on estates, but also laborers or tradesmen in the towns, the leaders, commonly called "daddies," were responsible for weeknight prayer meetings in class-houses on estates or in the villages, for the day-to-day spiritual oversight of class members, and for the collection of money for special purposes. It was a common occurrence for the people to form their own classes, select their own leaders, and have them accepted by the missionary, a procedure never followed by the Wesleyans. Indeed, the class-and-leader system was the seedbed for new Baptist congregations, which grew, as it were, from the ground up.

Tickets of different colors with biblical inscriptions were used as identification of either inquirer or full membership status. It was the usual practice for the ticket to be presented to the minister quarterly for renewal if the conduct of the holder warranted it. In most cases, the minister relied on the leader's information as to the spiritual and moral state of the holder. Ticket holders often made voluntary contributions at the time of renewal, giving rise to rumors of a kind of Baptist simony.[18]

The minister usually met with his leaders once a week. A meeting with the whole congregation (to be distinguished from worship services) was held monthly, at which the minister was chairman. This meeting was the final authority in matters of authority and discipline. There was no higher authority as with the Methodist District Meeting, or the complex Anglican system which could go all the way to the committee of reference in England.

The crucial difference, then, between the Baptists and Methodists was in the principle of congregational order. The Methodist system was more tightly knit and was more a church in the Anglican mold, with the district meeting acting as a kind of synod.[19]

The other missions fell somewhere between the poles of hierarchical authoritarianism and democratic congregationalism. The London Missionary Society (L.M.S.) was formed in 1795 as a nondenominational group but was supported largely at first by Presbyterians and Anglicans, then increasingly and mainly by Independents or Congregationalists. In Jamaica, the L.M.S. mission became the foundation of the Congregationalist church. The fundamental principle was to establish no particular form of church order and government but simply to preach the gospel. The churches formed in response were expected to choose their own form of government.[20]

This would appear to have made the L.M.S. missionaries the natural comrades of the Baptists in Jamaica. As it turned out, however, competition for converts and disagreement with the Baptist use of leaders led to a bitter conflict between the two groups. Moreover, the board of directors of the L.M.S. in London continued to control finances, to select and manage mission stations, and appoint and maintain missionaries. The Independents, therefore, were not as independent as their Baptist brethren/rivals.

The Unitas Fratrum, or Moravians, were formed in 1732, and their missions were perhaps the first to grow out of European pietism. They were certainly the first Protestant missionaries in Jamaica (1754). Although today they have an episcopacy and a carefully designed system of elders and catechists, in the eighteenth and nineteenth centuries the Moravian missions were little more than preaching stations. Moravians consistently worked under planter patronage and were allied with particular estates in the southwest region of the island. Although they had black leaders, or "helpers," as they were called, the small size of Moravian congregations ensured that the supervision of the missionary was complete and total.

The Scottish Missionary Society was formed in 1796, representing both the Established and Secession churches of Scotland. The Committee in Scotland set general policy for the missions. The first mission to Jamaica in 1800 failed because of the death of the missionaries. No more were sent until 1824, when Rev. George Blyth commenced a mission under the patronage of certain north coast proprietors. In 1836, the six missionaries on the north side came together in Montego Bay to form the Jamaica Mission Presbytery. The presbytery was divided into districts which, in 1847, became four presbyteries. They came together yearly as an all-island synod. In 1848 there was an amalgamation of the S.M.S. and Secession missionaries (who had begun to arrive independently in 1835) into the United Presbyterian Mission in Jamaica.[21]

The Presbyterian practice of congregational election of elders, which prevailed in Scotland, was modified in Jamaica. There were black elders in the Jamaican congregations, but they were chosen by the minister rather than elected. Hope Waddell, in fact, appointed his in pairs rather then singularly to restrain, as he put it, the tendency to black autocracy which stemmed from traditions of African kingship and village despotism, and from the example of black rulers and plantation drivers in Jamaica. His purpose was to prevent the Presbyterian elder system from resembling too closely the despised Baptist leader system. By 1836, election of elders was allowed for the presbytery, but not within estate congregations.[22]

The Roman Catholic mission was under the control of the English Province of the Society of Jesus (Jesuits). Jamaica at the time did not have a Catholic bishop but was under the ordinary jurisdiction of the vicar apostolic of the Antilles who resided in Trinidad. The English provincial was immediately responsible to the superior general of the Jesuits in Rome. Day-to-day decisions in Jamaica and long-term planning (liable to be overruled by the provincial) were left to the local mission superior, who resided in Kingston. Because a large number of Catholics in Jamaica, mainly in Kingston, were French and Spanish speaking, Jesuits were sometimes 'borrowed' from the French and Spanish provinces to work in Jamaica. They thereby came temporarily under the authority of the mission superior and the English provincial. Wealthy Catholic laypeople sometimes made representation to the provincial on certain matters of disagreement with the mission superior. This was completely at their own initiative, however, as there was no institutionalized system of lay consultancy in the Jesuit mission. There was no congregational principle at all operative in the Catholic church.

THE MISSIONARY PRESENCE

The Anglican role in Jamaican society was offset, often dramatically, by the presence of the Protestant nonconformist missionary groups.[23] From the first, they offered an alternative to the dominant white planter way of life. The Moravians, for example, expected their missionaries to support themselves by doing manual labor, a contrary policy in a society where such was not usually expected of Europeans. The Methodists began their work in the West Indies by deciding to work among the blacks, avoiding the whites, and criticizing white society for its moral laxity. The Baptists came to Jamaica originally not at the invitation of the whites but at the request of black religious leaders.[24]

In general, the approach of the missionaries to the slaves was one of familiarity and sympathy, unlike the approach of other whites. Moreover, they offered an alternative to the corruptions of planter life, so that, observed Elsa Goveia, morally the converted slaves became better persons than the whites of the established church.[25] In a letter from Kingston dated March 1825, the Baptist missionary William Knibb, newly arrived, exclaimed, "The poor, oppressed, benighted, and despised sons of Africa form a pleasing contrast to the debauched white population."[26]

The strength of the missionary commitment was a far different thing from the vocation of the ordinary Anglican clergyman. It was a life-or-death dedication, with little hope of status or financial reward. There is no reason to dispute the viewpoint of Colonial Secretary Goderich in 1832:

> They devote themselves to an obscure, arduous and ill-requited service. They are apprized that mistrust and jealousy will attend them, and that the path they have chosen leads neither to wealth nor reputation. . . . The great ruling motive must be in general that

which is professed, since in general there is no other advantage to be obtained, than the consciousness of having contributed to the diffusion of Christianity throughout the world.[27]

The Baptist missionary Thomas Burchell's either/or commitment is representative of missionary psychology: "I must either give up religion altogether, or yield to the dictates of my conscience and lay myself out for the extension of the Messiah's Kingdom in the world."[28]

The situation of the missionary in Jamaica was hardly one of peaceful coexistence. From the first conflict of the Moravians with the established order in 1763, when they pleaded exemption from militia duty, to the formation of the white vigilante Colonial Church Union in 1832, which violently persecuted nonconformists as fomenters of sedition, the Anglican plantocracy was in more-or-less open battle with sectarian missionaries and their black congregations. Even if they did not suspect them of being abolitionists, the planters were naturally suspicious of the missionaries for the power and following they could command; for example, the planters must have wondered and worried at the response given to the first Baptist missionary to Spanish Town, Thomas Godden, who arrived in April 1819: "His congregations were immediately large. The enthusiasm of the people was beyond description."[29]

The main work of the missionaries was conversion, the Christianizing of the slaves, and, if possible, the amelioration of master/slave relationships. But they were enjoined by their home committees from preaching abolitionism. The policy of the Methodist Missionary Society was representative of that of the other groups: while the home committee may campaign for abolition, missionaries in the field must be silent on the slavery question because in working with the slaves they were working with "inflammable materials." This position was expressed by Rev. Richard Watson at the Methodist Society's annual meeting in 1832:

> We have very properly imposed restraints on Missionaries: we
> have inculcated on them the most cautious reserve; nay, a total
> silence on the civil wrongs of the Slave, lest injudicious language
> should interfere with the great and all-important objects which
> the Missionary has in view, and which, however we may long to
> see the chains of the Slave struck off, we consider of still greater
> moment than his freedom.[30]

"Refrain from meddling in secular disputes" was a repeated Methodist injunction; circumspect behavior toward slave masters and civil authorities would gain the required toleration for the missionaries to pursue their work. A "heavenly calm" must be maintained upon "the stormy ocean of politics."[31] The Baptist Missionary Society was anti-slavery, but official instructions to missionaries in Jamaica advised them to have nothing whatever to do with the island's civil and political affairs; the gospel of Christ, "so far from producing or countenancing a spirit of rebellion or insubordination, has a directly opposite tendency. . . ." The B.M.S. was prepared to disclaim responsibility for agents who involved themselves in political controversies.[32]

The tense toleration of nonconformists demanded more than silence on the issues of slavery and abolition. Methodist missionaries were directed to conform even to the prejudices of the whites.[33] The pressure in Jamaica was for respectability according to ruling-class norms, the type of respectability that had minimum requirements such as getting from place to place by carriage or on a horse, never walking, and the retaining of at least two servants. Mary Turner observes that the Presbyterian and Wesleyan missions had special assets that could be exploited in the pursuit of respectability. Among these assets was the fact that both were related to churches that were already accepted in the established social order of Jamaica.

Although the Presbyterian mission drew its ministers from the United Secession Church of Scotland, it could appeal to the Scottish loyalties of those members of the planter class who identified with the Church of Scotland represented by the Kingston Kirk. The Wesleyans, rather than emphasize their break with the Anglican church, played upon their Anglican traditions to bolster their social standing. They sought to be ecumenical rather than adversative by standing in for Anglican clergy, holding joint services, and taking Anglican communion.[34]

By their anti-slavery testimony at home in England, and their Pauline injunction to slaves and missionaries in the West Indies to respect the status quo of social relationships, the missionary societies sent out a double signal. But even their witness in Britain against slavery was limited by the distrust and fear of the politics of popular associations caused by reaction to the French and Haitian revolutions. Nonconformists were careful to bracket slavery as a moral and religious issue for the British Parliament but as a civil and secular one for missionaries in slave colonies. In both cases, they warned that abolition had nothing to do with democracy, liberty, and equality in the radical political sense. Thus between the rise of evangelical- and nonconformist-based abolitionism in the eighteenth century and the popular agitation to affect the outcome of elections to the reformed Parliament in 1832, abolitionist activity was confined mostly within Parliament and shunned popular radicalism. The vocabulary of the "Rights of Man" increased in anti-slavery discourse in the 1820s and 1830s, but with the explanation that these rights were divinely ordained rather than secular endowments to be seized by secular means, and the evangelical and nonconformist abolitionists were adamant on avoiding what they posed as purely political controversy.[35]

As the year of emancipation approached, individual missionaries began to state their belief that full religious liberty could not exist without full civil liberty and addressed the question of sla-very in spite of official instructions. As the Wesleyan Mr. Crookes put it in 1833, "The slave question binds our hands. We *cannot* 'de-clare *all* the counsels of God.' We feel our manacles and are afraid that we shall be compelled to carry them until the oppressed go free."[36] The Baptist William Knibb stands out as the most eloquent representative of the missionary critique of slavery. He saw it as the basic corruption that touched everything in Jamaican society. "To proclaim liberty to the captive and the opening of the prisons to them that are bound, is a delightful employment, and here would I dwell that I may be thus employed."[37]

Generally, however, missionaries did not express consciousness that their work was bound to influence the balance of contradictory forces that constituted Jamaican creole society in the first third of the nineteenth century. Their anomalous presence, and much of their preaching, built up a conflict between ideas of equality and those of subordination that would eventually have to be resolved.[38] Their im-mediate concern, however, was to retain the toleration of the whites in order to achieve what they considered religious success.

Baptist Activists

In 1842, a common Presbyterian charge against the Baptists mission-aries was that they encouraged a "worldly and covetuous spirit" in the people.[39] The accusation was based on the general observations that Baptist laborers were more adamant in wage disputes with planters than were workers belonging to other denominations and that the Baptist ministers, in encouraging worker demands, were breaching the line between religion and politics.

The revolution in consciousness and commitment that was mani-fested in Baptist activity in Jamaica in the early post-emancipation period resulted in a phenomenon that was correctly called "Baptist politics," a term used by both its opponents and its defenders. Baptist politics involved, first, a developing theology of mission; second, a strategic use of the elective franchise; and, third, activity to augment the economic independence of the ex-slaves.

First of all, it stemmed from a Baptist sense of mission that went beyond that of most nonconformist missionaries to an appreciation of this world that inevitably led to political engagement. William Knibb and like-minded ministers did not see themselves as divided between two worlds, the Kingdom of God and that of man. The demands of the former bore upon the contingencies of this world. The economic and political lives of their congregation members were as much of concern as their interior state of soul; issues of labor, wages, and land were as important as personal morality. As Pastor Richard Merrick of Jericho put it in defending his election to the vestry of the parish of St. John in 1843, his purpose was to "show the poor people that I loved their bodies as well as their souls."[40]

This developing theology was not seen by Baptists as a secularization of religious concerns or as a kind of secular humanism. Thomas Burchell's brother and biographer set a keynote for an understanding of Baptist thinking when, in interpreting his brother's life as a Baptist missionary in Jamaica, he put forward a kind of historical theology:

> From the essential holiness of his [God's] nature he not only "loveth righteousness," but also "hateth iniquity." In accordance with the laws of his administration, therefore, crime has sooner or later entailed punishment. This, the colonists have proved through successive generations. Their anxious and ceaseless fears of servile vengeance, and the occasional outbreak of violence under the impulse of suffering, have proved to them a perpetual scourge, and successfully prevented their forgetting that at any and every time they slumbered

on the bosom of a volcano. Their apprehensions leading them to the adoption of severe measures, have not infrequently precipitated the crises they dreaded; and the violence they intended for others has "come down upon their own pate."[41]

The impulse of such divine judgment was behind much of the action taken by Baptists in attempting to vindicate the black people against centuries of that suffering and repression.

Although it was not systematic, their theology of human events that was developing out of their responses to emancipation and post-emancipation society made Baptists see a separation of religion and politics as too facile and artificial. They saw emancipation, for example, not simply as a change of legal status but as the opportunity for the ex-slaves to achieve, and to be recognized on, a new spiritual, human, and political level.

James Mursell Phillippo, in his autobiographical notes, wrote of the actions of Baptist missionaries in the 1830s to promote the social and political interests of the blacks in opposition to the oppressive exactions of their former masters. He defended the interventions of Baptist parsons on the principle that certain events and circumstances not only render it proper but impose it as a duty that religious ministers should express their opinions, "viz., whenever the prosperity and even existence of any portion of our Country or of our fellow subjects [are] threatened with poverty, wretchedness and annihilation by oppression and wrong." The Christian's involvement and duties in civil, social, and domestic relations are not dissolved by religion, but are, on the contrary, exalted and intensified. Moreover, the interference of religious ministers in some political questions is not only a duty but a right. Phillippo was speaking not only for himself but for his brethren in enunciating the principle that "the peculiar character of every divine disposition is adaptation to the circumstances of men." The same ideas were put succinctly by Walter Dendy: "There are times and seasons when ministers may legitimately step forward as advocates of the oppressed and as champions for the Civil and Religious Liberties of Mankind. . . ." A later Baptist chronicler, Leonard Tucker, wrote, "Were any justification needed for the strong political action taken by the Baptist Union as a whole, of District Associations or individual ministers, it would surely be found in the principles that animated the Baptist champions of freedom: 'We did it for the Gospel's sake.'"[42]

Secondly, "Baptist politics" referred to their use of the electoral franchise to affect the legislature. They worked to transform the lines of power within the political parameters allowed by the Jamaican constitution; they pushed to the limit of what was allowed within that system. Their use of the Jamaican electoral laws was perfectly legitimate, but it was pursued by them with a hard-headed vigor that irritated British authorities, both in the island and in the Colonial Office, who saw Baptist political activity as inopportune at a time when the imperial goal was not the advocacy of black ascendancy but the appeasement of the planter class.

The Baptists became a political force, or a party in an informal manner, in directing the ex-slave franchise toward the goal of shifting political power from the old plantocracy to the increasingly influential combination of colored lawyers, landowners, and merchants, wealthy craftsmen, and Jewish entrepreneurs. They approached a more formal institutionalization of their political involvement in 1839–40 with the formation of the St. Thomas-in-the-Vale and Falmouth Societies for Protection of Civil and Religious Liberty and in 1844 with the Anti-Church State Convention.[43]

One of their most notable efforts in the political arena was their struggle to extend the franchise and to campaign for the election of candidates to the Assembly who would be dedicated to legislation for the benefit of the black population. "If an Assembly of whites will not give relief, men of darker colour will be found to fill their places," was a Baptist prediction in 1842. The Baptist platform included such fundamental planks as decreased taxation (based on their criticism of nonproductive expenditures such as that for the ecclesiastical establishment), the withholding of grants for immigration, a decrease in the amount spent on law and order, and a redirection of funds to the social needs (e.g., health and education) of the ex-slave majority. The dilemma was the selection of candidates who would back wholeheartedly Baptist goals for the peasantry. The six-pound franchise gave the vote to many members of Baptist congregations, but qualification for candidacy (annual income of 180 pounds from land or real property worth 1,800 pounds or both real and personal property worth 3,000 pounds) excluded men like Baptist deacons whom Knibb, for one, was prepared to support for Assembly membership. Knibb complained that "with thousands of votes, we have not a man we can send in." The choice was liberal whites, mainly Jews, and wealthy coloreds, who, sympathetic as they might be toward many of the Baptist goals, never supported the Baptist platform in its entirety.[44]

The Baptists also targeted the class legislation of the Jamaican Assembly during the governorship of Sir Charles Metcalfe (1838–42)—a series of laws that sought to maintain the control of the planters over tenancy and the movement of labor, and, in general, to limit the legitimate pursuit of ex-slaves outside of the sugar monoculture. Related to their challenge to the legislature was their protest against the juridical weapon of the plantocracy, summary jurisdiction in the hands of the local magistracy. The well-organized pressure of Baptist-led agitation helped lead to the Assembly's modification of the harshest measures of class legislation during 1840–41. Baptist influence was also instrumental in encouraging the Colonial Office to continue the institution of the independent, nonplanter, "special" magistracy which, however deficient as a protection of ex-slave rights, acted as a check on the most extreme anti-black bias of the planter magistracy.[45]

Thirdly, the Baptists attempted to increase and fortify to a certain extent the economic independence of the ex-slave. The process of achieving this independence was not one that was initiated by the Baptists. It already had a material base within the slave system as the planter class had managed it, and as the slaves had learned to manipulate it: in the cultivation of provision grounds, the disposal of surplus produce within an internal slave-marketing system, the slow but sure accumulation of liquid capital, and the availability of land unused or unowned by planters. What the Baptists did was to assist the ex-slaves in using these social and economic conditions for their benefit. This was the aim of Baptist advice on land tenancy, rents, and wages, and one of the aims in the sponsoring of free village settlements. With this assistance, for example, the number of registered peasant freeholds increased from 2,000 to 27,379 between 1839 and 1845. This was the result of the campaign begun by Baptist parsons in 1839 to have small settlers register their titles and thereby become enfranchised under the electoral laws so as to influence future elections to the Assembly.[46]

As a result of Baptist political involvement, their actual influence was often equal to their intentions; the criterion for the exercise of this influence was what the Baptists conceived of as the well-being of the ex-slave.[47] In February of 1839, a group of Baptist missionaries sent an address to the former governor, Sir Lionel Smith, in which they acknowledged their influence over a large portion of the population. They also suggested that they could have led the people into open resistance and rebellion at any time. Instead, however, they used their power to keep the country peaceful. "So far from having employed the influence we possess to the disadvantage of the general interests of the country we have done everything in our power to promote them." They claimed as unfounded the charge that they were hostile to the interests of the proprietary class:

> ... the only pretext that we can conjecture for such a representation is, that the interests of the proprietors are considered inimical to the rights of the freeman,—to the diffusion of religious and general knowledge, and to the relief of the oppressed.

They were convinced that, if they as Baptists were to contribute to the well-being of Jamaican society, then they had to pursue their course and not be swayed by criticism. The signers of the address included the well-known names of Tinson, Phillippo, Burchell, Knibb, Abbot, Dendy, Clark, Clarke, and Taylor.[48]

It was the political involvement of the Baptists that drew upon them not only the opprobrium of the plantocracy but the united criticism of other missionary and church groups; any discussion of the Baptist system began or ended with a critique of Baptist politics. "The Baptist preachers, who have very great influence with the blacks, have done immense mischief. Many of the blacks refuse to work, and thus the crops have in some places been ruined," wrote a Jesuit in 1838, voicing the sentiments of many.[49]

In spite of criticism to the contrary, the Baptist foray into electoral politics was not a reckless adventure but was based on both a realistic assessment by the missionaries of their influence over the black peasantry immediately after emancipation and a projection of goals for their socioeconomic welfare. The success or failure of Baptist achievement must be assessed in terms of the limitations imposed by the system. Franchise restrictions as well as the realities of power prevented a full flowering of Baptist political goals.

While Baptist opposition did not bring about a radical reform in planter attitudes and legislation, it was nevertheless crucial in a balance of forces, which included Colonial Office scrutiny and Governor Metcalfe's mollifications, that prevented the immediate post-emancipation period from being one of extreme oppression and anti-black recrimination. This balance was maintained during the administration of Governor Elgin. But from about 1847 it began to break down, occasioned by such external factors as the new free trade policy in England as well as the erosion of humanitarian and anti-slavery opinion in the mother country, and internal factors such as conflicts among the Baptists themselves and the deaths of such stalwarts as Knibb and Burchell in the mid-forties.[50]

Baptist opposition was not, in the end, able to prevent the Assembly's financial neglect of education and health care in favor of expenditures on prisons, police, and immigration. A partial and paradoxical result of a combination of this neglect with planter antagonism toward anything that seemed to lead to the economic independence of the ex-slave was a hastening of that independence. For example, high rents and low wages tended to push the ex-slaves off the estates into free villages or squatter settlements over which planters had little direct control.[51]

The work to effect a change in the composition of the House of Assembly did not outlast the 1840s. Knibb's death in 1845 seemed to deflate the spirit of the Baptist attack. The effort was carried on, however, by many of the men, especially colored and Jewish politicians, whose candidacy the Baptists had backed. Partial success could be claimed in that by 1853 these new legislators, with a nonplanter base, accounted for over 40 percent of the Assembly's membership. The amount of progressive legislation that actually resulted, however, was minimal, as Edward Bean Underhill, secretary of the Baptist Missionary Society, observed in 1865.[52]

By 1865 Baptist criticism of Jamaican politics was mild compared to that of earlier years. By the same year, the most outspoken Baptist voice came from afar. Underhill is best known for his famous letter to Colonial Secretary Cardwell analyzing Jamaican conditions prior to the 1865 rebellion.[53] In private correspondence he is just as penetrating as he was in that published letter; he suggested to the missionaries in Jamaica, for example, that they organize defense associations to protect peasants and laborers against biased magistrates.[54]

In the early 1860s, different church groups in Jamaica were proposing cotton production and export as an alternative source of wealth for the country. Their expectations increased when the Civil War in the United States cut cotton production there. It was Underhill who warned them that Jamaica would not be able to compete once the war ended. He proposed instead that small cultivators concentrate on local crops other than sugar and cotton, and that they organize export cooperatives within their various congregations.[55] But as in so many matters, Underhill's wisdom was greater than local will or foresight.

Underhill's was the last progressive English Baptist voice on Jamaican problems in the period. After the Morant Bay Rebellion and the establishment of Crown Colony government, Baptist thinking in Jamaica became comfortably accommodated to the political status quo. The positions were summed up in the Baptist missionary D. J. East's pamphlet on "Civil Government," appearing in December 1865, in which he put forth a kind of biblical Hobbism defending strong government and strict maintenance of law and order as the only bulwarks against anarchic dissolution of society.[56]

Post-forties Baptist opinion (especially following 1865) was increasingly in support of Crown Colony government, a prospect that had been strong in the Baptist mind from 1839 but which did not have priority as long as there seemed to be a fighting chance that the blacks could become an effectual power base within the old representational system. Baptist ministers seemed to have lost faith not only in that chance but in the blacks themselves, who, after all, had wills of their own and did not consistently follow Baptist political advice. Moreover, it is problematic whether the temporary alliance of Jews, coloreds, and black peasantry that Baptist politics helped to form could ever have held in a socially and culturally fragmented society like that of Jamaica.

Methodist Moderates

It is obvious from a consideration of Baptist political action and criticisms of it that the approaches of other missionary groups to the same problems offer a different study. The most important group of missionaries after the Baptists were the Wesleyans. They consistently defended their policy of noninterference in "temporal" affairs. They claimed that their proper work was one of spiritual charity, which was of a higher order than material charity, such as that engaged in by the Anti-Slavery Society. Moreover, "We are persuaded that, to bring men under the full influence of Christianity, is the surest and readiest method of correcting all the evils which exist in civil society."[57]

The Wesleyan missionary John Williams, in a letter written in November 1837, compared Baptist and Wesleyan politics, which already sharply contrasted:

> Thus the Baptist Missionaries are engaged in perpetual litigation
> with the Magistrates, Planters, and others. They cry out the wrongs
> of the Apprentices both in public and in private, and the Negroes
> look upon them as their great defenders. Neither our excellent
> Instructions nor our Christian prudence would allow us to agitate
> and disorder a state of society established by laws, and which
> with all its defects would (if it were not for designing men) work

itself to a peaceful end. . . . Yet I believe the time is not distant when our conduct will appear to the Negroes in its proper light— when they will be able to distinguish between a Minister of the Gospel and a Political Agitator.[58]

The Wesleyans, in fact, supported the doctrine of laissez-faire. They were opposed to current (1830s) moves to organize workers in British cities, so they would naturally be against any similar type of movement in Jamaica.[59]

Whenever a Wesleyan missionary was seen to be becoming too outspoken on political issues, he would be disciplined into silence. One Mr. John Hornby, for example, joined with the Baptist ministers Dexter and Clark in 1838 to complain to the governor about the misapplication of justice under apprenticeship, thereby causing one magistrate to be removed. Hornby was summoned before a district meeting "to answer for breaking missionary instructions by addressing himself to a political question. . . ." He promised his brethren that he would maintain silence in the face of such questions. In his correspondence, however, he continued to express criticism of the apprenticeship system:

> and while I consider myself bound, by the pledge I have given, to be a silent looker on, I wish to be considered, *in principle*, bound to deprecate the system of apprenticeship, and I hope and pray that I may see its speedy extinction, and that my injured brethren of a different hue may enjoy the blessings of entire freedom.[60]

The Wesleyan district chairman in Jamaica at emancipation, Thomas Pennock, was also publicly outspoken against the apprenticeship system as prolonged slavery. He considered the slaves to be ready for immediate freedom; apprenticeship could only be for the satisfaction of the planters and no one else.[61] Pennock was considered a renegade by his brethren, however, and was soon to secede from the main Wesleyan body because of his refusal to be silenced on this and other issues, especially that of color prejudice within the Wesleyan mission.

Henry Bleby may be taken as representative of the majority Wesleyan outlook. Contrary to Hornby and Pennock, he did not observe much oppression under apprenticeship:

> I am perfectly satisfied that the apprentices generally felt so grateful from the benefits actually conferred by the laws which came into operation in 1834 that they would most cheerfully and peacefully have wrought to the termination of the specified period, had they not been tampered with, and rendered dissatisfied by weak, and interested, and popularity-hunting men.[62]

The Wesleyan chronicler Peter Samuel summarized the official viewpoint: "To be useful, the missionaries have been compelled to occupy neutral ground, and live and act 'as the *friends of all*, the enemies of none.'" District Chairman Edmondson, who succeeded Pennock, believed that the Baptists were intent on exacerbating the differences between planter and worker, whereas the Methodists would have the two classes "forget old grievances and . . . meet and unite in the common affairs of life." It was natural that the Wesleyans would be more amenable to the administration of Charles Metcalfe rather than to that of his predecessor Lionel Smith. They thought that Smith allowed himself to be entangled too much in conflict. They appreciated his support of missionaries but not his particular friendship with the Baptists, and the conciliatory policies of Metcalfe were more to their heart.[63]

The Wesleyans and Baptists, then, had fundamental differences of approach to the problems of post-emancipation society. Concerning agitation to shorten the apprenticeship, Edmondson reported that the "Baptists are taking a very active part in this work but we take our old stand and refuse to be mixed up in politics, although we ardently wish to see the negro perfectly free."[64]

On the problem of wage disputes after 1838, Samuel concludes: "Interference between masters and their labourers and servants on the adjustment of work and wages led to jealousies, feuds, and bickerings, injurious to the real temporal and religious welfare of all parties." It was consistent with Wesleyan laissez-faire policy that, as one missionary wrote, "we have considered it no part of our duty, and no benefit to the Labourer to interfere between him and his master on the subject of wages, judging it to be a business soly [sic] between the employer and the employed, with which a third party has nothing to do."[65]

The fact is that during the apprenticeship Wesleyan members defected to the Baptists precisely because, when apprentices complained to their ministers about abuses and injustices, they were told to bear their injuries in a spirit of Christian resignation. Lack of any positive action by the Wesleyans caused many members to leave them. Edmondson noted:

> In many instances the Negroes have been made to believe that Knibb, Burchell, and other Baptist ministers obtained freedom for them; . . . political agitation is a main element of theirs. . . . These things give them great influence with the Negroes and place us at a discount.[66]

It was this passivity that caused the Quaker commentator Joseph Sturge to accuse the Wesleyans of conniving at the evils of apprenticeship.[67]

One other illustration of the difference between Wesleyan and Baptist political style would be useful in this comparison. It is indicated in a letter by Edmondson endorsing a proposed Marriage Bill in Jamaica in 1837. The bill, it seems, was only a half-measure, and would not have totally removed the legal distinction which existed between dissenter and Anglican marriage.

> The Baptists I understand are rather bitterly opposed to it, in its present state; but I shall be glad to get a little now, and a little more by and by, and thus to advance till the law becomes what it should be; and think if we press too much they may send us empty away.[68]

For the most part, the Wesleyan ministers were obedient to their instructions. Occasionally, however, there were important exceptions. Whereas most of the Wesleyans blamed the Baptists for any disturbances after 1838, Hornby, again, was convinced that the source of mischief in Jamaica was otherwise: "I have known of no disturbance, except such as has been occasioned by the imprudence or injustice of the planter." On other issues, Hornby expressed himself like a Baptist: "The periodicals published here can in few cases be relied on, for giving a true statement of facts if those facts involve the condition of the labouring class, and the working of the free system."[69]

In spite of Wesleyan silence on political issues, we find, in 1858, a rare, hard-headed political critique from the Methodist missionary William Tyson, stationed in Brown's Town. In his correspondence to the home society in Britain, he complained in detail how the tendency of the entire course of the Jamaican Assembly's legislation was to keep the blacks in a state of dependency that was little removed from slavery. The legal settlement of land was too expensive; sometimes the cost of conveyance almost equaled the cost of purchase. Taxes were too heavy, and tended to be collected in the most vexatious manner. "They [taxes] fall most heavily upon the man who makes the most earnest endeavour at improvement. His land, his donkey, his horse, his cart, his house—all are taxed: and if he build a better house than his neighbours, his taxes are immediately increased." Public funds were wasted on fruitless schemes of immigration while the social needs of the existing population were ignored. Tyson, it is to be noted, later demurred, begging forgiveness for his correspondence, but stating that his observations nevertheless sprang from good motives.[70]

Surviving correspondence indicates that at least one other Wesleyan missionary in the late 1850s besides Tyson, Rev. Edward Fraser at Duncans, observed the political and social scene with a cold and critical eye. What is more, Tyson's and Fraser's letters contain not only political observation but analysis based on insight into the class relationship of planter and laborer. In Tyson's correspondence, for example, he considers the view of black laborers as a class who will not work, who are incapable of improvement, and who are sliding back into barbarism. He suggests that such characterization was not the result of any innocent or unbiased observation of the black man but a stereotype manufactured by "the Planting interest" to justify refusal to deal fairly and justly with creole laborers, and to "suit the design" of those who wanted to substitute immigrant labor.[71]

Fraser was an anomaly among Wesleyan ministers at the time in Jamaica, and his background might help to explain his insight and outspokenness. He was nonwhite (it is not clear whether he was colored or black), having been a slave in Bermuda. It was as a slave that he became a Methodist. The extreme segregation in the Methodist church in Bermuda, however, had prevented him from advancing in his desired clerical career there. Ironically, the Anglican bishop of Nova Scotia, in whose see Bermuda was included, was so impressed with young Fraser that he offered to ordain him. He was determined to be a Methodist preacher, however, and, thwarted in Bermuda, left for Jamaica and was accepted in the Wesleyan District there.[72]

Addressing his critique to Thomas Carlyle's "Quashee" image,[73] Fraser affirmed that the Jamaican peasantry was not a collection of vagrants and squatters and lazy cultivators of provision grounds but a people of integrity and willingness to work, whose main problem was their oppression in the plantation system. "A country subjected to revolution from bondage to liberty requires a full regeneration of corresponding changes in all departments," he wrote. But such a change could not occur with planter control of the Assembly and the magistracy. Such men had no long-term view of development, not even a plan to preserve the plantation system by placating the workers. They were interested only in the ready and quick return. "Hence it seems to be that the way of supplying labour full blown at the expense of the country by Immigration is so earnestly adopted, and nothing done to multiply and train our native population."[74]

Fraser went on to propose a Jamaican political economy that would work for the benefit of the whole population, not just for planters and their attorneys. As critical as Fraser was, he was by no means revolutionary. His final proposal did not amount to a fundamental change in the Jamaican class structure: ". . . the prosperity of a free country should be sought for its people as they make a whole, so that while the highest class should as is fit have the largest share, it should be a share consistent with free scope to be given to a lower and to the lowest class to secure their positions as well."[75]

In spite of their correspondence, Tyson and Fraser consistently maintained that it was not their intention to meddle in politics. The content of their letters made them exceptions among the Wesleyans. They wrote with voices that resembled those of the Baptists but with a nervousness and hesitation about their motives that was characteristically Wesleyan, not Baptist.

THE PLANTER COUNTER-OFFENSIVE

Insofar as the planters were religious, their adherence was mostly to the Anglican and Scottish churches. Some may have been true believers according to the norms of faith and practice of those churches. Many were thoroughly secular in that any adherence they gave to a church was purely out of motives of social respectability. But most were religious in the broad and degraded sense[76] that they accepted a theodicy of privilege that thoroughly justified subordinations of race and class, whether or not such subordination was legally designated as slavery. That theodicy was inherent in the ideology of the plantocracy, and they were not averse to using whatever means possible to preserve a society of masters and servants. One of the means used, aside from the exercise of their political prerogatives in the Jamaican Assembly, was the Christianity of the churches in Jamaica. And while it was most difficult to utilize the Baptists in this respect, the other churches proved more amenable to planter manipulation.

When the emancipation question was settled by Parliament in 1833, planters realized the futility of their harassment of religious groups. The use of religion for social control increased in importance as a strategy. Proprietors, legislators, and magistrates condescended to acknowledge that missionaries had been made to suffer without really deserving it, and that all who really wished well to the interests of the country should support them. This did not mean that political controversy involving religious groups would automatically disappear at emancipation. Apprenticeship brought new conflicts. But powerful people sought more than ever to control the influence of religious groups and leaders, so that one missionary could write, "instead of the brethren being annoyed by sounds of insult and threatening, they were beginning to have their principles tested by the more dangerous voice of flattery and applause."[77]

It was the Church of England and her missionaries that were the most favored by the majority of the planters who adopted the strategy of religious instruction. The planters did not have to assume the crude and abrasive postures of men like Rev. G. W. Bridges, rector of the parish of St. Ann at the time of the slave rebellion in 1831–32. Bridges, a major leader of reaction against the nonconformists' work among the slaves, was an extremist of the established order. Goveia described him as "intolerant, intransigent, and totally without charity . . . a militant partisan of the pro-planter, pro-slavery group [in whom] appeared, at its most naked, the particularistic justification of West Indian society and its institutions by appeal to the doctrines of racial inequality."[78] More respectable approaches were available that would not alarm moderate Christians in Jamaica and England. Thus in the 1830s, the Jamaican list of subscribers in support of the Society for the Propagation of the Gospel read like a Who's Who of the island aristocracy. The S.P.G. endeared itself to planters especially with its policy of hiring estate bookkeepers and overseers as catechists when none were available to send from abroad.[79]

Much more serviceable also than Bridges's approach was the outlook of Rev. J. M. Trew, rector of the parish of St. Thomas-in-the-East. His posture was apparently benign and apolitical.[80] In his view, the purpose of religious instruction was to qualify the negroes "for the discharge of their various relative duties." He belied his insistence that his intention was nonpolitical in statements such as this: "Remove the present means of religious instruction, and you remove the pillars which are the stay and support of the whole colonial fabric." Trew's words furnish justification of the Marxian critique of religion when he maintains that religion's value was that it could "tranquilize the minds of the many." Social tranquility could best be preserved by teaching the slave the "Christian duty of submission."[81] Increasingly, proprietors and overseers began to enlist as catechists and lay preachers, especially for the Church Missionary Society and the Wesleyans.

It was most clearly perceived as the duty of the established church to maintain the social subordination of the black population. Bishop Lipscomb, at the time of emancipation, was not hesitant in proclaiming this intention. He manifested his belief that one of the best results to be hoped for from religious instruction of the blacks was the cementing of good relations with the masters.[82] Another aspect of Lipscomb's plan was to keep the population distribution of the blacks from shifting too much from what it was in the final days of slavery. This could be done, he believed, by improving and expanding church facilities throughout the island in order to keep the negroes in estate areas by their attachment to the Anglican church there. This policy tied in with the custom of proprietors to establish plantation chapels so that laborers would not of necessity have to leave the estate for church or chapel attendance.[83]

The view of the church establishment was fully elaborated by Lipscomb in a sermon he preached while on a visit to England in 1840, at St. Michael-Le-Berry, York. He acknowledged a great change in public opinion as to the duty and necessity of religious instruction. He spoke of "the obvious truth, that religion must form the basis of all sound government." It was the result of religious instruction that "the conduct of the emancipated negroes throughout the West Indies has been remarkable for tranquil obedience to the law, and a peaceful demeanour in all the relations of social life."[84]

The teaching and preaching of the established church never deviated from this theme. Shortly after emancipation in 1834, for example, the Anglican church devised a special catechism for the instruction of the negroes, to teach them their divinely ordained duty to obey the authorities over them. The catechism was dedicated to the bishop.[85] At the laying of the foundation stone for St. Paul's Church, Annandale, St. Ann, in 1834, Rev. Henry Browne preached that, in the house of prayer, we are reminded that in heaven there are no distinctions between rich and poor, master and servant. But: "Constituted as society is here below, it is indispensably necessary that worldly distinctions should be maintained for its well-being."[86] At the termination of apprenticeship in 1838, the church published a special prayer for use by the negroes on the first of August; it had them pray to "dispose our minds to a cheerful and willing obedience to the Laws, after the example of Thy blessed son, who submitted Himself to every Ordinance of Man, and was subject unto all in Authority for conscience sake."[87]

The proprietor who set the pace for most others before emancipation in conciliating his workers through religion was J. B. Wildman, owner of several estates in Jamaica, including Salt Savanna in Vere and Papine in St. Andrew. He realized the advantages of incorporating religious instruction into slave routine in such a way that emancipation would make little difference to master/servant relationships on his estates. Wildman built chapels and schools on his properties and obtained resident C.M.S. missionaries. At Salt Savanna, for example, there was a day school for slave children; from 6:00 to 9:00 A.M., they did manual labor and then attended class for the remainder of the day. Adult instruction was offered at night. Sabbath school was also held along with at least three religious services a week.[88]

Wildman insisted on having only C.M.S. missionaries on his estates. As Anglicans, they helped to build up and maintain black membership in the established church, with its well-formed theodicy of social subordination. At the same time, because of their anomalous relationship with the Anglican hierarchy in Jamaica, the planter could attempt more control over them than over regular curates whose obedience to the bishop's authority was more clearly defined. In 1835, it happened that no C.M.S personnel were available for Papine, and an L.M.S. man, John Woolbridge, was allowed to serve in the interim. Woolbridge noted that Wildman imposed many restrictions on his ministers, among them that no Baptist, nor even Wesleyan, missionary was to be allowed near his negroes. Woolbridge was replaced by an Anglican clergyman as soon as one was available in the following year.[89]

Wildman's policy seemed to have the desired results. It was reported that his slaves would voluntarily give up their free time to do extra work such as building and machinery repair. In the words of one observer, his negroes became "the most respectable, enlightened, industrious, moral, and well-behaved that can be found in the country." At emancipation, more proprietors began to adopt the policies of Wildman, applying for the services of C.M.S. missionaries to become private or domestic chaplains on their estates for the purpose of instructing the blacks.[90]

Planters who could overcome their distaste and distrust of missionaries began to hope that, if the slave system could absorb Christian preaching rather than be undermined by it, then emancipation would have little effect on the social order forged during slavery. Planter patrons of missionaries accepted them with the understanding that they should have limited access to the slaves, that they should show every respect for the established church and the magistracy, and that they should shun association with critics of slavery. More and more slave owners followed Wildman's lead in grasping the idea that Christianizing the slaves could make them internalize the attitudes of humility, patience, and obedience, which would allow the master to rule by "love" instead of force.[91]

The overtures of proprietors to the various denominations were noted in private correspondence and in official missionary publications. Even the Baptists observed that men who once persecuted them were now offering them facilities and respect.[92] Even though Baptist ministers tended for the most part to resist, most missionary societies—Anglican evangelicals as well as nonconformists—met these overtures enthusiastically and were able to match planter intentions with their own policies of social control.[93] At emancipation, a prevailing analogy was that, as the planters were to receive compensation money, the ex-slaves should be given more religion as their compensation. Echoing the views of other societies, a Wesleyan Missionary Committee report allied the work of the missionary with that of the magistracy and military in preventing insubordination.[94] The Catholic position on social order as expressed in the *Jamaica Courant* on 13 March 1833 was useful: "It is the province of religion—whenever any portion of the people groan under social or political disabilities—to admonish and preach submission, never, on any account, to counsel active resistance to the laws."[95]

Wesleyan policy drew the support of the planters who saw the advantages in it. "Most of the planters are by this time," wrote Wesleyan John Green in 1842, "convinced that our purposes are good, and that we wish not to injure them, but that we desire the welfare of all. . . ." Wesleyans seemed proud to notice that their teachings had results that contrasted with those of Baptist work, especially during the apprenticeship. The Baptists, it was claimed, were not for the welfare of all, and their backing of the interests of the laborers against those of the planters had the dire result of causing "insufferable impudence" among the blacks. It is little wonder that, during the administration of Charles Metcalfe, it was Wesleyan laborers who were chosen to sit on that governor's "Courts of Reconciliation" throughout the island.[96]

Even Baptist activity, separated from the disdain with which planters in general viewed it, contained adjustments that could be useful for the preservation of plantation society. The greatest and most successful experiment of the Baptists among the freed slave population, the free-village system, even though it contributed to the independence of the ex-slave peasantry, was not a revolutionary groundwork for a new society. In many ways, the system was meant to shore up the plantation system. The missionaries endeavored "to convince these simple-minded people [the ex-slave inhabitants of the free villages] that their own prosperity, as well as that of the island at large, depended on their willingness to work for moderate wages, on the different properties around them," as Phillippo put it.[97]

Phillippo may have been apologizing for his more radical-sounding brethren when he wrote:

> In numberless instances the [Baptist missionaries] prevented the occurrence of insubordination. . . . At considerable personal inconvenience and risk of health, with the certainty of being reputed by calumny and misrepresentation, they travelled from one estate to another, for no other purpose than to stimulate the peasantry to cultivate feelings of kindness and goodwill toward their employers, and to exemplify their Christian character by a steady and conscientious performance of their duties, whatever the circumstances in which they might be placed.[98]

Phillippo especially was courted by planters as the termination of apprenticeship approached. He wrote that nearly all the planters in his district were encouraging him in the work of imparting religious instruction to the people. A dozen "of the most influential individuals in town and country" were inviting him to establish schools and preaching stations near their estates, and offering land and materials for the necessary building.[99]

The shift of the planters to support of religion was given various interpretations by missionary writers. The Wesleyan chronicler Peter Samuel offered an idealistic interpretation:

> During the existence of slavery, honourable members of the Assembly were wont to regard and treat the missionaries as unprincipled men of sinister designs, whose presence in the island was its bane! So that one is apt to conclude that the mental and moral emancipation of the free colonists was as striking as the liberation of the slaves from their civil bondage.[100]

The Congregationalist missionary historian Gardner similarly remarked on the changed attitude of the whites towards missionaries at emancipation and their willingness to assist financially in religious instruction. He did not offer much of an explanation of this change, other than proposing that a "liberality of sentiment" was brought about by the removal of "the moral and mental incubus of the slave system."[101]

Some of the other missionaries were closer than Samuel or Gardner in understanding the real reason for the change in the planter mind. The Wesleyan Richard Harding wrote in 1837:

> Many in the higher circles of life, who do not attend our preaching nor concern themselves about the salvation of their own souls, going upon the principle that religion is good for servants, and the lower orders of society, and judging that those doctrines inculcated by the Methodists are more useful than those taught by some other bodies, wish prosperity to us.[102]

A Baptist missionary, Henry Taylor, put it most succinctly when he remarked that Mr. Bravo, a white proprietor favorable to the Gospel, was so *"more from policy* than anything else." Bravo insisted that missionaries associate with him and attend his dinner parties.

Taylor refused to be wooed, knowing that the result would be loss of confidence with the blacks.[103] The Presbyterian Hope Waddell, who himself had gotten started in his mission in Trelawny with the assistance of several planters, reported that Richard Barrett, custos of St. James, clearly stated his motivation in acceding to Waddell's request to preach on his property: "I must in candour own that I am not influenced by religious principles myself in this matter, but simply by self-interest."[104] The editor of the *Royal Gazette* summed up planter hopes for Christian education for the blacks when he proposed that such instruction would eventually supersede the necessity for a police force.[105]

At any time during the latter years of slavery, examples of planter patronage of religious instruction for the slaves could be found, in spite of the general hostility of the planter class towards that instruction. Wildman is the most outstanding example. The change in planter policy at emancipation, then, could not be considered a totally sudden and unexpected occurrence.[106] Nor can it be claimed as unanimous. There was never, within the white sector of society, complete acceptance of the idea of religious instruction for the blacks. There was continuing debate after emancipation as to its desirable or undesirable effects.[107] It could not be expected that all white estate personnel, with attitudes forged during slavery, would change their minds that religion was dangerous in the minds and hearts of black laborers. Indeed, it was not until 1860 that Phillippo felt he could put aside all caution and proclaim that opposition on the part of planters to the progress of the Gospel had entirely ceased.[108]

Sufficient numbers of Christian ministers, however, had been compromised by planter patronage to make their relationships with the blacks more complicated than they might have been; the credibility of the Christian message had been weakened. To attempt to separate their work from the "secular" had blinded many missionaries to the secular manipulation of their teachings.

One great incentive for missionaries to ingratiate themselves with the wealthy was pressure from the home societies to become as financially self-sufficient as possible. After emancipation, the Methodist Missionary Society urged missionaries in Jamaica to live as much as possible on private subscriptions. The contributions of the poor, through regular collections, were not sufficient for this purpose. Subscriptions of any size could be obtained only from planters and merchants, the class that had formerly been the persecutors of missionaries.[109]

For all the support promised by the proprietors, however, their actual assistance proved to be a disappointment to missionary groups. Phillippo found himself heavily in debt with extra school and chapel construction undertaken on the basis of planter pledges that were never fulfilled. Many of the planters, continuing to believe resentfully that nonconformist missionaries were responsible for emancipation, reserved their support (through Assembly and vestry expenditures) for the established church, hoping that it would draw most of the ex-slaves. Even the C.M.S. could not collect on planter pledges. The committee hoped in the early 1840s that sufficient subscriptions would be raised from planters to enable them to carry on in Jamaica, "without any undue demand upon its general funds." These hopes were not fulfilled, and lack of local support was a main reason for the phasing out of C.M.S. work in Jamaica in the later 1840s.[110]

Even considering the importance of religious instruction as a tool in social control, and the support of such instruction by a pro-planter newspaper like the *Royal Gazette*, the Assembly spent very little on education. To the extent that the legislature had any interest in the subject, it focused on so-called "industrial education," which was not interpreted in a broad and liberal way as constituting the increase in skills and economic options for the ex-slaves and, consequently, the economic diversity of the island; the Assembly's view of it was of minimal instruction on the elementary level and the inculcation of habits of manual labor.[111]

If the attitude of the Assembly can be taken as a measure of the majority planter viewpoint, then the fear of an educated black population seemed to overcome the realization of the usefulness of education in the control of the population. Nine years after full emancipation, the reluctance of the Assembly to support education caused the Colonial Office to remind the Jamaican legislators of the benefits to themselves of proper education of the lower class; necessarily including religious instruction, it would help create a population that would be orderly, stable, respectful of authority, and imbued with new wants and desires that could only be satisfied by constant and steady employment.[112]

Increasing fiscal difficulties can be claimed as one reason why religious groups were disappointed with the actual support given by planters. All denominations that were receiving at least some assistance from the planter class began to suffer even more around 1848. By that year, planters who were affected by the financial ruin they attributed to the Sugar Duties Act were discontinuing subscriptions. It was not only nonconformists who were affected this time but the established church as well. For months on end, curates on the island payroll went without salaries because the Assembly insisted that the treasury was empty. Bishop Spencer, Lipscomb's successor, was perturbed by this situation because he saw the church as "the most hopeful amulet" in the preservation of "industry and order" among the peasantry. But fiscal difficulties alone were not sufficient to explain the actual reluctance of the Assembly to support education for the ex-slaves, whether religious or "industrial" education. The idea was never really relinquished that the best means of controlling the blacks was coercion. Compared to expenditures on education and even on the church establishment, vastly more was spent on police and prisons.[113]

In 1850, the Assembly resumed legislation for scourging as punishment, ten years after it had been abolished. It was revived not only for serious crimes like rape but for every felony after a previous conviction, even for larceny of produce. In 1852, it was enacted that, while estate cattle that trespassed on the grounds of the small farmer were to be taken to the pound, the small farmer's livestock could be destroyed at once by planters or overseers when they strayed onto an estate.[114] These enactments, for whipping and the destruction of the poor man's livestock, were the result of relentless campaigning by pro-planter newspapers, more relentless than any campaigning for education had ever been. The principles and prejudices of slavery had not ended with the legal abolition of that system. In the words of the *Jamaica Standard* in 1842, whipping was necessary for blacks because they had "no other feelings than the physical sensation of the beasts" and therefore could only "be flogged into tameness and submission."[115] In the end, repression was the only method for social control that the planters thoroughly understood.

CHAPTER 2

White Ministers in an Afro-Creole World

In the 1830s, the Baptists recognized that the interests of the ruling class and the apprenticed laborers were often not reconcilable, and they made no spurious claim to serve all regardless of class. Phillippo wrote, "Being wholly independent of local influence, the missionaries were almost the only individuals on the island who *dared* to interfere between the oppressors and the oppressed." Another Baptist, John Clarke, in his published *Memorials*, acknowledged the same recognition of a class of oppressors and one of the oppressed in moderate but firm words.[1] The continuing enmity of most planters towards Baptist missionaries, long after they began to cooperate with other nonconformists, is testimony to the truth of the observations of Phillippo and Clarke.

The influence of the Baptist missionaries among the free peasant population is undeniable. It was not just gratitude on the part of the blacks for the abolitionist commitment of the Baptists; they continued after 1834 to defend the reputation of the ex-slaves as a hardworking and industrious people to counter the calumnies of the planters against the freed population. And in spite of earlier disclaimers about their ability to influence the people for or against rebellion, after the mid-1830s the Baptist ministers had become more certain of their power. Early in 1839, all the Baptist missionaries of the island informed the governor, Sir Lionel Smith,

that at any time, if they so wished, they could lead their congregations into open resistance and rebellion against planter or government oppression.[2] Their refraining from leading their people into
any such resistance was due to their fear, it seems, that to do so
would coordinate with the plans of some of the planters to pro-
voke rebellion, in order both to use it as a pretext for suppression
of the freed population and to present it as evidence to the British
government that emancipation was a mistake and could not work.

The Baptist missionaries perhaps gained the confidence to proclaim their influence for rebellion from a demonstration in August
of 1838, an occurrence which also provides an outstanding example of the closeness and affection between a missionary and his
church members. On 19 August the report spread that William
Knibb had been shot. The news "flew like wild-fire, and the effect
was electrical. . . ." The Baptist peasantry were in a mood to elimi-
nate all whites and mulattoes, it was reported, and indeed they
supposedly claimed that they would do away with all white ministers except Baptists. The appearance of Knibb safe and unshot
was able to quell a second "Baptist War," as the 1831 Christmas
rebellion had been called.[3]

Even if some of the missionaries saw some benefit in seeking
planter patronage, they had to pay the price of not doing so in
order to maintain their leadership among the blacks. Another Baptist, Henry Taylor, noted that, if any minister were to become too
intimate with the white people, the blacks would become very shy
of them, and confidence would be lost. His influence among the
blacks was the cause of much excitement against him from "those
wretched white people."[4]

Taylor expressed this to the head of the London Missionary Society (probably by way of advice on the commencement of L.M.S.
work in Jamaica) and soon gained some support for his viewpoint
from the L.M.S. missionaries. One of them, W. G. Barrett, wrote to

his chairman that too close an association with planters would cause the people to lose confidence in the minister. Barrett, however, was at the same time critical of the nature of Taylor's influence among the people, claiming that he baptized too indiscriminately. Barrett was later to lead a pamphlet attack against the Baptist ticket-and-leader system. In any event, it was a truth generally acknowledged by all missionaries that, once a minister was labeled a "Busha's Parson," it was very difficult for him to communicate with the people on any intimate, personal level.[5]

One student of missionary work in Jamaica, Dorothy Ryall, criticizes the motives of those who volunteered to leave England or Europe for such work in the West Indies. Many of them, she asserts, were seeking to escape their low status in the class system in their home countries in order to establish a social dominance in a colony which they could never achieve at home. "In the exercise of the paternalistic functions of the missionary among the unlettered and heathen natives of some foreign country," she writes, "they would be assured of a feeling of self-importance which was denied them by the rigid social hierarchy at home."[6] Ryall's explanation of missionary motivation must be modified on at least two counts when we consider the actual experience of the missionary in the West Indies. First, although there was a certain amount of social prestige to his position, the hardships, mental and physical, of adjusting to a tropical colony were a high price to pay for any rise in social position he may have experienced. And second, the native response to and relation with the missionary was much more psychologically complex than a simple child-parent relationship. Contact with the Jamaican blacks was at times a humbling experience for the missionary. In reflecting on private visits and conversations with his members, the Methodist missionary Curtis wrote of this most difficult aspect of his duties: "It shows me, more than anything else, my ignorance in theology, and my deficiency in Christian experience, while much, very much, may be learnt."[7]

From the missionaries of the Church Missionary Society we get some of the clearest testimony as to the nature of the less visible, day-to-day work of these men. Rev. Jacob Sessing, who in 1838 was stationed at Birnam Wood in the parish of St. George, wrote of the difficulties of doing his missionary work while caring for his child and an ailing wife and having to do the housework in his cottage. Such domestic obstacles forced him to reflect on the nature of his work. Were such mundane tasks perhaps a vital part of missionary activity? He concluded that they were, that such living example of family solidarity was every bit as important as preaching, among a population in which he perceived a lack of marital dedication:

> Many of the Negroes were heard to explain, "Ah! we never see Buckra (the Negroes' expression for White Man) do so!" and some would say to Mrs. Sessing, "Massa good to you: he mind you well." These expressions show that they watch us closely; and make their comparisons between the Europeans, in general, and the Ministers and Teachers sent to them.[8]

It is often mentioned in missionary correspondence that one of the minister's duties was the settling of domestic quarrels among the members of their congregations. While there is little indication of the results of such ministerial intervention, it is obvious that, in a mission country like Jamaica, the minister was called upon to be much more than a spiritual pastor alone. This was especially true of the Baptist minister, whose myriad duties and commitments made him a magistrate and solicitor in settling property disputes, physician and dispenser of medicine, domestic adviser in family disagreements, and government agent in the management of day schools and in the work of parochial and government boards.[9]

What is problematic is the directness of understanding on the part of the Jamaican blacks of what the missionary was attempting to communicate. Ambiguities, misunderstandings, and reinterpretations could occur which might not have been readily apparent to either party. Missionaries wittingly or unwittingly played upon the prescientific perceptions of the blacks. One night in October 1837, Rev. D. Seddon, a church missionary at Elstree, Manchester, told some of his congregation, "Tomorrow night you will see something the matter with the moon." He was announcing an eclipse. Seddon did not expect much from his announcement and in fact claimed that he forgot all about it until the following evening when, near sunset, people from all over the district congregated on the mission premises.

One old woman said, "Me come up to beg Massa to gib me prayers."

"Why?" answered Seddon.

"Because ever since Massa tell de people 'bout de moon, last night me bin 'fraid; me tink we all going to die."

Upwards of two hundred had congregated, according to Seddon, all overcome with fear and showing "symptoms of unusual dread." They were as silent as death.

As the moon was eclipsed, Seddon took the opportunity to sermonize. It seems that he did not make much of an attempt to explain the eclipse in any scientific way. Instead he used the occasion

> . . . to call on them to forsake sin, and all evil, for the service of God. I
> showed them that it was the want of faith in Christ, and of love of
> God, which made them so terrified; otherwise, why should they fear,
> though the heavens were on fire, and the earth destroyed.

He did interject a simple explanation of the eclipse, but the people were probably unable to absorb any rational explanation after being so shaken by this religious experience. "They departed like prisoners released from death," not because they understood the eclipse but because the minister had prayed with them in their fear.[10] No literary telling of the story from the viewpoint of the blacks exists, of course, and missionary anecdotes of this sort are probably behind much of the paternalistic interpretations of missionary/native relations offered by students such as Ryall.

For ministers who did not possess the personality and charisma of a Knibb, the success of acquiring a large congregation soon led to a failure of communication. The larger the congregation, the more remote the minister was likely to become from most of his people. For example, at Siloah in 1844, the C.M.S. missionary Redford had three thousand members in his district, "12 miles by 14—far too much for one weak Labourer."[11]

Phillippo remarked that the people were drawn to a missionary by the style of his preaching and that they valued the preaching according to the degree of feeling awakened in them by it. However, diligent missionaries realized that sermons in themselves were of little use in communicating religious ideas to masses of people. Only patient, persistent, and personal conversation, it was admitted, could begin to accomplish such a task.[12]

The only other solution, of course, was the appointment of native leaders to be responsible for the spiritual care of sections of large congregations. But this was eschewed by most non-Baptists. And in any case, both solutions could not prevent, and with the latter solution actually ensured, the reinterpretation of the "pure" Christian message into categories of meaning that made sense to the Afro-creole mind.

It cannot be denied that there was often deep affection on the part of the blacks towards their ministers, and not just for outstanding ones like Knibb.

Oh were it possible for me to describe the intensity of delight, with which the Natives hear of the arrival of a Missionary, the rapidity with which the tidings spread from village to village, and the warmth of affection with which we are received.[13]

This remark of the Methodist William Sinclair in 1842, probably written to impress the general secretaries of the M.M.S. with the success of the Methodist mission, is nevertheless not a total exaggeration. On the other hand, there were many ex-slaves who either shunned association with white preachers or carefully managed that association to suit their own needs, tendencies that increased as time went on.

The frustrations inherent in the contradictory relationships of white ministers and black Jamaicans in the nineteenth century are illustrated in the case of the most assertively independent group of Afro-Jamaicans, the Maroons. Those of Accompong in the parish of St. Elizabeth were a special challenge, and their case cannot be explained readily in stark terms of either affection or rejection of the person of the white missionary.

Formed around ever-increasing corps of runaway slaves—whose militancy, communal organization, and religious worldview were built on the basis of Akan cultural survivals—the Maroons battled the British in eastern and western mountain areas in the seventeenth and early eighteenth centuries until they were granted a somewhat circumscribed autonomy by the treaties of 1739. Four official settlements—Moore Town, Scotts Hall, Charles Town, and Accompong—consisting of a total of about eleven hundred Maroons were in existence when the Church Missionary Society began its catechetical and educational mission among them in 1828. While difficulties were encountered in Moore Town and Charles Town (no agents were sent to Scotts Hall), the recalcitrance of the people of Accompong, the most remote of the settlements, appeared to bear out most dramatically the resistance to

Christian preaching anticipated by the pro-planter historian of the Maroons, R. C. Dallas, in 1803.[14]

After ten years and four catechists,[15] the Corresponding Committee of the C.M.S. recorded their exasperation with "the little effect which has attended the long course of Christian instruction afforded by the Society to the Maroons of Accompong; and the almost hopeless case of persons who under such long and patient moral culture refuse in general to submit to its outward decencies and restraints. . . ."[16] Faced with the decision of the society to withdraw their catechist once and for all, the Maroons petitioned that he be allowed to remain in Accompong. With this evidence of possible conversion, the society delayed withdrawing the catechist until 1839, when it became obvious that the Maroons had no intention of changing their ways.[17]

Encouraged once again by signs of response to the promptings of divine grace among the Maroons, the C.M.S. sent a visiting missionary for a few years in the mid-1840s, but it reestablished no residential mission in Accompong before the society's departure from Jamaica at the end of the decade. By 1880, only a minister of the Church of Scotland had resided in Accompong, for a year in 1875–76, sent at the request of the Maroons.[18]

The C.M.S. catechists who had worked in Accompong neither described in detail nor analyzed coherently the frustrations they encountered, beyond general statements concerning the recalcitrance and heathenism displayed by the Maroons. Some explanation is possible in the light of what is known of Maroon society and values. In attempting to assert their leadership, the white missionaries assaulted the independent spirit of the Maroons that was based in their history of militant resistance and in the concessions granted by colonial authorities in the eighteenth-century treaties. C.M.S. catechists and missionaries, although Anglican, were itinerants, and even the ordained ministers among them had a problematic relationship with the established church and its bishop; they were not accorded the same prestige that rectors and curates directly under episcopal authority would have been granted by rank- and title-conscious Maroons. A comparison of the Accompong expe- rience with what is known of the relatively less severe difficulties en- countered by the C.M.S. in other Maroon towns suggests that educa- tional and property disputes were also at issue. The leaders in those communities complained of the low standards of the C.M.S. school- masters; Maroon parents may have been largely illiterate, but they nevertheless had intelligent expectations of academic achievement for their children, and C.M.S. teachers were not fulfilling these expecta- tions. This problem was compounded by their having to teach under a tree or in rented premises, as the legal arrangement of Maroon au- tonomy prevented the alienation of communal land to individuals or outside agents such as the C.M.S., whose control over educational procedures was constricted by lack of title to school property.[19]

When C.M.S. missionaries entered Accompong they entered an Afro-creole religious world the essential elements of which were what Christian preaching was intended to eradicate, and which were bundled together by white minds in the nefarious and catch- all term of *Obeah*. Major aspects of African traditional religion, creolized according to the peculiar features of Maroon history, predominated: the belief in a high creator God who was remote from daily concerns; a spirit world consisting of the founding an- cestors, more recently departed members of the community, and lesser nature spirits—all of whom were intimately involved in the practical affairs of the physically living; and specialists who ex- pertly channeled communication with the spirits in private ritu- als or public ceremonies of dancing, drumming, libation, and pos- session. Missionaries, bearing "true religion," hoped for a total conversion away from this cosmology. Maroons, living in a spiri- tual world of their own understanding, accepted what they could in the Christian religion without abandoning their own. What in Protestant Christianity could supplant the necessary services provided by the spirits, such as helping to identify community thieves, punishing anti-social behavior, ensuring fidelity in human relations, and curing illness?[20]

What seemed to irritate and exasperate the missionaries most was the instrumental nature of the relationship that the Maroons appeared to demand of the missionary, an arrangement that becomes increasingly obvious in further examination of the role of white ministers in the Afro-creole world on the whole. Blacks who listened to Christian preaching or accepted baptism often saw their relationship to the church, school, and catechist or minister as a contractual one: for the time and attention they gave to the minister, they desired some concrete return; for attending to Christian instruction, discipline, and routine, some material compensation was expected. This was explained by one C.M.S. missionary:

> Many of the people, when exhorted to attend prayers, ask what I will give them. Sometimes they promise to come if they get their dinner, in one instance, an old woman told me, she would not come without getting her dinner every day in the week. Most of those living in fornication, promise to get married whenever I please, provided I lend them the money to get the victuals and clothes.

The last C.M.S. catechist in Accompong, Mr. J. Gillies, echoed this observation when he reported how the Maroons tried to bargain with him for food as compensation for allowing their children to attend his school.[21]

Barbara Kopytoff, a recent student of Maroon society with special reference to the history of Accompong, has noted that the social, psychological, and material concessions that the people of Accompong expected from C.M.S. personnel in return for their limited compliance derived from "a cultural pattern of mutual aid in which the obligation to reciprocate acted as a constraint on excess." Gillies and other missionaries, however, saw it only as a nagging, covetous, and ungrateful begging, and they were unable to enter into the mutuality of Afro-creole communal life.[22]

The difficulties of the C.M.S. among the Maroons resembled those found in some evidence provided by the Roman Catholic Jesuit mission in Jamaica. At first glance, a consideration of relationships within the Roman Catholic church would seem to contrast with the problems encountered in the Protestant churches. Both the unique hierarchical structure of the Catholic church and its concentration in the city of Kingston suggest this difference. It was not, after all, a church of the black peasantry but of relatively well-off Europeans and white or brown creoles in Kingston and Spanish Town, generally of Spanish or French background. The Catholic church in Jamaica was known as the French church well into the nineteenth century.

Upon closer examination, however, it seems apparent that the Catholic laity were as independent and demanding, in their own fashion, as the black peasants of their Protestant ministers. Relations between the Jesuits, who almost exclusively formed the Catholic clergy, and the laity were never consistently cordial and were, in fact, often stormy and bitter; Fr. Joseph Woollett, the Jesuit Superior in 1873, characterized the Catholic population as "our conceited ignorant Jamaican creoles."[23] Indeed, relations among the Jesuits themselves were often as bitter, reflecting arguments about the most effective way of evangelizing.

Woollett continued to call Catholic church members "our vain, conceited, half-educated, self-sufficient Creoles."[24] This remark was occasioned by what he considered the failure of the more established Catholic membership to appreciate the hard-working Fr. Hathaway, another Jesuit. Hathaway, it seems, did not allow himself to become a sycophant to the Catholic elite but devoted himself to pastoral work that took him outside of their circle. As Woollett observed,

> He goes through an immense amount of work, but of course his humility at the poor school is scoffed at, his zeal at the penitentiary is disregarded, his devotedness to the sick in hospital is unknown, his attention to soldiers at Camp is slighted, his piety is scarcely valued even at the convent, and his beautiful sermons are unheeded, and all because the good old man stops nowhere to gossip.[25]

Fr. Hathaway was indeed aware that he was breaking a mode that was expected both in Jesuit training and by the creole elite who tended to see the Jesuits as little more than their personal chaplains. He was critical of other Jesuits in Jamaica for a style of preaching that could not reach the poor. He wrote to a young Jesuit concerning seminary training: ". . . all that sort of thing has to be unlearned afterwards, if preaching is to be of any use beyond showing that you are learned—which is about the worst use it can be put. . . ."[26]

The catalyst that brought the increasing enmity between the Catholic elite and Fr. Woollett to the boiling point, apparently, was Woollett's unwillingness to have the Jesuits commit themselves to running a college, which the Catholics wanted for the education of their sons. Woollett saw much more of a need to emphasize the type of work that Hathaway was doing: pastoral work among the poor rather than elite education.[27]

Woollett's refusal to entertain petitions in support of a college exacerbated the resentments of the prominent Catholic laity. In a letter to the Jesuit provincial in London, they made certain accusations against Woollett and the Jesuits who supported his viewpoint: they were too casual and friendly with Protestants, they had extravagantly dissipated mission funds, and they were "against morality." Woollett's reply to the accusations was undetailed and dismissive. He wrote that, if he had more time, he would be found even more frequently at the homes of Protestants, and that he had had difficulty staying at the homes of Catholic families, "so flagrantly scandalous were their lives." Concerning mission funds, Woollett claims that, on the contrary, he was busy depositing all that he could in the savings bank. The anti-morality charge seemed to have had a nebulous beginning in a ribald joke someone had started about the priests, which had no basis in fact but which had been fanned by the winds of verandah gossip.[28]

Perhaps the best general explanation for the discontent of the Kingston-based Catholic laity was the refusal of Fr. Woollett to allow the Jesuits to serve them as a Catholic elite or to shore up their assumption that the Catholic church in Jamaica consisted solely in themselves. The priests were not conforming sufficiently to the role that these Catholics had defined for them: thus a list of "charges," considered spurious by Woollett, was sent to Jesuit headquarters in London. The Catholic elite, among whom the most prominent names were Chavannes, Garcia, Henriques, Figueroa, Feres, Desnoes, Duquesnay, and Vendryes,[29] saw the purpose of the Jesuit mission as almost exclusively a ministering unto themselves; and it was probably this attitude that prompted Woollett to characterize them as conceited, ignorant, and self-sufficient.

At the same time, the Jesuits were beginning to devote some attention to a ministry among the Jamaican peasantry. The effort seems insignificant when compared to the years and volume of Protestant nonconformist work. It has provided us, however, with one of the best documents we have for understanding the approach and assumptions of a European missionary and the responses of Afro-Jamaicans in the post-emancipation period. The most complete and candid document we have to illustrate the relationship of a Catholic missionary priest with Jamaican peasants is the diary of James Splaine, S.J., kept during the years 1872–73.

This is a sketch of a cane press, for makin
sugar, cut on the trunk of a mango tre
by an African. The lever passes through th
tree & rests on a projectin table on the top edg
of wh. two teeth are left (one is visible in
the drawing) to keep the cane in its place
while being squeezed. The liquor runs over
the table & down the side into a gutter
by wh it is collected & directed into a
ARCH. PROV. ANG. S. J. OCTOBER. 1968

1. Sugar cane press in the trunk of a mango tree. From the diary of James Splaine, S.J., with entry dated 18 February 1872. Reproduced with permission of the Archivist of the English Province of the Society of Jesus. Photographed by Irwin Arthur.

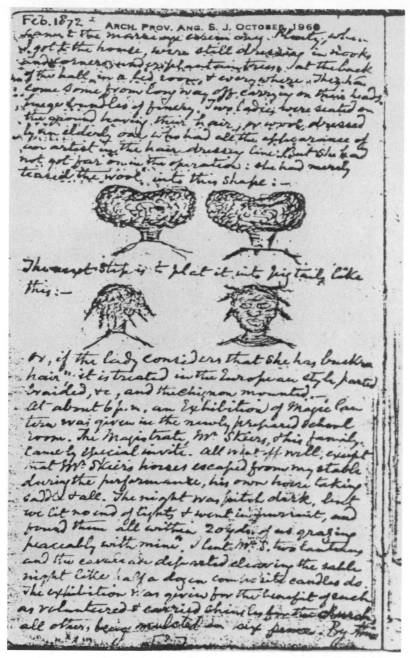

2. Afro-Jamaican women's hairstyling. From the diary of James Splaine, S.J., with entry dated 28 February 1872. Reproduced with permission of the Archivist of the English Province of the Society of Jesus. Photographed by Irwin Arthur.

Ordained in England in 1867, Splaine received his mission assignment in 1869 and departed for Jamaica in November of the same year. His first mission station was at Agualta Vale, about one mile south of Annotto Bay. By 1872 he seems to have been based at Avocat, a Roman Catholic church property in the village of Silver Hill, overlooking the Buff Bay River in St. George parish. The name Avocat recalls French Haitian families, refugees from the Haitian revolution, who acquired coffee properties in the area around 1800. Splaine's mission territory formed a crescent, from Annotto Bay on the west to Hope Bay in the east, but he occasionally celebrated the Catholic liturgy outside of this area. He wrote most of his Jamaican diary at Avocat.[30] By the time he arrived there, the Catholic church no longer relied on the membership of the old white and colored French-Haitian families but on the allegiance of former slaves and their descendants.[31] They continued to live mainly as tenant farmers, cultivating food crops for their families and for the local market and growing coffee and later bananas for the Silver Hill proprietor. Splaine's diary refers to some small-scale sugar cane cultivation for domestic use and contains a drawing of a small sugar cane press constructed within the hollow of a huge mango tree trunk.[32]

The diary's underlying theme, the issue to which Splaine's observations repeatedly draw attention, is the nature of the relationship between the missionary and the black farmers and tenants in the hills. Splaine probed that relationship with a constancy that, in comparison, is not communicated in C.M.S. journals on that society's work among the Maroons. Splaine's diary becomes a kind of prism in whose fractured light we glimpse elements of late nineteenth-century Afro-creole religion and ethics. The diary is replete with the contradictions and ambivalence of a thoroughly European man trying to deal with a Jamaica that was more African than European. In spite of Splaine's ambivalence, however, a symbiotic relationship developed between the priest and parishioners to whom he rendered material and spiritual services. Much of Splaine's ambivalence and frustration resulted from the total lack of correspondence between what Jamaicans and Africans demanded from him and his own sense of mission. Splaine's experiences with Afro-Jamaicans and Africans can only be understood in the context of their own conception of the functions of religion and priesthood, which they framed in African, not European, terms. In this sense, the relationship is comparable to that between the Accompong Maroons and the frustrated C.M.S. missionaries.

Three aspects of Splaine's relationship with his congregation are especially noteworthy. First, he was called upon to be a medical doctor as often or perhaps more than he was called upon for his priestly services. Second, as a spiritual leader, the relation of the blacks to him was often as to a Myal man, an Afro-Christian religious specialist (which in the minds of the blacks undoubtedly was related to the first role); his sacramental powers as a priest were seen in this light. Third, and again relatedly, the people unselfconsciously revealed their Afro-creole customs and religious beliefs to him, beliefs which he considered mere superstitions. In general, his advice and services were called upon in every conceivable situation; not only was he a doctor and a priest, but also a useful and necessary link with the other Jamaica, the official Jamaica of white and colored creoles and Europeans.

Splaine did not anticipate, when he arrived in Jamaica, that Catholic symbols could assume significance within an African religious context. He seemed unaware that, in dispensing these symbols, either as sacraments or sacramentals, he was reinforcing African beliefs. His diary contains an account that aptly illustrates the point:

A man named Davy who came to me here a couple of months back to be relieved from duppies [ghosts or "shadows"] and bad dreams and whose wife left on account of the disturbance created by the evil spirits has been telling the people that I worked a wonderful cure and dispelled them all. The fact is I gave him a Catechism, and perhaps a medal or a cross, and told him to come again, as he wanted to be received into the Church. . . . But he seems to be perfectly satisfied with what he has already got for he never came back.[33]

On another occasion, Splaine was called to a house where duppies were harassing the inhabitants by throwing stones at them. Even though his attitude was condescending, his apparent compliance with Afro-Jamaican expectations cast him in the role of Myal priest: "very well said I, I am fond of ghosts and so I am going to ask them all to come home with me & now I trust no lady or gentleman will throw stones—Peace was thus reestablished & I got home all safe."[34]

They particularly valued Extreme Unction, the anointing with special oils of the seriously ill and dying, accompanied by special prayers. Like Catholics, they associated the ritual with the restoration of good health, and the sick were likely to show an interest in conversion in order to receive Extreme Unction. Splaine was told: "dem all want to be Catholic when dem sick, sake of hearin Ext. Unc. make dem hearty." He observed that several cases of recovery "from the point of death" had occurred in St. George parish.[35]

What is even more striking in the relationship was the frankness with which the black people displayed their African religious culture before the priest. Two examples demonstrate this. One day after Mass, some men whom Splaine identifies as Africans came to lay a complaint before him. One of the men had discovered that some yam heads, which he had stacked and which were ready for planting, had been stolen from his ground. The men knew of another African named "Saalwata (salt water)" who had means of finding stolen goods along with the thief. This man had been sent for, and he soon arrived. In Splaine's presence, Saalwata proceeded to enact his divining ritual. He had a bowl with him

> on which was chalked some marks and then three men took hold of the bowl and kept moving it to and fro to see whom it would knock and it knocked the fellow who had first told of Saalwata's skill. He at once denied having stolen them. His opponents naturally asked him why, if that was the case, he had said the bowl always *told the truth*, and as he could not give any satisfactory explanation, it was agreed that he was the thief.[36]

It is possible that these Africans felt that the efficacy of the fetish was somehow augmented by its being used in the presence of the priest. In any event, it is noteworthy that they seemed completely without guile in having the priest witness a ceremony that he could only view as superstition.

Another example concerns the African and Afro-Jamaican belief in a dual soul. As one woman explained to Splaine, the human soul was really two souls, a big one and a small one, big when going to heaven, small when bound for hell:

> "as him tek de road," she said, "him come down small so," holding the palms of her hands concave towards each other; "but when he go a heaven him big, bi-i-ig so," stretching her arms out as wide as she could. When questioned as to how she knew all that, she exclaimed, "hy! my own judgement tell me. De glory no mek him so? No one person when him happy, look bigger 'an somebody?"[37]

The Jamaican belief in a dual soul is old, persists to this day, and probably derives from multiple African sources. In Splaine's time both Afro-Jamaicans and Africans would have subscribed to it. The dual soul consists of a personal spirit and a duppy or shadow. At death the personal spirit departs this earth, but the duppy or shadow remains with the corpse and, if not properly buried, can wander around, haunting people for various reasons, and perhaps behaving like the poltergeist exorcised by Splaine. One function of Myal practitioners was to capture wandering shadows and force confessions from anti-social people who tampered with them. The version of the dual-soul belief recorded by Splaine, with its references to heaven and hell and its description of the changing size of the two souls, appears to be a creole variant influenced by Christianity.[38]

Besides his medical and religious functions, Splaine acted as an intermediary with white and colored officials and arbitrated marital, family, and village disputes. Yet, for all this, little affection existed between Splaine and his Jamaican congregation. The people themselves determined what role the priest should play in their lives. The role was very important to them, but it was not what the priest wanted it to be. This accounts for his initial ambivalence, and for the bitterness and disillusionment that is increasingly evident as his journal proceeds. When Splaine realized, rather soon in his labors, that the people had no intention of accepting what he conceived as pure Christian doctrine with its attendant morality, he accused them of a combination of dullness and vanity that was impervious to any instruction or correction. The diary reveals that his close and constant work with Jamaicans never led to success as he understood it, and be blamed his failure on the immorality and superstition of the "niggers"—a term he used with increasing frequency. He concluded that black people were mentally dull and vain and observed that the acquisition of a little knowledge made them resent further teaching.[39]

Resistance to Splaine's preaching on sexual morality was particularly strong yet was neither covert nor disguised by outward

conformity. Without any sign of shame or confusion, his parishioners calmly offered counter-arguments, especially to his condemnation of the "sin" of concubinage. He observed that Afro-Jamaicans considered it less sinful to live together before marriage than
to marry first and have to separate later on. Men explained to him
that it was necessary to live with a woman before marriage in order
to discover whether their tempers were compatible. In response to
his persistent condemnation of their living in sin, they replied that
God was merciful and forgiving.[40] Splaine was

> particularly struck by one girl who said she was not living with
> any man, & backed me up when I urged on Wilson that he ought
> to get married, especially as he had tried his lady for three years.
> Then she added that she would not give any man more than *three
> months*. I took her to task for that & asked her if it was not a sin to
> live for three months in concubinage. She only turned her eyes
> sideways to the sky and asked me no mus' beg de Lard?[41]

When a visiting priest asked a man who had deserted his wife for
a widow if he was living in sin, the man responded, "Es Massa,
but God' eye too pure fo' look upon sin."[42]

Splaine's experiences were not unique. Protestant missionaries
also failed to instill a sense of sin and guilt. Black Jamaicans were
especially skeptical of the Protestant emphasis on man's inherent
sinfulness and on the essential depravity of the human heart. A
Wesleyan missionary observed that Jamaicans always told "the
same story and they are always doing well, never *mourning for sin*,
never *struggling with temptation*." A common Jamaican reply to
Protestant attempts to convince them of the corruption of their
hearts was "Heart quite good, Massa; heart quite good."[43]

Splaine was not entirely negative toward black ethics. As a Catholic priest he was bound to condemn concubinage, but in one remark-

able passage he acknowledged that, although black Jamaican morality was not influenced by Christianity, it nevertheless existed. He commended the fidelity of many common law unions, admitting that Jamaicans disapproved of infidelity and that marriage was indeed the ultimate goal of cohabitation. Splaine also observed that Jamaica had none of the "unnatural sins" of Europe, and he judged the species of immorality he found in Jamaica superior to that of Europe.[44]

Jamaicans' indifference to Splaine's moral teachings resulted not from an amoral attitude but from a different value system. For one thing, many African religions conceive of the Supreme Being as remote from everyday life, and the Afro-Jamaican unconcern with the judgment of God regarding concubinage may stem from this belief. Moreover, morality, in a traditional African context, is horizontal rather than vertical, and the prime determinant of an act's morality is its effect on relationships—hence the nineteenth-century Jamaican Myal notion of sin as an offense, not against God, but against society.[45]

Splaine perceived, however dimly, that Jamaicans had their own reputable value system, but he never conceded its authenticity. In the final analysis, Splaine was paternalistic and racist. He concluded:

> They [black Jamaicans] never will take any interest, any "disinterested" interest in their master's work, and they have not the ballast to be masters. Therefore they must be slaves or servants and they must be held by pain of belly or by pain of back. Beat them or starve them. . . .[46]

CHAPTER 3

Race and Class

Anglican clergymen who were able to remain in the West Indies were those who were the most able to accommodate themselves to the way of life and ideology of the ruling elite. Association with the upper class determined their ambitions and social sympathies. The Anglican church was the white man's church not because only whites belonged—that was not the case. It was the white man's church because the clergy in practice showed that white leadership and membership were its only social legitimization.

Caldecott, the historian of the West Indian Anglican church, claimed that, at the establishment of the See of Jamaica in 1824–25, the new bishop and his clergy were a means of healing the breach between the upper and lower classes by the bond of Christian fellowship.[1] He did not immediately confront the most obviously connected question, which would have been a test of the validity of his claim: did the church heal the breach between white and black?

He distinguished the issues of class and color and dealt with them separately. He stated squarely that, at the time of writing (1898), "The most prominent question in social life in the West Indies is that of the Races"; yet the whites were, "in the orderly and recognized relationships of life, at least, farther than ever from mixing with the humbler races here as in South Africa." Indeed, the church never suggested that the separation of the races be broken down, beyond the "general respect for each other's 'talent' in the present order of things." The church was content with asserting spiritual equality but was laissez-faire with regard to racial equality—or, as Caldecott put it, it "leaves the relations of race to work themselves out in the light of a belief in a common destiny."[2]

Caldecott displayed his racial outlook in his references to the "humbler races." With regard to the Anglican ministry, while claiming that there was open access to its ranks, there was still special caution with black aspirants because of the "known weakness of stability in the lower races, and consequent necessity for longer proof of sincerity on the part of each individual before he is entrusted with grave responsibility." He unabashedly explained that, just as the "mixed race" is immune from some serious forms of disease, they also just as certainly are prone to lives of ease and luxury.[3] These were the operating prejudices in considering nonwhite candidates for the Anglican ministry.

Color prejudice, Caldecott admitted, was not very quickly being worn down in the offices and employments of the church in the West Indies. Indeed, nonwhite as well as white members of Anglican congregations had internalized this prejudice to the extent that, claimed Caldecott, they preferred white men as priests. To belong to a congregation with a nonwhite minister would not carry with it the same prestige. Even in public worship there was still racial segregation at the end of the nineteenth century. Caldecott explained this as really based on distinctions in social class, similar to the social distinctions that would be found in an English parish church.[4] But by making this analogy, he failed to confront the unique relationship of class and color in West Indian life. English social distinctions could not go very far in explaining the divisions of West Indian society, which had their basis in slavery. Furthermore, to attempt to pattern West Indian society along the lines of English social distinctions could only have served to reinforce color as the criterion for determining social class. Thus fixed by this most visible of social symbols, West Indian society could never move toward the equality of a "common destiny." Caldecott was thus being either insincere or naively sanguine in anticipating in 1898 that at least another generation would pass before nonwhites would become an ample source for a native clergy.[5]

A critique and summation of the church's class position during the period was neatly given in a pamphlet entitled *Jamaica in 1866* by the English quakers Thomas Harvey and William Brewin. Harvey was well known as the coauthor, with Joseph Sturge, of *The West Indies in 1837*, a book that was critical of the abuses of apprenticeship and which contributed to the early ending of that system. The authors of the pamphlet argued for disestablishment of the Anglican church in Jamaica, and a major part of the argument was that it was not the church of the mass of the people but of the minority wealthy class:

> The Established Church has far less excuse for its position in Jamaica than in England. It never was the religion of the people: it has no territorial nor historical claims, and its services to the common cause of Christianity, either in regard to the black or white population, have not been conspicuously great. We do not believe in the permanence of the status quo, nor do we think the interests of the Church of England in Jamaica would eventually suffer by its being thrown on Voluntary support.[6]

Whatever Caldecott meant in his claim that the church in Jamaica would be able to heal the breach between the upper and lower classes, it could have meant only one thing to the planters who adhered to the Anglican church. The "bond of fellowship" to them could never have meant the obliteration of the class structure. The social purpose of the church in their eyes was to maintain the hegemony of the master class. This helps to explain the bitterness of the mainly white masters toward those other whites, the Baptist missionaries, who, by their obvious commitment to the freed slaves and their desire to raise the blacks in the social scale, could cause nothing but social chaos. Indeed, the image we receive of the Baptist ministers as allies of the black lower class is due as much to planter definition of the Baptist role as to Baptist testimony itself.

Planters saw the Baptists as involved in a plot or conspiracy to abolish the class distinctions of Jamaican society—"to reduce to their own level every man who is their superior . . . who desire to promote their own interests at the expense and to the injury of every other class in the community. . . ." The Baptists, therefore, were really harming the black ex-slave class as well as the planter class because the consequent disruption of social order could only cause the unhappiness of all classes. The Baptist intent was, according to planter opinion, "to crush entirely the robbed and calumniated planters, to trample them remorselessly under the cloven hoof, and to erect the Baptist Creed as the established Church of Jamaica!"[7]

Two of the clearest expressions of the viewpoint of the Baptist ministers on their endeavors can be found in the sympathetic *Morning Journal* in the issue of 12 February 1839. This issue contained two Baptist addresses to the outgoing governor, Sir Lionel Smith; one was from the pastor of the congregations at Rio Bueno and Stewart Town, Benjamin Dexter, and the other from the Baptist missionaries assembled at their all-island meeting in Montego Bay. Dexter's stated purpose was the extension of the political franchise to the new peasant freeholders. He felt that, if this was thwarted by the legislature, then the Assembly should be abolished and Jamaica governed directly by laws passed in the British Parliament.[8]

In the eyes of the former slave masters, such a suggestion was subversive. While the British government reserved the constitutional right to legislate for the colonies, it had hardly ever done so in those colonies that had wrested from Britain concessions of local legislatures in the seventeenth century. Such legislative freedom had built up in the West Indian colonies that enjoyed it a sentiment of independence similar to that in the North American colonies which led to the actual independence of the United States. Because they were an archipelago of plantations and not a solid land mass well endowed with natural resources that would support industrial self-sufficiency, the islands had never been able to do more than bluff about declaring themselves independent. Nevertheless, the abolition of the slave trade, followed by the abolition of slavery itself—both measures of Parliament in Britain— had been seen by the island plantocracies as death blows to West Indian prosperity. Parliament was the enemy, and many planters in the 1830s entertained themselves with the notion that they might be taken over by the United States and saved from British tyranny. In thus appealing to Parliament as the benefactor of the oppressed peasantry of Jamaica, Dexter was touching a raw nerve, and must have realized that the response to his suggestion would hardly be a moderate one.

The address to Smith by the assembled Baptist missionaries asserted the willingness of the freedmen to labor if treated like human beings and awarded just and reasonable wages. The rebelliousness of the people, the missionaries believed, was caused mainly by planter harassment. They defended themselves as friends of the oppressed and advocates of civil and religious liberty against the misrepresentations and calumnies of their enemies. They also claimed, however, that the charge that they were hostile to the interests of the proprietors as a class was unfounded.[9]

The Methodists, on the other hand, carefully propagandized their image as a middle way between the extremes of class and color, criticizing the Baptists for becoming too identified with one class interest. They lost their respect for Governor Smith because he similarly had become "entangled." Echoing the policy of Governor Metcalfe, the Methodists in 1839 claimed to be "the friends of all and the enemies of none."[10]

They did not, however, criticize the established church for being too closely identified with a certain class interest. Nor did their claims of peace and harmony prevent controversy and defection over the issue of color within the Methodist fold. In spite of themselves, Methodist ministers did betray a bias. It is clear from a reading of their correspondence that the gaining of new members from among the black lower class was never cause for as much jubilation as when the least interest was shown by gentlemen of a higher class. Thus in March 1838, when they commenced open-air preaching in the Kingston parade, one of their ministers happily observed that "not fewer than one third of the whole assemblage were of a class who would have reckoned entering one of our chapels little less than downright fanaticism, and tantamount to sacrificing their proper caste in Society."[11] Many of these gentlemen, no doubt, were drawn out of curiosity. But the Methodists chose to see their presence as a sign of hope of a new respectability for their church after the emancipation controversies they were unwillingly drawn into.

In spite of the disclaimer about being allied with any particular class or color, sheer financial considerations meant that the interests of those who had more to contribute would gain more attention from the Methodist ministers. A large part of Methodist membership in the 1830s consisted of colored small proprietors who were the masters of apprentices. In the absence of figures, an indication of Methodist reliance on this sector was the expectation of a serious falling off of contributions after 1838, when these proprietors would lose their apprentices and have to pay wages.[12]

Consideration of the interests of these proprietors was also perhaps one reason why the Wesleyans attempted to remain aloof from controversies over the term and abuses of apprenticeship. While it is true that Methodist congregations probably contained the greatest variety of skin colors of any other denomination, and in spite of that church's claim to be the friend of all and enemy of none, the feeling existed that they were not quite on solid ground unless they were able to attract the more respectable colored and white proprietors.

In comparison, the question could be asked: why did the Baptists not adopt a policy of seeking to gain membership from all classes and colors? They did not dismiss Christian doctrines of fellowship and reconciliation; instead, their commitment to working for what they perceived as the spiritual and material welfare of those who had been recently emancipated showed them in practical terms the difficulty of reconciliation in the class structure of Jamaica. They realized that they had to emphasize a certain class and color affiliation in order to retain the confidence of the freed population. As Henry Taylor put it in 1835, "If any of the Brethren are too intimate with the white people, the Black people will be very shy of them."[13]

The L.M.S. missionaries were confronted with the same social realities. W. G. Barrett, who at first viewed Baptist efforts favorably but later was to attack their ticket-and-leader system, was told by a black man in 1836 that "Mass minister was too near Busha."[14] This was a warning that he could not hope to be effective among the blacks if he associated too closely with the planter class. Barrett was new to Jamaica in 1835, and he soon learned that he had to make a choice concerning which group he could work with in the class/color spectrum of Jamaica. He deliberately chose to emphasize his work among the "brown" students in his school at Four Paths in Clarendon. Seventy-five students were enrolled in the school; the average attendance was sixty-four. Fourteen of these were brown boys and girls who, Barrett claimed, constituted a distinct class. "These will on account of their parentage occupy hereafter a more respectable and influential station in life than many, and in hope that that influence might be directed in a proper channel I have devoted my attention more especially to them. . . ."[15]

Indeed, Barrett found it necessary for his purposes to teach the children of free coloreds separately from the children of apprentices. Otherwise, he explained, they would have been deprived of religious instruction because the free colored parents refused to have them mix with the children of slaves.[16] Another L.M.S. missionary, Hugh Brown in Mandeville, also felt compelled to segregate black and brown students in his school. Of his sixty-two students, twenty-six were brown and of free parents. He taught the browns in classes separate from the blacks. If he had not, the fathers, most of whom were overseers, would not have sent their children to the school. Brown's curious explanation was that the free colored parents were not motivated by considerations of color but felt that the black children had "filthy habits" which they did not want their colored children to learn.[17]

In any case, a comparison of Baptist and L.M.S. commitments shows that both groups shared the experience of having to adapt to the social fact of class/color conflict in Jamaica if they were to be effective among a particular segment of that society. They chose different groups among which to focus their labor: the Baptists committed themselves to the majority, the emancipated blacks; and the London missionaries made their preferential choices for brown skin in the light of their perception of the structure and conflicts of Jamaican society.

No matter how progressive some nonconformist missionaries appeared to be on social and economic issues, their response was generally incoherent and defensive on matters of race as such. As white-led churches became more concerned with social order, racial controversy was decreasingly an issue they would confront. Where the social structure was symbolized by layers of color, the majority of the missionaries would be reluctant to champion victims of racial discrimination if such advocacy threatened to shake an already precarious social order. Ryall writes that many nonconformist missionaries openly deplored the disdain in which whites, browns, and blacks held each other, and that they tried to dissolve it by fostering friendly association in church and social functions.[18] But association by those who accept their different (superior or subordinate) class positions, and a revolution in the structure of class and race relations, are two different things. Without the latter, fellowship and friendship are fragile and ultimately fail.

Three dramatic developments in the churches illustrate the issue of race. The first two were significant nonconformist secessions, one within the Methodist Conference, the other within Phillippo's Spanish Town Baptist congregation. The third was the controversy surrounding the ordination of the first black Jamaican in the Church of England.

METHODIST SCHISM: PENNOCK'S PROTEST

Mahlon Day noticed during his journey through the West Indies in 1840 that there was a greater class and color mix in Methodist congregations than in Baptist ones.[19] He no doubt was impressed by what would have seemed, without deeper investigation, to be a fortunate example of Christian fellowship. This appearance of reconciliation also compelled the recently appointed governor, Metcalfe, to choose the Welseyan church as the most favorable institution in Jamaica for implementing his moderating policies.

However, the ranks of the Methodists, stereotyped as occupying some stable middle area between Anglicans and Baptists, were actually undergoing some depletion because of controversies of color prejudice. By the time of emancipation, the Methodists were on the verge of internal disruption. During the slave period, colored Methodists resented both the slow promotion of colored ministers and church opposition to the marriage of white English ministers to colored creoles. With the demise of slavery, the issue came to a head rapidly and burst into a two-phased secession movement; the first was led by Edward Jordon, colored publisher and politician, the second by Thomas Pennock, a white Methodist minister. Both phases eventually merged into the Jamaican Wesleyan-Methodist Association.[20]

In March 1834, the missionary Isaac Whitehouse observed that for several years past "the work of God" had been declining in the Kingston circuit of the Wesleyan mission. Referring to the reports of other missionaries, he explained the cause of the decline to be "the prevalence of a political spirit amongst the members of this Society." Whitehouse was probably referring to the increasing free colored discontent with Methodist moderation, for he wrote that "the columns of *The Watchman* [Jordon's newspaper at the time] may throw some light on the subject." He went on to mention that at the time a group wanted to secede and call themselves "Independent Methodists." One colored leader was openly accusing the Wesleyans of color prejudice.[21] About the same time, Thomas Pennock, who was Jamaica district chairman, gave the first indication of the direction he would take. He sided with the coloreds in the growing controversy.[22]

Pennock was clearly in sympathy with the coloreds, and he wrote that because of his views he was losing the affection of the other brethren.[23] But in 1834 he was unsure about what he should do, and he certainly was not ready for any secession over the issue. In fact, he was grieved by Jordon's initial breakaway move: "I am very sorry to inform you that some of our respectable coloured and black people in Kingston, the Editor of the *Watchman* for one, have withdrawn themselves from our Society," and he feared that the whole of them might do so.[24] The colored plan was to form an Independent Wesleyan Methodist Society, with their own ministers. Two or three of the regular missionaries who were not suspected of color prejudice were invited to join. At that time, February 1834, Pennock, still maintaining an ideal of Methodist unity, felt able to assert that they "very properly" refused to join. About the same time also, another missionary reported that "our Chairman had a formal request to be its head, which I am happy to say he indignantly spurned."[25]

One issue was that of romantic association with ladies of color. During the year two young missionaries, Walters and Rowden, fell out of favor with the majority of their brethren because "both these young men were supposed to be paying attention to young ladies of colour—the coloured people have seemed resolved to defend them at all hazards," wrote Isaac Whitehouse, a senior missionary.[26]

Methodist records do not say much about what happened to young Walters, beyond his having been put on probation because of his engagement to a colored lady. Pennock had been overruled at the last district meeting in his defense of Walters. His appeal to the home committee that Walters's full connection with the society as a missionary be confirmed and that he be permitted to marry immediately appeared to be in vain.[27]

When Walters was called upon by the district publicly to exonerate the member missionaries from color prejudice, he at first declined to do so. Then he decided otherwise. Choosing, of all media, the *Watchman* to publish his statement, he wrote, "It devolves upon me to observe that the Rev. Gentlemen so maligned, have condescendingly disavowed being actuated in the discharge of their important duties and determinations in my case, by any feeling or principle but that of justice, prudence, affection, and discipline." The irony of the statement, compounded by its having been printed in the dissident Jordon's *Watchman* (1 Feb., 1834), was not lost on the missionaries.[28]

It is recorded that Rowden was not given a circuit, the reward for a successful probation. It was officially claimed that the reason was ill health, not his attachment to a woman of color. Nevertheless, all the Methodist missionaries, except Pennock and the younger brethren, were accused by the coloreds of showing prejudice in the affair. Missionary authorities suggested to Rowden that he should remove from the scene of "excitement and temptation" in Kingston to Spanish Town, under the "care and superintendence" of the missionary there, Mr. Corlett. Rowden refused. Instead, he moved into the residence of Edward Jordon.[29]

In the several cases of white Methodist missionaries becoming engaged to, or actually marrying, colored ladies, not once were they successful in acquiring or maintaining full standing as district missionaries.[30] No cases are revealed in the correspondence of any 'respectable' Methodist missionaries marrying outside of their own color.

After the Walters and Rowden cases, Pennock began to lean more and more toward the colored cause:

> ... the feeling on the part of the coloured people towards some of your missionaries is as strong as ever. I do very much fear that a split among the members of our Society will be the result. Much however depends on the steps the Committee take in this painful and unpleasant affair. I am blamed by the accused brethren for not coming out publicly and defending them against the charge of prejudice. But I have candidly told them that I neither can nor will act contrary to my own conscience.[31]

In July 1834, the Committee in England received an anonymous and undated letter from Jamaica. The letter was written specifically to support the charge of prejudice in the Walters case. The missionaries had shamefully lowered themselves in this affair, the writer affirmed. They were determined to prevent Walters from continuing his attachment to a colored woman. Every person of color in and out of the society felt the insult. "The result is that several of respectability have left the Society, among which is the Editor of the *Watchman* who must feel himself much aggrieved after all that he has suffered in the cause of Methodism, and Religion in general." One of the missionaries, the writer reported, had accosted Walters "and advised him to keep up his respectability and character as he was genteely brought up and he must not let himself down." The writer especially blamed the missionary wives; Mrs. Corlett and Mrs. Whitehouse are mentioned in particular. The women of color, he asserted, were superior in every respect to the missionary wives.[32]

Pennock grew increasingly disillusioned with his brethren in Jamaica. By 1837, his break was clearly imminent. Jonathan Edmondson had been appointed district chairman by that year, and in May he chaired a meeting to consider the case of Pennock, who was then openly criticizing the character of many of the brethren as well as Wesleyan doctrine and discipline in general. He refused to answer a summons to the meeting and sent only the note: "I have come to the determination of resigning at once and I do hereby this day resign all connexion with *Methodism as it is* ."[33]

Pennock's break gave impetus to a renewal of the separatist movement led by Jordon. Edmondson would concede nothing to them, calling them only "backsliders" and "factious members." He refused to enter a newspaper war, thinking that the issue would die quietly. He desperately tried to maintain some optimism in the face of what promised to be a large defection from the district's congregations.

The Grateful Hill congregation had already shown that they would accept no district missionary and would choose their own minister instead.[34]

The Methodist missionaries put up a self-righteous defense, and one of their most respectable spokesmen, Henry Bleby, accused Pennock of being a traitor, with all the cowardly connotations of that word.[35] But a more telling way of countering accusations of color prejudice was turning them around by claiming that the whites were actually the objects of prejudice on the part of the coloreds. The Rev. Mr. John Randerson wrote from Kingston in October 1837: "The most influential people in this City are colored men. They are closely united together and do not possess the most kind feelings towards the whites." Randerson claimed it was part of the strategy of the coloreds to circulate the idea that the missionaries hated them. However, his explanation why coloreds had not yet achieved ministerial status in the Methodist church lends itself to criticism on the grounds of certain prejudicial ideas as to the personality of coloreds:

> Many of the coloured young men in our society were wishful to become preachers, but they had neither gifts nor graces for the work. In fact as I have observed again and again, when a young man of this class was made into a prayer leader, an exhorter, or a Class Leader he became so proud that he was unmanageable and was continually taking offence. The opposite party have taken advantage of our prudence in keeping such persons in their place which we did for their own sakes and the good of the Society— and they say that we do not encourage native talent and our object is to perpetuate a race of white preachers in the island.[36]

Randerson exempted some coloreds from his judgment—"we have many who are humble, devout, zealous, and ornaments to our cause. . . . They do not meddle in politics which has been the ruin of the others."[37]

Wesleyan policy on a native ministry had been put to the test by the case of T. E. Ward, a colored leader. The district had refused in 1834 to accept Ward's application to become a full minister. It was Pennock's opinion that racial discrimination was the explanation for this. In March 1834 Ward himself wrote to the Committee in London about his treatment at the hands of the Jamaica District Committee. He had been waiting fourteen months for a decision from London concerning his acceptance as a missionary and had just received the reply that he had been put on trial, a period of probation previous to examination and confirmation as a missionary. In his letter, Ward asked to be allowed to work in Jamaica or at least somewhere in the West Indies, "as a great, and an effectual door is on the eve of being opened in the West Indies, by the expected change in the vast Negro population. . . ." It seems that he was being considered only for work in West Africa. It is remarkable that a prospective creole colored missionary had to request specifically to be allowed to remain in the West Indies. At the same time, at least one Methodist missionary, Mr. Wedlock, suggested that Ward be kept in Jamaica to counteract the increasing claims of color prejudice against the brethren.[38]

In June 1837, Pennock acknowledged that he was setting up his own society in Kingston. Jordon and Osborn "and a considerable number of backsliders and disaffected members," as Edmondson put it, espoused Pennock's movement.[39] They collected between three and four hundred pounds toward a chapel and burial ground. Ten colored leaders and about three hundred members, chiefly from Parade Chapel, left to follow Pennock. Edmondson was still adamant on refusing a public confrontation, claiming that he could kill the adversary with silence. Encouraged by what they saw as Pennock's courage, black and colored local preachers began to strike, on the ground that they were not appreciated by the white missionaries. "It is evident they have been influenced by Pennock's proceedings, as he talks largely about selecting and employing native ministers, etc.," wrote one missionary.[40]

The missionaries tried to downplay the significance of Pennock's protest, but they were clearly nervous about the admittedly powerful colored group. Edmondson wrote to England about these "brown men, Members of Assembly, Aldermen or Common Council men in the Corporate Body, having partial control over different public funds, and as they took an active part in obtaining the Civil privileges of the colored and black people, they are possessed of great influence."[41]

These influential coloreds insisted that some of the leading men of the British Methodist Conference were pro-slavery in their hearts. They offered to support Pennock's movement because the secessionists proposed to raise funds to support the poor, to bury the dead without charging fees, and to turn the financial management of the movement over to colored stewards and leaders.[42]

Edmondson tried to be optimistic that the secession would fail— inconsistently at the same time offering evidence that it was not abating. In August 1837, he reported that the Pennockite movement was spreading from Grateful Hill to Spanish Town, Vere, and the north side of the island. Jordon and Osborn continued to exhort the coloreds to abandon the Methodist Conference, and leaders continued to leave. The conference admitted losing one thousand members in 1837 to Pennock in Kingston alone.[43]

The secessionists raised issues that the missionaries were not willing to confront. Loyal ministers in the Methodist Conference explained the defections by referring to the weakness and gullibility of the negro character—and thereby, in a sense, corroborated the secessionists' charges of prejudice. The secessionists were considered to be acting from malevolent motives or blindly, with no motive at all. Some of the missionaries were in fact terrified by the secession and feared attacks on their lives. But there seems to be no evidence that the secessionists threatened violence.[44]

Nineteenth-century missionary historians and chroniclers gave very brief or hostile attention to Pennock and the Jamaican Wesleyan-Methodist Association. The significance of the secession was either ignored or missed by them.[45] Such dismissals of the case do not confront sufficiently the passion of Pennock's protest: "I do in my conscience most firmly believe that many of your Missionaries are deeply prejudiced against *Colour*," he wrote.[46]

The movement calling itself the Wesleyan Association did not subside. In 1845, it was still strong enough, in fact, for a missionary to be sent from England explicitly to combat the influence of the Pennockites.[47] The association lasted as a separate group until 1864. An item in the *Falmouth Post* in May of that year read:

> We learn that the Jamaican Wesleyan Methodist Association, is about to amalgate with the United Methodist Free Church in this island, of which the Reverend Abraham Hyamns is the Superintendent, and which is a branch of the church in the Mother Country, bearing that designation. The Association is purely a native body, has three ministers, and seven chapels, and numbers about eleven hundred members. It was founded by the Reverend Thomas Pennock.[48]

While the association provided for a time a haven for disaffected black and colored Methodists, many nonwhite Methodists, following the motivations of social striving that led them to the Methodists in the first place, defected to the Anglican church. Philip Curtin, who comments on this in his study on the divisions within nineteenth-century Jamaica, observes that these defections served to strengthen the desire of Methodist ministers to disassociate themselves even further from the black mass of the people and to strive more than ever for respectability in the class and color terms of mid–nineteenth-century Jamaican society.[49]

DISSENSION AMONG THE BAPTISTS: DOWSON AND PHILLIPPO

Thomas Dowson, sent out from England by the Baptist Missionary Society, arrived in Jamaica early in 1842 to assist J. M. Phillippo, the pastor in Spanish Town.[50] The relationship between these two English missionaries was initially cordial, even affectionate. Later in 1842, Phillippo went to England to recover from a throat ailment that had threatened to end his preaching career. Dowson wrote to him from Spanish Town:

> I love the people more and more in proportion as I know them
> and I flatter myself that they love and respect and have confidence
> in me increasingly in return. The two or three wicked white mon-
> sters whose deeds of darkness you have exposed are trying to vex
> the people by speaking disrespectfully of you.[51]

All of the early letters from Dowson to Phillippo have the same tone of respect for him. There was no indication that there would develop between the two one of the stormiest conflicts among Baptist missionaries in nineteenth-century Jamaica. The importance of the conflict is not only that it deeply shook Baptist optimism and unity but that attitudes toward race and native leadership were involved.

Phillippo returned to Jamaica in March 1844. The simplest explanation for what followed is that, during this two-year absence, Dowson's relationship with the people had developed to the extent where many of them preferred him to Phillippo for pastor. According to a later *Morning Journal* summary of Chancery Court proceedings, the dispute was over whether, in May of 1844, Phillippo announced his intention of making Dowson "co-pastor," and whether as part of this arrangement Dowson would remain in charge of Spanish Town while Phillippo would remove to Sligoville. Phillippo and his supporters claimed that this never happened. In any event, during the year following Phillippo's return, the congregation divided into the two factions; and in March 1845, the Dowsonites claimed, a majority of the Spanish Town congregation voted to remove Phillippo and replace him with Dowson as pastor.[52]

Phillippo maintained that there was no such thing as a Baptist congregation retaining the right of deposition, and that a minister, once approved and admitted, holds his office for life, and no civil or ecclesiastical authority can remove the pastor, except by injunction from the lord chancellor based upon substantial evidence of immorality. Other missionaries, however, in support of Dowson, claimed that the Baptist system was entirely democratic, that the power to depose was inherent in the power to elect, and that a minister had no right to continue if voted out by a majority.[53]

A separate chapel or "booth" was erected by the Dowsonites in January 1845. The election of Dowson on 5 March took place there, presided over by a Mr. Harry, a trustee under the foundation deed of 1821 but not a member of the congregation. It appears that other nonmembers were present also. Phillippo locked the Dowsonites out of the burial ground. On 25 March, they entered it to bury a deceased member of their group. On 26 March, in Dowson's absence, his people seized the chapel. The militia was called in to persuade them to leave. By April, nine black deacons had gone over to Dowson; four remained with Phillippo. Dowson, whose followers amounted to about twelve hundred, maintained that the erection of the booth and the seizure of the chapel were not suggested by him but were spontaneous moves on the part of his people.[54]

Most of the missionaries supported the older and renowned Phillippo. Thomas Abbott showed himself neutral and offered the suggestion that both Dowson and Phillippo leave the Spanish Town mission entirely, "there being *no* prospect of their working together, and but little of either being able to reunite the divided Church." Messrs. Hands, Lynch, Reid, Evans, Wood, and Taylor arranged themselves on Dowson's side; and Phillippo suspected that Samuel Oughton was also pro-Dowson.[55]

The case against Phillippo, as developed by these pro-Dowson missionaries, was that Phillippo had dismissed Dowson in opposition to the wishes of the majority, thereby violating the principles of dissenting congregations. He refused the people a meeting to discuss the matter, thus precipitating their withdrawal and the erection of a separate booth. Phillippo also refused burial on the chapel grounds of a Miss McLean, identified as Dowson's sister-in-law, a course of action "calculated to influence the passions of the people—which in fact it did." According to Evans, she had been one of the most respectable members of the Spanish Town Baptist congregation. Phillippo called out the police to guard the burial ground and obstruct the burial. When the people successfully carried out the burial, Phillippo allegedly raised a party to exhume the body at midnight. It was this that "so influenced the people as to cause them to proceed 'en masse' to the mission premises and finding the gate open to proceed to occupy the Chapel."[56]

In his own defense, Phillippo maintained that he had throughout attempted to avoid all strife and resentment. Dowson and his followers, he asserted, did exactly the opposite; they spared no artifices to accomplish their "unworthy purposes." Phillippo claimed support by "numbers of the most respectable inhabitants of the town." (About two years later, however, he wrote that Custos Ramsay was "almost the only avowed friend I have of respectability.") Concerning Baptist ministers who supported Dowson, their conduct was "cruel," "vacillating," and "dishonest." Phillippo attacked his attackers: "The Committee may rely upon the statement that, with but one or two exceptions, the leaders of this cabal are the most uninfluential and disreputable characters in the church." He quite firmly believed that he, his wife, and family were in jeopardy of their lives from the Dowsonites, who, claimed Phillippo, were "rabble," "dregs of the church," "scum," with no other motives than excitable passions.[57]

Only a little less viciously, but more informatively, he also described them as "surrounded by cunning and rapacious legal advisers, by a base political faction of which they are the tools, and encouraged by men calling themselves Christian Ministers." His accusations were broadly scattered: the sole object of the Dowsonites "is to get possession of the *premises* to which they are urged by a base political faction and a combination of high Churchmen, Jews, and Infidels.— By the former in the hope that the result may prove a death blow to voluntaryism and dissent—to the Baptist influence by the rest with a view to the banishment of real religion from the land—."[58]

Dowson was not without influential and "respectable" support. The prominent solicitors W. W. Anderson and W. J. March were his legal advisers. March, a colored member of Assembly, was mentioned in a letter of a Mr. C. Harvey, who was Phillippo's solicitor; Harvey concludes in his letter: "I cannot help thinking that this controversy is but a political contest of *colour* of which Mr. Dowson is made the scapegoat." Phillippo iterated Harvey's accusation when he wrote that Dowson was "the tool of a political faction whose object is to revolutionize the island."[59]

Racial feeling was an integral element in the whole controversy.

The Dowsonites accused Phillippo of being two-faced: of speaking well of the black people in their presence but abusing and vilifying them when speaking about them in England. They also felt that a strong anti-black bias came out in his history of Jamaica, *Jamaica, Its Past and Present State,* published in 1843 before the Dowsonite challenge arose. Phillippo responded:

> The latter has been one of the most serious charges against me. It was first made by Duggan (I think a deacon in Dowson's party) who was in the habit of reading all the portions of it which, though they might be quotations I introduced in order to disprove what was unfavourable to the black and coloured people, he wished to be believed were my sentiments. Mr. Dowson has followed in the same track although he once spoke extravagantly in its praise. He denounces the book and has raised such prejudices against it as that some of the people are ready to burn it, whilst he has quite succeeded in stopping the sail [*sic*]. The prejudices of the mass, indeed, are so general on this account that many of my own people have expressed their regret that I should have written it. . . . Thus the general opinion among the black people is, that I have abused them in a shameful manner in the book and they look upon me as a traitor to themselves and the country.[60]

Another of Dowson's ploys, according to Phillippo, was his telling the people that the regular Baptist missionaries were robbing them, whereas he would preach to them for nothing and would help provide them with money when they needed it.[61]

The B.M.S. Committee in England gave detached support and sympathy to Phillippo, but he constantly expressed his disappointment at their lack of more positive moral and financial support. He repeatedly asked the committee to disavow Dowson publicly, but they took no action in this regard. The B.M.S. did give

Phillippo power of attorney over the chapel and mission premises. But Cornford, a Baptist missionary who otherwise supported and defended Phillippo, argued that, because the Baptist system was congregational, and because the Jamaican Baptists had become independent in 1842, the B.M.S. had no right to interfere in the controversy. A B.M.S. deputation to Jamaica in 1846–47 consisting of the Revs. Angus and Birrell attempted but failed to bring about a reconciliation between Phillippo and Dowson.[62]

The whole affair almost succeeded in driving Phillippo from Jamaica. He actually wrote of the probability of his resigning and asking for a mission in another part of the world, "a more quiet and retired sphere. . . . Probably the Committee would accept me for China." What held him back, he claimed, from retiring immediately was his certainty that the mission premises would fall to the Dowsonite "rabble."[63]

The case went through almost seven years of litigation. It reached its end on 4 November 1850 in the High Court of Chancery of the island. The vice-chancellor decided for Phillippo on the grounds that Dowson could not prove that the meeting in March 1845 that elected him to replace Phillippo was a clear and democratic majority of the members of the Spanish Town Baptist Church. Even though the final decision was in Phillippo's favor, the Dowsonites on the whole did not return but set up the Independent Baptist Chapel in Spanish Town. And in the following year they twice attempted, without success, to gain possession of the mission property.[64]

The Dowsonite controversy gives occasion to examine more closely Phillippo's attitudes towards blacks. The reputation of the Baptist missionaries as champions of the rights of the emancipated people is well established. And Phillippo's well-deserved part in that reputation cannot be denied when one studies his activities and views prior to the 1840s. Rather than going into detail on the point here, it is sufficient to note his expression of his own political theology.[65]

Yet however admirable Phillippo's principles of political involvement were, and however beneficial for the blacks were actions based on those principles, they nevertheless rested partially on values that were culturally imperialistic. For Phillippo, they were based on his idealization and exaltation of British history, specifically in his apparent reduction of progress to the oppositions of the Protestant forefathers and their spiritual children to despotism and darkness: ". . . through their political exertions England is now a land of liberty and of Bibles, the recipient and the almoner of God's best Gifts to man."[66] The ex-slaves, abstracted from their blackness and the specifics of an Afro-creole culture, were worthy of these gifts precisely (only?) as British subjects.

Phillippo's ideas, then, did not prepare him for manifestations of black self-assertion, especially when his authority would be directly challenged. How could the receivers of gifts dare to be ungrateful? The Dowsonite conflict was a turning point in Phillippo's judgment of negro character. His previous optimism had eroded. Before, he had seen the blacks as grateful, docile to those in authority, and peculiarly impressionable to religious instruction. But he came to see that liberty had not corrected the tendencies of barbarism and savagery—almost (in the thought that Underhill puts into his mind) as if Homer's words were verified: "Half our virtue is torn away when a man becomes a slave, and the other half when he becomes a slave let loose."[67] Whatever the validity to the charge that Phillippo's book was anti-black, in the wake of the Dowsonite challenge his characterizations of blacks became vituperative: blacks had no endurance, they were subject to extremes in emotion, and they were inconsistent in duty. He claimed that among the followers of Dowson "the worst passions of half-civilized men were let loose. . . ."[68]

It is not possible from documentary sources to cite the specific passages in *Jamaica, Its Past and Present State* on which the Dowsonites based their charges of anti-black abuse. Yet it is instructive in consideration of their accusation to review Phillippo's views on Africans and their culture as these views are either implied or stated in his book. Baptist confidence and optimism had not yet been seriously eroded when the book was published, Phillippo had not yet reached the midway point of his career in Jamaica, and he had not yet undergone the Dowsonite challenge. In his apocalyptic view, Christianity was at battle with the gods of the heathen nations. He had two paradigms, the depraved African and the redeemed Christian.[69] With these in mind, he interpreted his experience in Jamaica.

Phillippo cannot be accused of biological racism. He considered the African, as a human being abstracted from all historical conditioning, to be equal physically, mentally, and emotionally to the European. Yet his bias against the inherited African culture of the Jamaican blacks was extreme. Their relationships were licentious; their music was rude and monotonous, and their singing consisted of hideous yells and discordant sounds; their dance was various contortions with strange and indecent attitudes; their religion consisted of barbarous customs, numberless incantations, and dark and magical rites; their funeral practices in particular were unnatural and revolting in a high degree. What we might see as a rich and varied religious tradition is demeaned in Phillippo's account of it: "Most of the negroes appear to have possessed some notion of a Supreme Being; though, like all uncivilized nations, their ideas of the Deity were very confused and unbecoming." Further: "Some of them were Papists; some professedly belonged to the Coptic or Abyssinian churches; some were Mohammedans; some Polytheists and Atheists: but most of them idolaters—worshippers of the sun and moon, of the ocean, of the rocks, and fountains and rivers, of lofty trees, and images of various forms and dimensions." The abolition of the slave trade

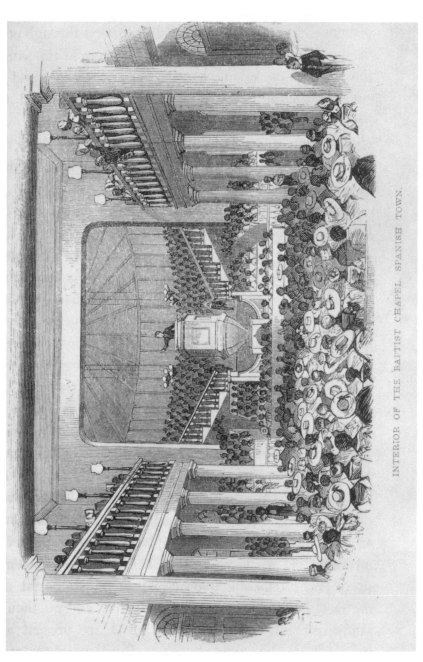

INTERIOR OF THE BAPTIST CHAPEL, SPANISH TOWN.

3. "Interior of the Baptist Chapel, Spanish Town." From J. M. Phillippo, Jamaica, Its Past and Present State, 1843. Reproduced with permission of the General Research Division of the New York Public Library and the Astor, Lenox, and Tilden Foundations.

HEATHEN PRACTICES AT FUNERALS.

4. "Heathen Practices at Funerals." From J. M. Phillippo, Jamaica, Its Past and Present State, 1843. Reproduced with permission of the General Research Division of the New York Public Library and the Astor, Lenox, and Tilden Foundations.

had been fortunate for the Christian mission in Jamaica because the cutting off of the supply of Africans had also cut off the source of "ignorance, superstition, and profligacy" in Jamaica.[70]

All of this, Phillippo asserted, had virtually disappeared in Jamaica by 1842. And the cause of disappearance had been Christian teaching:

> What else [but the spirit of the Christian God] could have influenced the poor African slave, accustomed from his youth to superstition and idolatry, to rioting and mirth, to licentious indulgence and secret abominations, to cast off the works of darkness—to surrender his beloved lusts—to "live soberly, righteously, and godly."[71]

This, then, was Phillippo's stereotype of the African and Afro-creole, in his mind a reality which had been conquered by a new reality, the Christian blackman, which, in effect, was a new stereotype.[72] He was soon disabused of his optimistic view of the redeemed African by the challenge to him by that same Christian black under the aegis of Mr. Dowson.

It is ironic that Phillippo listed the Rev. Samuel Oughton among his opponents in the Dowsonite controversy, because there were at least two similar occurrences in Oughton's congregation, in 1843 and 1854–55. Concerning the earlier case, Phillippo himself included in one of his letters a note written by the solicitor Harvey about an action in the Court of Common Pleas involving a Mr. Lagourgue, "a Native Baptist preacher against Mr. Oughton, the Baptist Minister, for an assault, and false imprisonment. The action originated out of the late differences respecting the possession of the class house in Beeston Street. The jury found for the plaintiff with £20 damages."[73] The second incident involved a similar challenge from a native preacher, and is recounted by Clarke in his *Memorials* . In both cases, the black people felt that the church or mission premises belonged to them because they had subscribed toward the cost of building and maintenance. They were encouraged by black leaders to insist on being able to choose their pastor and conduct their own financial administration. It was because of incidents such as these that the Baptists would begin to accept criticism by other missionaries of their leader system and admit drawbacks.[74] For in these cases, black leaders did not simply drop away and form their own congregations, which was the usual procedure, but challenged white Baptist leadership directly.

RACISM IN THE ANGLICAN CHURCH: THE CASE OF ROBERT GORDON

The split between the white-led churches and native religious groups might not have occurred to the extent that it did had there been more positive efforts by white ministers to encourage a native ministry. By 1860, the Baptist Union had fourteen native ministers out of a total of thirty-six, with five more still in training at Calabar College; nevertheless, the predominant Baptist view at the time was that it would be many years before it would be possible or wise to rely on a native ministry. Indeed, a visiting deputation in 1859, headed by Edward Underhill of the B.M.S., recommended the recruitment of more Europeans.[75]

The Methodist-initiated normal seminary of 1842 attracted only four students in its first three months and was closed only a little over a year after its establishment. The reason given was the spirit of insubordination among the students, "encouraged by the radical opinions and prevalent spirit of opposition to things legitimately constituted," wrote the outgoing administrator, "which even in our own Society is unbecomingly in the ascendant."[76] The purpose of the Methodist seminary, in fact, had not been to create a native ministry but simply to train native teachers.

The seriousness of any Methodist claims that they would welcome a qualified native ministry was challenged by the case of one of their local preachers in 1842, a Jamaican native named Cyrus Francis Perkins. The missionaries of the western section of the district refused his request to be accepted as an assistant missionary. In fact, he was to be superseded by candidates sent out from England and was told to return to his secular trade, and this after five years as a preacher. The Methodists claimed that they simply did not have time to work on the training of a native ministry.[77] Congregationalist opinion on the question of a native ministry resembled that of the Baptists and Methodists. W. G. Barrett of the L.M.S. expressed the opinion that if the home committee had to choose between colored and white ministers for Jamaica, it could not hesitate to choose the latter. The blacks, he observed, disliked coloreds extremely, and the whites "have the most inveterate prejudice against the least vestige of African blood."[78]

It was only because of the C.M.S. that the Anglican church can be said to have fostered native leadership, and even then only as teachers and catechists, in the years after emancipation. The experience of the C.M.S. led that society to acknowledge the inability of young European teachers to communicate effectively with the Jamaican peasantry.[79] Bishop Lipscomb, however, had no intention of encouraging native leadership and was busy searching England for graduates of Oxford, Cambridge, and Dublin to build up his curacy in Jamaica.[80] Bishops Spencer and Courtenay likewise ignored black Jamaicans as a source for their clergy.

Had he known of it, the Anglican historian Caldecott, writing in the 1890s, would have concurred with Barrett's 1835 observation on the extent of color prejudice in the Jamaican churches. He would have added that the situation had not changed by the end of the century. He did observe that, as long as qualified men could be found in England for the West Indian episcopacy, there would remain in Jamaica a preference for Englishmen, just as—he asserted in a pointed aside—there was a preference for Englishmen to be principals of the Baptist Calabar College, or conference presidents and pastors in the Wesleyan and Congregational churches.[81] In the light of Caldecott's observations, the ordination of a black man in the Anglican church in Jamaica would have been revolutionary. Yet Caldecott, as well as the chroniclers and historians of the other denominations, ignored the case of Robert Gordon, the first black Jamaican to become a priest in the Anglican church.

"I am a native of Jamaica, and of pure African blood. . . . I was the first man of my race, in Jamaica, who had ever reached the priesthood. The Bishop's treatment of me has considerably tended, as I can prove, to facilitate the present prostrate condition of the Church."[82] In these words from a letter written in January 1868, Gordon indicated what he perceived as the turmoil caused by his ordination. In this and other writings, he also showed that he was specifically conscious of himself as a black man and aware of the important social and political statement made by his being ordained. The documentary evidence concerning Gordon is not clear on all of the issues involved in what was an important crisis in the history of the Anglican church in Jamaica; that race was a major issue, however, is undeniable.

Gordon was born about 1830 to black creole parents who were probably free, although Gordon's correspondence is unclear on this point. In spite of his parents being Methodists, the young Gordon found himself "instinctively inclined" to the Church of England. As a ten-year-old boy in Kingston, he vowed to devote himself to the Anglican ministry.[83]

At the age of seventeen he became a catechist and went on to teach at Highgate in St. Mary and at the East Branch Episcopal School in Kingston. It was also at the age of seventeen that he determined to educate himself for the clergy. He presented himself for examination on arriving at the canonical age of twenty-three, in 1853. It was at this point that Gordon's story takes on a wider significance, beyond being merely an interesting personal memoir: "As it has ever been the policy of the Jamaican church to exclude the black man from preaching the Gospel, obstacles were ever after studiously raised to prevent the realization of my object."[84]

In 1853, Gordon applied to Aubrey Spencer, the Bishop of Jamaica, for ordination. Spencer's response was to offer Gordon a place at Codrington College in Barbados, to prepare to be a missionary to West Africa. He was immediately suspicious of this offer, which meant that, if he were to be a priest, it would not be in Jamaica but somewhere else, and rejected it.[85]

Spencer soon thereafter retired to England because of poor health, leaving the administration of the diocese to his auxiliary, Reginald Courtenay, bishop of Kingston. Gordon repeated his application for the ministry in Jamaica to Courtenay. The bishop did not initially discourage him, "though," wrote Courtenay, "I had grave doubts concerning him . . . he had forfeited all claims to special indulgence by his refusal to undergo a regular training."[86] This training, however, had been specifically presented to Gordon as preparation for the ministry outside of Jamaica, whereas he was applying for a ministry in the island.

In 1857, or shortly thereafter, Gordon left for England because of the frustration of his plans in Jamaica. There he was appointed by an Anglican missionary group, the Colonial Church and School Society, to the mission of London in Canada. It appears to have been a black or at least racially mixed community, as Courtenay identified it as "a place of concourse for refugees from Slavery in the United States,"[87] most likely an end station of the Underground Railroad. Six months after arriving in Canada, he was ordained deacon, and a year after that a priest, by the bishop of Huron.

It is probable that Gordon's intention from the first was not to remain abroad but to return and work as a priest in Jamaica. Most of the facts of the case are available through a printed circular headed "To the Clergy of the Island of Jamaica" from Courtenay, dated 6 December 1861, and so are colored by the bishop's interpretation of them. He wrote that, on the grounds of ill health, Gordon "unannounced and uninvited came to this Diocese, and again applied to me." Courtenay outlined his case against Gordon. He had no letters of recommendation from the Bishop of Huron or the Church and School Society. He had precipitously and irresponsibly abandoned his Canadian post. Courtenay advised Gordon to apply again to the society for employment. "I find, however," wrote the bishop, "that the Committee of that Society have formed a very unfavourable opinion of Mr. Gordon, regret his ordination, and would not employ him again."[88]

Subsequently, Gordon did produce a letter of recommendation from the bishop of Huron, who spoke of him kindly and favorably and expressed his hope that he would be "usefully employed, as a Minister of the Church, amongst his people."[89] The context of Courtenay's mention of this fact allows interpretation of it as a suggestion that the bishop of Huron was saying politely that he did not wish Gordon to return to his diocese.

Courtenay's circular was an attempt by him to vindicate his judgment in refusing employment to Gordon in Jamaica. The bulk of the circular was a reproduction of a previous response of the bishop to a petition, received in April of 1861, in favor of Gordon. The bishop felt compelled to answer because the memorial bore the signatures of "several gentlemen of consideration in Kingston"; the list was headed by the name of Edward Jordon, who had played an important part in the Methodist schism, a crisis centered on charges of color prejudice against the Methodist missionaries. Courtenay's response was addressed to Jordon as the chief spokesman of those who supported Gordon in the present controversy.

The petitioners had alluded to Gordon's previous history, and it can be inferred that from their viewpoint they found no overwhelming fault in that history to prevent their wholehearted recommendation. Courtenay began his response to them by announcing his formal policy—that it had always been "at once to raise the standard of qualifications in Holy Orders, and to encourage youthful candidates for the Ministry wherever they could be found if apparently pious and sincere."[90] He followed with the declaration that he had no personal prejudice against Gordon, and explained, "I was very far from insensible of the advantages I should acquire, by proving myself superior to all prejudices, and by assisting merit in its efforts to rise, and, in fact, I have in more instances than one, rather gone beyond others, than fallen behind them in the measure of encouragement that I was disposed to afford Mr. Gordon."[91]

The bishop cited some popular feeling against Gordon, in order to counter the unconditional recommendation of the petitioners and to support his own adverse opinion of the man. The inhabitants of Highgate, for example, where Gordon had worked as a catechist, had sent the bishop "a very energetic protest" when they heard that Gordon was seeking ordination, a protest based "on certain immoralities of his, which had caused scandal in the district." There was other agitation against Gordon's ordination, but the bishop was not explicit on the nature of it. The signers of the petition in support of Gordon later referred to Courtenay's response as "a tissue of frivolities."[92]

The bishop left Jamaica on 25 June 1861 to visit England. "Scarcely had I left the Island before attempts were made in some of the Newspapers to represent Mr. Gordon as a much injured man, the victim of prejudice on my part on account of his colour." To strengthen his own defense in the controversy, he made further inquiries and found "that the representation that Mr. Gordon had left his employment in Canada, with an unblemished character, in consequence of the coldness of the climate, was false." He was, claimed the bishop, given six months' salary in advance, dismissed, and asked to leave the country.[93] Courtenay, however, could not adequately explain away the positive endorsement of Gordon by the bishop of Huron. He was adamant in demanding that, as the indispensable condition for employing Gordon, he wanted from him formal acknowledgement of the truth concerning Canada, a "necessary humiliation." He wrote, "Mr. Gordon has shown the greatest reluctance to do this; a reluctance which justifies my decision, and confirms me in my determination to adhere to it."[94] Throughout Bishop Courtenay's correspondence, Gordon is characterized as being insolent, unwise, and immoral, although a dearth of information is presented to verify the characterization.

In January 1868, Gordon wrote an autobiographical letter to the secretary of the S.P.G. He gave his own viewpoint on the Canadian adventure. Unfortunately, he was as vague on details as the bishop of Kingston was in his circular. For some reason that Gordon did not describe, the local committee in Canada of the Church Society objected to his efforts. On this point, Gordon's information coincided with that of Courtenay. He admitted that the committee recommended, in a resolution to the parent society, that he be given six months' pay, and that someone else be put in his place. He defended himself in writing, but they adhered to their resolution.

In spite of the committee's stand against Gordon, it seems clear that the bishop of Huron himself continued to support him. In fact, it was when the trouble started that he offered to ordain Gordon as a full priest; he had previously ordained him deacon. "The Bishop [of Huron], who, although Chairman of the Committee, yet took no part in their hostile action, voluntarily offered to hold a special ordination to ordain me Priest, in order that I may be convinced that his feelings towards me had undergone no change."[95]

Gordon admitted that in Canada his labors had been "tinctured" with "imperfections and shortcomings." Nevertheless, he experienced "no ordinary degree of happiness" there. Upon his departure, his congregation presented him with an address of their personal affection, a purse of money, and various kinds of souvenirs. All of these things, "which were given me, on my leaving Canada, by black, white, and coloured, testify to my worth."

The bishop of Kingston had written of Gordon's return to Jamaica as "unannounced and uninvited." The harshness of attitude suggested by his choice of words is confirmed by Gordon's own account of his return:

> . . . having returned to Jamaica, in the early part of 1860, I threw myself, *ad miserecordiam*, on the Christian consideration of the Bishop of Kingston. The recollection of the studied indignities and cruel unkindnesses which, it seemed, Dr. Courtenay felt an unenviable pleasure to subject me to, because I did not think with him that "Africa was my proper sphere of duty," must ever be bitterly coeval with the existence of my memory. I appealed to him when I was suffering from the want of the necessaries of life, and he treated me, not for the first time, as if the God whom we both serve had explicitly told him that He had not created me "after His own image," and that the treatment which he should give to a bad dog would be too good for me. . . . I need not say that I was the first man of my race, in Jamaica, who had ever reached the priesthood. The Bishop's treatment of me has considerably tended, as I can prove, to facilitate the present prostrate condition of the Church.[96]

Gordon mentioned the petitions on his behalf in Jamaica, and his description of his support there counters the bishop's claim of earlier popular agitation against his ordination. Gordon maintained that the communicant members of three churches in Kingston, as well as thousands of all denominations in other parts of the island, petitioned for him—but without success.

Between the time of Courtenay's circular of 1861 and the letter of Gordon to the S.P.G. in 1868, the general line of events of Gordon's life can be gleaned from his letter, although time periods are vague. There is no indication that he ever responded to the bishop's demand for a letter of "humiliation" concerning the Canadian situation; and he was not given a church or pastoral ministry in Jamaica. He was, however, elected headmaster of Wolmer's Grammar School, a post that he held for a period of five years from 1862.[97]

In June 1867, he sailed for England. He carried with him a letter of introduction to the colonial secretary, the Duke of Buckingham, from Sir Henry Storks, chairman of the select committee investigating the Morant Bay Rebellion, and acting governor for the duration of the investigation. With the colonial secretary's assistance, he acquired the license of the archbishop of Canterbury, and subsequently that of the bishop of London. Desirous of obtaining an English degree, Gordon asked the S.P.G. to give him work at Oxford, where he could prepare for examinations. The bishop of Oxford had written a testimonial on Gordon's behalf, and it was received by the S.P.G. simultaneously with Gordon's letter of 31 January.[98]

Informed of Gordon's letter to the S.P.G., the bishop of Kingston was quick to respond. He wrote to the S.P.G. on 22 February and included his 1861 circular. His attitude toward Gordon had hardened. Of Gordon's career at Wolmer's, the bishop accused him of "insolent and overbearing behaviour" and "undue familiarities with a young female teacher in the girls' school" and suggested that his dismissal from Wolmer's was due to general incompetency. The bishop did not attempt to reconcile these charges with

Sir Henry Storks's kind letter of introduction of Gordon to the colonial office.[99]

The conflict between Gordon and Courtenay, then, remained
active after Gordon's removal to England. In 1872 there arrived in
England a deputation from the church in Jamaica consisting of
Archdeacon Campbell and the Rev. Enos Nuttal.[100] The bishop of
Jamaica, Aubrey Spencer, retired in England since 1856, had died
a few months previously. The two clergymen bore a petition from
the bishop of Kingston that the stipend of the bishop of Jamaica,
drawn from a Parliamentary Consolidated Fund, be continued to
Courtenay in Jamaica. Informed of the deputation, Gordon wrote
to the secretary of state for the colonies, Lord Kimberley, to protest the petition. He was subsequently informed by the Colonial
Office that they had no intention of requesting the continuation of
the bishop's allowance. But Gordon developed this correspondence on the matter into a vigorous tract against the Jamaican
church, which he published under the title of *The Jamaica Church—
Why It Has Failed*. Gordon was identified on the pamphlet as curate of the parish church of St. John of Wapping in London. The
pamphlet was a critique of colonialism in general and of the anti-
black policies of the Jamaican church in particular. It is worth
quoting to appreciate the style and logic of Gordon's protest:

> I hold that the Anglo-Saxon race having, during many genera-
> tions, used their superior knowledge and physical power in injur-
> ing, oppressing, and degrading the black race, it is their moral
> duty to do everything in their power—now that slavery has been
> abolished in the countries which their "auri sacra fames" had
> caused to have been its miserable strongholds—to assist in elevat-
> ing them to whatever stations in life they may have all the qualifi-
> cations for filling with honour to themselves and advantage to

society; at any rate, to place no insuperable bar in their way, on the ground of colour, for which you and I, my Lord [Kimberley], are just as responsible as for the changeable weather that we have been experiencing from the beginning of the year. The hateful policy of the Jamaican Church, persistently carried out by the Bishop of Kingston, has ever been to make an invidious distinction between the white and coloured subjects of Her Majesty, and the black inhabitants, who are as loyal to the British Throne and Constitution as are any of the former, in the systematic exclusion from the ministry of any candidate of pure Negro origin, thereby nullifying an important part of the political, social, and legal rights of three-fourths of the population.[101]

It was Gordon's view that, if the church had sincerely wanted to become an indissoluble part of society and the state, "it would have taken special pains to have encouraged the training of one black clergyman in each of the twenty-two parishes into which the island is divided." Such a creation of a black clergy, believed Gordon, would have helped to remove the contempt for blackness that was a source of division in Jamaican society. The example of an educated black clergy would have been an impetus to the educational improvement of the rest of the black population. Gordon did not have much respect for the only fully black religious congregations, the native churches. He considered their influence to be a backward one. If the established church had raised up a black clergy, "The occupation of most of the uneducated, self-ordained native ministers—who were of the same class as the people whom their presumption made them think themselves qualified to teach—would certainly have gone."[102]

Gordon suggested that the church was working against time, and that it actually reinforced those prejudices and jealousies which should have been gradually disappearing. Indeed, he saw the church as far behind all the other institutions of colonial society in its attitude toward blacks. To make his point, he cited the cases of blacks who had become magistrates, justices, members of the House of Assembly, a coroner, an alderman, and common councilmen in the Corporation of Kingston, and vestrymen in the various parishes. Compared to this record in civil and political life, the church was a fortified castle of exclusiveness. The specific burden on the church, Gordon concluded, was the paying of the moral debt owed by the entire English nation for the crimes committed against Africa and her descendants.[103]

The view of Jamaican society that emerges from Gordon's activities and writings should be noted. After emancipation, the black people continued to find their religion in dissenting missionary congregations, but as time went on, more and more independent native congregations developed, forming a Christianity that was more African. The Church of England took more interest in spreading religion among the black population, but the rationale of the church's interest was the maintenance of social control; religion was seen as the force that would keep the freed blacks docile, tranquil, and industrious, a ready labor force in harmony with plantation society. White dissenting missionaries vacillated between two emphases. Most of them veered toward the ideology of social control, while others, especially Baptists, saw their congregations as places of resistance against the oppressions of plantation society. Generally, this describes the situation when Gordon appeared upon the scene. He represented a different development. He was to religion in Jamaica what the black assemblymen, vestrymen, and magistrates he cited were to civil government. He was drawn to the church rather than to these other offices because he saw the church as the soul of the nation and considered that Jamaican society would not be redeemed until the established and white-controlled church became a black church. He saw himself as the vanguard of that black redemption of the church. This may not have been explicit in his mind when, at the age of ten, he decided that he wanted to be ordained. But it certainly became his philosophy after the conflict started upon his application for ordination in 1853. Indeed, the first evidence we have of Gordon's as a public voice, a lecture on education delivered in 1856, emphasizes the task of education in combatting racism in Jamaica.[104]

Gordon was not of the peasantry and had no part in the independent native religious tradition; he excoriated such elements of Afro-Jamaican folk culture as duppy stories and Anancy tales.[105] He saw that tradition as backward, although he implied that it was a development caused by the main institutions of Jamaican society, especially the established church, being closed to the mass of black people. He was conscious and proud of himself as a black man, a son of Africa. Yet he was primarily an Afro-creole nationalist who did not see a productive future for blacks in Jamaica either in white-controlled colonial institutions or in the ex-slave folk tradition. What had to be done, he believed, was the complete opening of the institutions of society, especially the church, to black initiative. Robert Gordon's vision and vocation were thwarted in Jamaica. It testifies to the peculiar dynamics of colonialism that his ideas and determined career led to a metropolitan exile.

The Jamaican Anglican church's treatment of Gordon was consistent with the Establishment's attitudes and policies toward the idea of a local black clergy. Bishop Lipscomb had not entertained the notion of a creole clergy—black, brown, or white—and relied on the importation of young English curates.[106] By the time of Courtenay's episcopacy, the policy had only been slightly modified. In general, Courtenay did not see any worth in the local population as a source of clergy. Native catechists were accepted, but only in strict subordination to the clergy. When John P. Grant became governor of the island in 1866, Courtenay wrote to him to make sure that he saw the situation clearly:

> . . . it is extremely difficult to procure men to suit our purposes. The Clergy have been repeatedly called upon to recommend to our Missionary Society persons in whom confidence could be placed, but with very partial success. And when your Excellency has resided long enough amongst us to acquire a personal knowledge of all classes of the people I am confident that you will perceive that the difficulty of procuring an adequate supply of persons worthy to be entrusted with the solemn responsibilities of an ordained Minister of the Gospel out of any but the highest classes will be all but insuperable.[107]

This letter was dated 15 November 1866, when Robert Gordon was still headmaster of Wolmer's and was probably very much on the bishop's mind.

The most readily available form of ecclesiastical function for the black Jamaican was the institution of native catechists. This, however, was not perceived as a positive step but as a necessary evil. As the bishop wrote to Governor Grant on 24 November 1868, "I regard such substitutes of Catechists for Clergymen as is contemplated even in my own scheme as a serious evil, though perhaps in the present financial condition of the Island it be inevitable. For our Catechists are little to be depended on, and need more frequent supervision than the Clergy can give them. . . ."[108]

By the year 1866, the S.P.G. had withdrawn its financial support of the Jamaican church. The society had by then dedicated itself to the ideal of a native church, led by native ministers. But race distinctions in Jamaica, fortified by the church's refusal to encourage a native ministry, had defeated the hopes of the society for the island. Without native ministers, the S.P.G. argued, local

congregations would never feel themselves sufficiently independent and self-reliant, and it was not the intention of the society to
continue to subsidize dependence.[109]

Faced with this challenge, Bishop Courtenay pleaded with the
C.M.S. to resume its work in Jamaica, which had been discontin-
ued in 1850 in the hope (frustrated up to that time) that the Jamaican
church would become increasingly self-sufficient. The reply came
from the secretary of the C.M.S., the Rev. Henry Venn, in the form of
a lengthy criticism of the Jamaican church's failure to encourage black
leadership. Venn also explained that the society's commitments in
Asia and Africa prevented their resuming the Jamaica mission but
that they would always be available for advice. His advice to the
bishop was not exactly what Courtenay wanted to hear. He put it to
him that the chief cause of the failure of the Jamaica mission was the
deficiency of black teachers for the black race. He was equally critical
of the earlier work of the C.M.S. in this regard: "The congregations
were not organized *upon the principles of a native Church*, but under
the false idea expressed by the Committee that they would 'fall naturally, as it were, into the general ecclesiastical establishment of the
island.' . . . race distinctions, not sufficiently understood at the period
of Missions, introduced an element which defeated the best hopes of
the Society."[110] With regard to the white missionary among black
people, Venn outlined this policy:

> . . . he must not attempt to be their Pastor; though they will be
> bound to him by personal attachment and by a sense of the ben-
> efits received from him, yet if he continues to act as their Pastor
> they will not form a vigorous Native Church, but as a general rule
> they will remain in a dependent condition, and make but little
> progress in spiritual attainments. The same congregation, under
> competent native Pastors, would become more self-reliant, and
> their religion would be of a more manly, home character.[111]

Venn saw the answer to Jamaica's religious problems as: "A LARGE, WELL-ORGANIZED SUPPLY OF NEGRO PASTORS TO MINISTER TO THE NEGRO CONGREGATIONS [emphasis in original document]."[112]

Courtenay's opinion of black people did not predispose him to a sympathetic consideration of Venn's advice. In 1858 he voiced his opinion of blacks as ". . . without instruction, without external control, unintellectual, immoral—the baser impulses of human nature are indulged without restraint either from a sense of shame or religious obligation."[113] Courtenay was also known for avoiding situations in which he would find it necessary to stop overnight in the homes of colored people, not to mention blacks—and this extended to the homes of colored ministers of the Anglican church.[114] An editorial in the *Falmouth Post* for 30 June 1876 remarked on the reputed racial prejudices of Courtenay and specifically connected this with his refusal to give Robert Gordon a curacy.[115]

In the light of Gordon's objection to Courtenay's original suggestion that he go to Africa as a missionary, Venn's final piece of advice is ironic: ". . . eventually the society might give one or more of its Native Pastors on the West Coast of Africa the opportunity and means of visiting the coloured congregations of Jamaica, with a view to their mutual comfort and encouragement."[116] Courtenay wrote and politely thanked the C.M.S. for their advice, and the matter seemed to end there.

CHAPTER 4

The Black Church: Memory, Identity, and Resistance

The frustrations experienced by the European churches in attempting to implant a system of religious and moral practice among the ex-slave population that corresponded entirely with European ideals of religious culture did not mean that the blacks rejected that culture in preference for a secular and amoral society. On the contrary, the other side of the coin of missionary frustration was the triumph of Afro-creole religious practices and social and personal norms. This triumph constituted not a total rejection of missionary Christianity but an adaptation of it on the basis of customs, values, and perceptions that began in Africa and were modified in the blacks' experience of slavery and an emancipation that largely preserved a system of class and color relationships forged during the nearly two hundred years of Jamaica's status as a British slave colony.

It may be the nature of creole identity always to be in formation, having no settled condition in the present. It is always in tension between memory and expectation, much more so than is social identity in relatively stable and traditional societies. Memory among black Jamaicans after emancipation would not only have been of slavery but of an African past, remote for most but immediate for many. How was Africa remembered and imagined among freed slaves and descendants of slaves? How did they relate to Africa in conceiving their own (individual or group) identity? There is some evidence that sheds light on these questions in nine-teenth-century Jamaica, specifically in the context of the religious mentality and affiliation of the blacks. Most of the information is in the form of missionary reports and journals, and a few news-paper accounts. This material most readily provides the image of Africa projected to black Jamaican congregations and their ob-served response to this image.

Missionary societies, the anti-slave trade movement, and cam-paigns for the "civilizing" of Africa kept alive a concern for that con-tinent. One of the best recorded of these campaigns was carried out by the Rev. Mr. J. M. Trew in Jamaica in 1842 on behalf of the African Civilization Society.[1] He was assisted by his fellow Anglican, the Rev. Richard Panton, and the solicitor William Wemyss Anderson.

The report of the society on the campaign stressed that the vari-ous congregations visited by its agents paid deep attention to the accounts of the sufferings of Africa and that many of the blacks "knew from bitter experience what those miseries were which we endeavoured to picture to them." The accounts of the different meetings during the campaign repeat the pattern. At one con-ducted by the rector of Portland, the Rev. Mr. Griffiths, at the church in Port Antonio on 17 April, some of the listeners offered to go and teach their brethren in Africa. A group of black children brought up an offering "for their fatherland." These particular children were African, for it is noted that they had recently come to Jamaica as part of the cargo of a captured slaver.[2]

At a Manchioneal meeting, the African-born blacks identified themselves by nation. Trew reported: "It was amusing to see the especial interest taken by several tribes, as their countries were named. The majority of those present were from Ibo. . . ." As he talked of their countries of origin, "many of them were standing on tip-toe, fearful that one sentence of the last news from their country should be lost. While we continued the narrative, we overheard them calling the attention of others. 'Dat for *we* country—you hear dat now?—what you say to dat?'—and similar expressions."[3]

These and other responses observed by Trew of the blacks upon hearing accounts of Africa were corroborated in many independently written missionary reports; they noted the alertness and delight of the people when it came to news of Africa:

> The Negroes are very fond of hearing anything about Africa: and I have read them some accounts of Sierra Leone, which made so deep an impression upon them that, I believe, if I had had strength to have read it all night, they would have been glad to have heard it. [One] was so overpowered with joy at hearing about his own country that he could not refrain from laughing aloud.[4]

Missionary journals from Africa were often read to Jamaican congregations. Both the Baptist missionary Mr. Reid and the L.M.S. missionary Barrett were reading such a journal, "Freeman's journal among the Ashantee," to their Clarendon congregations in 1840. Barrett reported his members as showing great excitement because of their recognition of and acquaintance with "Ashantee" customs.[5] All the reports suggest that responses toward Africa varied depending on whether African-born blacks or creoles were responding.

The obvious observation to be made about religious and philanthropic campaigns for Africa is that the attitude that the religious leaders attempted to foster among the people was one of benign condescension toward a related but more benighted people. In the early years of free society in Jamaica, some nonconformist missionaries, especially the Baptists, included *Africa* in their religious vocabulary in a somewhat less condescending manner. William Knibb's usage of the term provides the most obvious example. The full name of the weekly paper he began in 1839 was *The Baptist Herald and Friend of Africa*. He himself always referred to, and referred to himself as, "friend of Africa." He consistently called the black people "children of Ethiopia" and used the phrase "your countrymen" when talking about Africans to his congregations. It was probably under Knibb's prompting that his people, in an emancipation celebration and procession in Falmouth in August 1838, carried banners with slogans like "Africa is free, August, 1838" and the constantly used abolitionist proclamation "Ethiopia shall stretch forth her hands unto God."[6] Knibb's outlook on Africa was expressed when he prayed:

> O my Heavenly Father! work by whom thou wilt work, but save poor, poor, benighted, degraded, Europe-cursed Africa! My affection for Africa may seem extravagant. I cannot help it. I dream of it nearly every night, nor can I think of anything else.[7]

Generally, however, missionary comparisons of Africa and Jamaica were intended to persuade the blacks that Jamaica was a better place—happier, more comfortable, and blessed with true religion. The post-emancipation outreach from Jamaica to Africa, using creole volunteers, was presented as a phase of the anti-slavery movement. Black and colored missionaries would go to the African fatherland to redeem heathen souls who were being physically saved from the slave trade. The devotion of Jamaican blacks to the African cause was also posed by missionaries as a test of the authenticity of their embrace of Christianity.[8]

But missionary records make it clear that many Jamaicans regarded Africans not as distant pagan relatives but as part of a black family. And some preserved testimony indicates that, in the precariousness of their situation in a polity and economy like that of Jamaica, some ex-slaves perceived Africa as an alternative: "If the Governor [Metcalfe] was displeased with us, let us write to the Queen, and tell her that we and our ministers will go away to Africa, and leave the island to the governor and his friends," testified one former slave on behalf of his brethren at a Bethtephil Baptist meeting in 1840. The same political and economic pressures served to keep alive the desire of post-emancipation African immigrants to return to Africa.[9]

The post-emancipation importation of Africans into Jamaica, through captured slave ships or immigration, kept alive an awareness of Africa among creole blacks. Questions concerning the quality of this awareness and the dynamics of African/creole relationships are difficult to answer, as most of the immediate observations were written by missionaries who, in general, were outspoken against the immigration of laborers, African or otherwise, who would compete with the creole workers in their congregations for work, wages, and land. A minority viewpoint among missionaries was that of Mr. C. W. Winckler of the C.M.S., who considered African *arrivants* to have personalities superior to those of creoles, "for they know nothing of that cunning which slavery has produced in these Islands."[10] But most missionaries disapproved of the presence of Africans. They felt that they brought with them habits of superstition, barbarism, and immorality that the missionaries were working hard to root out of the lives of blacks in Jamaica: newly imported Africans "engage in their African customs and dances to the very great injury and corruption of the young people who are led to follow their example," wrote a Methodist missionary in 1845.[11] Almost every missionary letter on the subject contained a judgment similar to this one in 1858:

> The introduction of still pagan Africans would most certainly promote the very extensive revival of still lingering and terrible superstitions of Obeah and Myalism, the practice of which is considered by the Legislature [deserving] of severe punishment, and which is even now declared to be fearfully prevalent.[12]

Some missionaries saw a direct connection between the immorality of the Jamaican blacks and the number of Africans with whom they were in contact:

> The moral condition of the people on this side of the island [St. Ann] appears in advance of that in St. Thomas-in-the-East.
>
> The importation of Africans and Coolies into the Eastern part of the Island has tended very much to corrupt the minds of the young people in the East.
>
> The absence of such people here is an advantage.[13]

Sometimes a missionary would even go so far as to attribute entirely to the influence of newly arrived Africans any persistent elements of "immorality" or "superstition" among the creoles, without acknowledging their prior existence in creole folk culture. Peter Samuel, for example, defined Myalism as "a species of *Obeah*, a pernicious African superstition, which was introduced among the people at this time [1842–43] by a number of Africans, who were rescued from a slaver by a British ship of war, and located as apprentices on some of the estates."[14] Myal and Obeah were actually Afro-creole religious forms that were noticed by commentators in Jamaica at least as early as the 1770s.

The importance of the churches in the introduction of African immigrants to creole customs and institutions, and as centers of interculturation, is suggested by reports of the incorporation of newly arrived Africans into existing congregations: "Some little time ago, two slave ships were brought into one of the ports of this island: they had more than 1000 Africans on board," wrote a Jesuit missionary in 1838. This large group of Africans was not dispersed randomly among the creole population but was immediately taken into the Baptist congregation in the district where they arrived: "In less than a week the parson administered to them all the sacrament of baptism. I suppose he has the gift of tongues and something more, to convert and prepare for baptism so many ignorant and probably vicious foreigners, in so short a time."[15]

In 1833, the Methodist Henry Bleby recorded a similar incident, in which 226 Africans were brought ashore from a Portuguese slave ship wrecked off the south coast; they were immediately indentured and baptized.[16] Another Methodist, Mr. Sergeant, wrote in 1842 from the Port Royal Mountains: "Here you have 24,000 members of the [Methodist] society. The majority of them bear the interesting appellation of liberated Africans [liberated from the illicit Spanish and Portuguese slave trade]."[17]

Available reports hardly remark on how members of missionary congregations related to newly arrived Africans after emancipation. It is fortunate, therefore, to come across an entry from the journal of the C.M.S. missionary Mr. Sessing who, besides merely noting that in September 1837 he took fifty *emancipados* into his church at Birnam Wood (in the parish of St. George then, Portland now), went on to record that some of his regular church members,

> retaining a little knowledge of their native languages, began searching for their countrymen; and some of them were very successful, especially a Congo man, who soon made himself intelligible to some of them; and of the joy which now ensued, no one can form an idea, but those who saw their countenances. A hearty shaking of hands commenced; and a very interesting conversation followed, not less interesting to the bystanders than to themselves.[18]

Several groups formed, "Congos, Mandingoes, Bassas, and a few from unknown tribes of the interior. These looked very sad, as they had nobody to whom to speak." Sessing was predisposed to make these observations because he had worked in Africa before coming to Jamaica, and in the particular scene that he wrote about he momentarily thought himself back in Liberia or Sierra Leone. Sessing was still at Birnam Wood in 1842 when a small group of Yoruba immigrants were settled in the district. At least one of these immigrants was known personally by Sessing, who had taught him in Bathurst.[19]

Waddell's experience was similar to that of Sessing when in 1839 about 400 *emancipados* from a Spanish slaver captured near Cuba were brought to Jamaica and apprenticed. A large number of them were brought to Cinnamon Hill, where Waddell had a congregation. They were given Christian instruction by Africans already on Cinnamon Hill Estate who spoke the language of the arrivals. Later these liberated Africans would contribute toward sending a mission to Africa.[20]

The 1872 Preston Census [21] of a Catholic mission station is an example of the balance of Africans and creoles that could have occurred in different Jamaican communities as late as 1872. It stated the number of "Emancipados & their families" as 57; the "Adults received by me since 1869" as 12; "Infants Bapt^d under 14 yrs., by me," 135; "Adults Bapt^d by Fr. Jones," 6; "Infants [baptized by Fr. Jones]," 34; "Old Catholics, their children, servants, etc.," 9; with a total of 253. Within this particular Catholic mission community, the proportion of *emancipados* was quite high.

Besides documentary sources, oral history gives some insight into the process of the incorporation of African immigrants into the Christian churches. Monica Schuler, a modern academic historian who has utilized what remains of the oral tradition, observes, for example, that older residents of Abeokuta in Westmoreland in the 1970s remembered African-born ancestors as Baptists and Baptist deacons in Jamaica, indicating rapid creolization through Christian conversion and church membership. A similar memory was absent among Schuler's informants in St. Thomas, which is understandable since mission work was not highly concentrated in St. Thomas-in-the-East before 1866, when African immigration had ebbed. The Baptists, for example, did not establish a mission in Morant Bay until that year.[22]

Arrivals of Africans—regardless of their numbers in the nineteenth century after slavery—were at least continuous throughout the period. Dr. K. O. Laurence, working from official immigration figures, gives the number of 11,391 Africans arriving in Jamaica between 1834 and 1867. He also remarks on the persistence of African identity among them:

> . . . the process of assimilating the newly arrived Africans, drawn as they were from many different tribes, took longer than has sometimes been thought. Although often regarded by the planters as forming one homogeneous population group with the Creole immigrants and native Negroes, African immigrants when they eventually left the estates sometimes tended to congregate in tribal groups and form their own villages.[23]

This cohesiveness among the African born was not a new phenomenon after emancipation but stems from the time of slavery itself. Planters noticed the fact, as can be seen in the testimony of John Baillie, resident proprietor of Roehampton Estate from 1788 to 1826, before the House of Lords Select Committee of 1832. The Africans called each other brother and sister and other titles of family or tribal relationship. And in Baillie's experience, if an African slave died with no children, whatever property he had managed to acquire was claimed by his countrymen. Fr. Splaine in 1872 also observed that "The Africans are clannish and they keep their own secrets, even from the Creole blacks."[24]

The most elusive aspect of the question of African memory is the image of Africa preserved in black folk memory, independent of missionary influence. The literary clues are thin and indirect, and usually exacerbate the question without providing much by way of answer.

It had long been a religious belief among the slaves that after death they would return to the ancestors. This was a belief held especially by the African-born slaves. With them, death meant a return to the ancestors to live a way of life remembered in Africa. The missionary teachings on heaven and the afterlife were often reinterpreted in this way; it had more appeal than the European Christian heaven.[25]

Monk Lewis observed that the Africans generally believed in a life beyond this world and that it consisted in a return to their own country—thus the frequency of slave suicides. But this was mainly among the newly arrived, and since the abolition of the slave trade "such an illusion is unheard of." Lewis claimed that the seasoned slaves lost the desire to return to Africa, yet offered observations which showed that this was not entirely true.[26]

African reinterpretations of Christian ideas on the afterlife, of course, were met with the disapproval of those missionaries who were alert to them. A Scottish missionary in 1834 noted the difficulty of instructing a "blind watchman," whose imperfect English compelled the missionary to enlist "another negro as the organ of communication, but he so misrepresented what I told him to say, and employed similes so inapplicable, as convinced me of the very defective nature of religious instruction carried on, sometimes, among themselves." To the missionary's chagrin, his temporary assistant mingled with his account of the future happiness of Christian believers the African notion that the blind watchman would also, after death, go to see his father and mother and eat victuals with them. The missionary noted it as a common pre-Christian belief among the blacks that the departed soul returned to Africa and was there entertained by its friends. He was sanguine that Christianity had largely defeated this "prejudice," yet had to admit that "it requires no ordinary degree of moral force to make the negro forego the hope of returning to his own country" and to seek heaven instead.[27]

Toward the end of slavery, the C.M.S. missionary Mr. Collins reported a contention in his congregation between the older slaves and younger ones over burial customs. The younger relatives of a deceased slave were willing to allow a Christian burial service whereas "the old people, who are still wedded to old customs, strove hard for the observance of ancient rites, maintaining that, unless they were observed, the spirit of the departed would trouble them."[28] A question here is whether there was an explicit connection between these customs and an awareness of Africa in the minds of the blacks. Collins did not say. But Gardner, in discussing slave funerals in 1872, wrote that in the ceremony one or two slaves played the "goomba," another blew a conch shell, while another chanted or "wailed" a solo recitative, the words usually referring to the return of the departed to Africa.[29]

Phillippo mentioned the vivid memories of the African born, how they recollected the scenes of African childhood, remembering the circumstances of their captivity as if it were only a recent occurrence, and expressing concern for any family members who might yet be alive in Africa. Gardner, in his well-known passages on the African origins of the Jamaican blacks, mentioned that traces of the original "stock" might be observed in 1872 among the settlers, but he did not indicate the extent of their memory of these origins.[30] In our time, Schuler has utilized the oral tradition most fruitfully not only for understanding the present experience of Central African descendants in St. Thomas and Yoruba descendants in Westmoreland but for extrapolation into the past to understand the original experiences of their *arrivant* ancestors. She has shown that Africa is an integral element in the consciousness of those descendants.[31]

Native religious groups or movements that were not a part of any missionary or European church network did not leave written evidence of their thinking or attitudes. We have a clue, however, in a placard, containing a long, apocalyptic proclamation, found posted to a wharf gate in Lucea in June 1865. It began:

> I heard a Voice speaking to me in the year 1864, saying, "tell the Sons and Daughters of Africa, that a great deliverance will take place for them from the hand of Opposition; for said the Voice, they are oppressed by Government, by Magistrates, by Proprietors, and by Merchants." And this Voice also said, "tell them to call a Solemn Assembly, and to sanctify themselves for the day of deliverance which will surely take place; but, if the People will not hearken, I will bring the Sword into the Land to chastise them for their disobedience, and for the iniquities which they have committed. And the Sword will come from America. If the People depend upon their Arms, and upon our Queen, and forget Him who is our God, they will be greatly mistaken, and the mistake will lead them to great distresses."

The correspondent who found this placard, which was signed "A Son of Africa," sent it to the *Falmouth Post* and identified it only as the production of some persons of heated imagination who resided in or near Lucea. The fact that this document appeared when it did, in the summer of 1865, invites speculation on its connection with the conditions of the island that led to the Morant Bay struggle of that year. But the point for us here is that the prophet or prophets involved assumed an identification with Africa. It suggests the existence of a connection of prophetism, politics, and Africa consciousness that is commonly thought to have

come about later in the colonial history of Jamaica, in the twenti-
eth century with Garveyism and Rastafarianism.[32]

Still, the question of the consciousness of Africa among nineteenth-century Afro-Jamaicans remains an enigma; the answers
are both diverse and difficult. One reason is that the question cannot really be separated from the presence of Africa in the subcon-
sciousness of the people. It has to do with what G. M. Foster has
called "cognitive orientations," which perdure long after specific
cultural forms and institutions have been fragmented, dispersed,
or modified. These orientations involve basic assumptions about
social relations and the way the world works phenomenologically
that can be distinctly African as opposed to European, assumptions that may be more important than overt and explicit cultural
continuities.[33] Within the religious matrix, these assumptions are
more resistant to acculturation than more observable cultural
forms. At a subconscious level, they provide the foundation for
the creation of new worlds. That Africa as an explicit memory and
image for the building of a new black world has never disappeared, however, is indicated in Schuler's observation that to this
day in Jamaica descendants who retain an ancestral religious culture refer to themselves as having "come up in the African world"
and to their spiritual leaders as doing "the African work."[34]

The Africa that persisted in the consciousness of black Jamaicans has, over time, been progressively mythologized: birthplace,
motherland, home of the ancestors, and, in Rastafarianism, Zion.
As a concept, an emotion, and a "cognitive orientation," it formed
one element in the formation of black creole identity and in the
process of black resistance against the cultural and political dominance of European Jamaica. This process, however, was perceived
by its Afro-creole movers not as cultural and political but rather
as religious. Black religion, in its unique and several Jamaican syn-

theses of African and European elements, provided communities of cultural cohesion and spiritual motivation for political protest.

There were three degrees of independence of black religious groups, both during and after slavery, from church and mission groups: mission members on estates, whom the missionary visited infrequently; groups formed by mission converts, most often prayer and class leaders, among blacks who did not attend mission churches; and native religious groups having no connection with mission groups. What the three categories had in common was the power of black leaders, regardless of whether these leaders were "legitimized" by membership in mission churches and selection by a white missionary.

The different missionary societies had varying policies with regard to the native leadership system, but most of them, either by force of circumstance or policy, provided positions of responsibility to blacks as assistants, deacons, and prayer or class leaders to oversee those aspiring to membership in the congregations. The Baptist Missionary Society, for example, reported at least 250 leaders as of the end of 1830. And by 1832, there were 456 Wesleyan slave leaders.[35] During slavery, prayer and class meetings under these leaders provided an experience of humanity, dignity, and brotherhood which no other institution could provide. Of more political importance is that this arrangement served as a more-or-less legitimate means of organization and communication in a society that depended for its continued existence on the disunity of the blacks and their absolute subordination to white rule.

The Baptist class-leader system is perhaps the most well known (even though the system was a Wesleyan innovation), not the least because it was the most notorious in nineteenth-century Jamaica. The missionaries would set up a class house in each area where church members lived and appoint a black member of the community as leader. Prayer meetings were held in the class houses, and at any time the leader could call the class members together for special business. This system provided a means of communication and independent action for the leaders, and the leaders could decide what constituted "special business." Their position gave the leaders a sufficient sense of importance to dispute, on occasion, the authority of the missionary himself. "They resented any interference with the size of their classes, any questioning of their reports on members' conduct, and their meetings with the missionary tended to be quarrelsome and aggressive," wrote the Baptist missionary John Clarke.[36]

The apparent success of the system in augmenting Baptist membership was one reason for the criticism from other missionaries of the Baptist use of it. But more than this, most non-Baptists agreed that the influence of these "half-pagan" leaders was corrupting and subverting real Christianity. The leaders, it was claimed, made impossible the preaching of "pure and undefiled" religion. "As to spiritual oversight of the ministers over their people, they have none, but what they obtain thro' their leaders. . . ."[37] The C.M.S. put forth their case against the Baptist system in 1839:

> . . . all the Negroes in Jamaica now call themselves "Christians"—
> generally "Baptists," though their religion differs little from their
> old African superstitions. The bulk of them are enrolled in Classes
> under some black Teacher as ignorant as themselves; and they are
> connected by the purchase of a ticket with the Baptist Congrega-
> tion in the nearest Town, where they go, and receive the sacra-
> ment once a month, or once a Quarter; but they are utterly igno-
> rant of the simplest and plainest of God's commandments. They
> are too ignorant to understand and profit by the Public Preaching
> on the Sabbath; and they never see the Missionary at any other
> time; for they live far away from him and he has thousands at-

tending him whom he does not know. They are perishing in their sins, and stand as much in need of instruction as the Zooloos![38]

Wesleyans and Presbyterians joined with the Independents and the Anglicans in the attack. Gardner observed, "A discussion as to the purity of these large [Baptist] churches was commenced by the Rev. G. Blyth, a Scotch missionary of great experience." By 1842 the controversy was full blown.[39]

The Presbyterian missionaries organized their system in such a way as to forestall what they saw as the anarchy of the Baptist system. In the Scottish congregations, black elders were chosen by the minister, a departure from practice in Scotland where the elders were elected by the congregation. To cover up this anomaly, they were called "deacons" and not "elders" in Jamaica. Hope Waddell observed that he chose his in pairs, in order to prevent black autocracy and despotism, a tendency he believed was allowed free rein in the Baptist system.[40]

Mr. Milne of the L.M.S., in criticizing the Baptist system, in effect offered a clear and reasonable explanation for its necessity: the black people claimed that they could not understand a white man, and that they had to rely on their daddy or leader to explain the minister's sermons; the people would attend the minister's services, but without the slightest intention of hearing or understanding for themselves, meeting afterwards to get the sense of the sermon from their own black spiritual guides.[41]

The Baptists defended their system as long as they could, and as long as it ensured large congregations. John Clark of the Brown's Town mission, for one, was not ashamed to admit allowing the people to form their own prayer and worship groups with their own leaders, with no interference from the missionary.[42] It is not inaccurate to say that Clark saw this as a sign of religious vigor.

Waddell's criticism of the system, however, and his method of preventing it within his congregations, were based on the recognition of its important function in black religious self-determination. Among the Baptists, it served as a ratification or confirmation of an already existing system of relationships among the people. As the L.M.S. missionary W. G. Barrett described it:

> A man whom the Missionary found exercising a headship over a number of people, whom he called his "children," and who called him their "daddy,"—and being received by the Missionary in the character in which he presented himself, together with "his children," he was thenceforward recognised by the Missionary, and by the church under him, as the leader of those people whom he had brought, and of as many more as he could induce to join them.[43]

In other words, the Baptist missionary did not usually choose a man he thought would make a good leader and then present him to the people. More often, he would accept as leader a man already acknowledged by the people as a chief among them. The important point is that simply being chosen by "buckra" or the white minister was not sufficient to create a leader's influence among the people where there was none before. Moreover, the leader system came to be seen by the blacks as one that belonged to them, and even the white ministers could not modify it without protest. Mr. Reid, a Baptist missionary, tried to do so and consequently lost some of his congregation to Native Baptists. Reid was one of the first of the Baptist missionaries to join with the critics to disparage the system. His readiness to criticize the system and his brethren's use of it perhaps had something to do with his being the brother-in-law of the L.M.S. missionary Barrett, who was the main spokesman of the critics of the Baptist system.[44]

As long as the daddy remained loyal to the missionary, his people would remain in the congregation. But Reid's experience and later developments, after 1845 especially, would show the tendency and power of the leaders to break with the white missionaries. In a sense, the critics of the Baptists were correct; the system would become one cause of the failure of white ministers to hold onto their vast memberships. The Baptist ministers showed by a decision in 1845 that they had by then acknowledged this as a reality. They resolved that no congregation in the Jamaica Baptist church could choose leaders and deacons, as Clark seems to have allowed, or nonwhite ministers, unless the man chosen was approved by at least four Baptist ministers. By this method of accreditation they hoped to curtail the growing tendency toward separation under black leadership. It had, of course, little effect, and may even have accelerated the proclivity of black leaders to ignore the authority of the Baptist ministers.[45]

It is important to note that the Baptist acceptance of black leaders who brought their followers with them repeated the original pattern of the Baptist Missionary Society's entry into Jamaica. The first Christian preaching that a great many of the slaves heard was from black preachers, not from white missionaries. These preachers were forming congregations before the arrival of most of the missionaries, being preceded only by the few Moravians who began working in Jamaica in 1754. The English Baptists came to Jamaica only after correspondence with these preachers, who needed assistance with their growing congregations.[46] The Baptist church in Jamaica was historically a black-initiated church, and white ministers like J. M. Phillippo and William Knibb are preceded in time and importance as pioneers by George Liele (or Lisle), Moses Baker, George Lewis, George Gibb, and Nicholas Swiegle, the ex-slave preachers who laid the foundation for the Baptist edifice on the island. Moreover, the use of class leaders was also a part of the system of the black Baptists before the arrival of the first English Baptist missionary in 1814. This helped to create a precedent wherein white ministers did not have full control over the criteria for selection of the leaders, nor over the criteria used by the leaders in their assessment of class members. It was one of the leader's functions to recommend to the minister that certain inquirers were ready for baptism. Often, however, his values in selection were not the same as those that were operative in the mind of the white minister. Where the minister looked for expressions of conversion and change of heart with concomitant moral reform the leader often relied on interpreting the dreams of the inquirers as signs that they possessed the proper spirit for baptism. The people's belief in dreams and visions and in the leader's power to interpret them not only reinforced the influence of the leader but served to maintain "old and hurtful superstitions among the people," as the critics put it. It was under the leaders that the people felt free for more African types of religious expression, called "wild extravagances" by white observers.[47]

This is what Waddell was referring to in his claim that Moses Baker "initiated them [slaves] into a strange system of mingled truth and error, which his leaders carried to the length of monstrous superstition." Waddell implies that the English Baptists simply absorbed this superstition, beginning in 1824 when Thomas Burchell in Montego Bay accepted the Baker Baptists into his congregation—leaders, classes, and all. This caused, in the view of Waddell and other critics, "permanent injury" to the Baptist system in Jamaica, an injury that continued to be manifested in the tendency of Baptist inquirers and members to convulse, fall, and "tumble about" under the influence of black leaders.[48]

Not all of the Native Baptists, however, were absorbed by the Baptist mission. Outside of St. James, they tended to remain independent, a constant reproach to the "purity" of the mission churches. Waddell wrote of these "self-constituted ministers" and remarked that in 1838 in Kingston alone there were six or seven of them (they did not seem to warrant a precise count), chiefly Native Baptists ordained by George Liele. An L.M.S. missionary told Waddell of a party that had come to him for admission into his congregation if he would accept their native minister as his colleague on an equal footing.[49]

In general, the class leaders in the Baptist system manifested more of a spirit of independence than did those in the other sectarian churches. The Methodists, however, could not boast that their black leaders were totally passive. In 1834 there was the dramatic case of James Beard, an apprentice on Bogg Estate and a Wesleyan class leader. On religious principle, Beard protested against the apprenticeship system. It is doubtful that any Methodist minister would have defended Beard's biblically inspired rebellion:

> Mr. Laidlow, one of the special magistrates, informed us that he attended the Bogg Estate on the 4th of August, when James Beard stepped forward and spoke nearly as follows. He inquired "were the Israelites made apprentices when they came out of Egypt?" and being answered in the negative, he asked, "Will you swear upon the Bible that *God* has made *us* apprentices?" The magistrate immediately did so, when some of the negroes said *that* is not the king's Bible. The magistrate then informed them that the next day he would bring his own Bible and swear upon *that* which he did; . . . Many of them seemed satisfied and went away. James Beard again asked "has *God* made us apprentices?" and on being answered in the affirmative he exclaimed, "then God has done us injustice!" Afterwards, on their refusal to comply with the law two or three of them were, by the magistrate's orders, laid down and flogged, and James Beard, who thinks himself suffering for righteousness' sake, and a few others, were sentenced to hard labour with the penal gang in the workhouse, for six months.[50]

District Chairman Edmondson expressed his fear in 1838 that his more influential leaders seemed prepared to form societies on their own, and indeed there was an increase in incidents of Methodist leaders forming their own independent congregations at that time. However, this did not occur among the Methodists to the extent that was observed among the Baptists. The only remedy that the Methodists could think of was to request more missionaries from England.[51]

Many of the slaves, however, resisted Christianity entirely, whether it was preached by white or black ministers—not because they were religionless but precisely because they had their own religion. The slaves developed their own Afro-creole religious forms, which were often disguised or hidden from the whites, who had outlawed any manifestations of the "superstitions" of Myal and Obeah. They used their religious beliefs and practices "to regulate relationships among themselves, placate the unseen forces that guided their fortune, and ensured that their dead, free at last, were launched with proper ceremony into the spirit world," as Mary Turner has put it.[52] Each person was a priest (not exactly in the way understood in the Protestant tradition of the "priesthood of all believers"), for through the guidance of the specialists and the ceremony of the dance and the sacrament of the drum he or she "could not only communicate with the gods," in Brathwaite's words, "but become and assume the god."[53]

The paradox was that the slaves' African religiosity often facilitated conversion and yet enabled them to reinterpret and undermine orthodox Christianity. This remained the missionaries' greatest and most baffling problem.

An essential feature of Afro-creole religion, in its Christian form as well as its pre-Christian or non-Christian forms, was its practicality and worldliness, its readiness to deal with the world when the mechanisms for doing so of the planter's Jamaica were either closed to or used against the blacks. One of the most important manifestations of this in Baptist congregations, whether native or missionary, was an alternative system of justice, the creation of "people's courts." Moses Baker himself described it: "We appoint judges and other such officers among us, to settle any matters according to the Word of God. We think ourselves forbidden to shed blood, or to go to law one with the other before the unjust, but settle any matters we have before the saints."[54] The missionary historian Gardner noted:

> Wills were made and property bequested by slaves, just as among white men, without the legal formalities, but with quite as much certainty of the wishes of the testator being observed. In some places the slaves established courts of justice among themselves. Three judges were usually appointed, and decided all disputes.[55]

The system described by Baker and Gardner as carried on during slavery was continued after emancipation. The black laborers could hardly, if ever, get a favorable hearing in the Jamaican courts. Judicial reforms in 1840 did little to change the situation, mainly because they were limited to the higher echelons of the judiciary. While the reforms restricted the admission of ignorant and prejudiced magistrates onto the higher courts, the courts of petty sessions remained under the control of the planter magistracy. It was these courts that the vast majority of the ex-slaves had to face with problems of vagrancy, recovery of petty debts, contract, trespass, and tenancy. Moreover, even if there had been little anti-black bias on these courts, the demands of the judicial system on both plaintiffs and defendants, e.g., costs and fees, paperwork, travel, etc., were objectively unjust. As a result, in many districts, the black people simply gave up taking any cases into court and instituted a private court system composed of their own community leaders, who were usually religious leaders, to handle disputes among themselves. These people's courts were of two kinds: those described by Baker as based in religious congregations to settle disputes before the saints (black Christians) rather than the unjust (planter magistrates); and mock courts, especially prevalent before the 1865 rebellion, to rehearse for the inevitable confrontation with the official judicial system.[56]

Besides native courts, other types of expression of the connection between religion and material liberty in ex-slave consciousness can be found in missionary sources, similar to the Methodist leader James Beard's protest against the apprenticeship system. At a meeting at the Baptist station at Salter's Hill in 1841, for example, the former slave Robert Scott addressed himself to his brethren: "Try to get all you can for self, and for your wife, and for your children, and try to get it that you may serve God. . . . Yes, and the time is coming when black people will get rich and ride in their carriages as well as white people."[57] A similar connection between spiritual dignity and material well-being was expressed at an 1839 meeting at the Baptist station at Maldon by the former slave John Grey: "We must have a strong fence around our privileges, and around our hearts. Watch over your rights, and pray to God that Satan may be kept out of your hearts."[58]

The native courts as well as these oral expressions indicate a sense of solidarity evidenced by the realization, among Baptist ex-slaves at least, that there were blacks who recoiled from the burdens of the struggle for a free society. At the same Maldon meeting mentioned above, Robert Scott, who had been born in Africa and bought his freedom in Jamaica, raised the accusation:

> Some headmen say, that slavery is better than freedom; this they say to please their masters, and get favour from them. If slavery is better let them go to Cuba. Do not carry two faces. Do not wear sheep's

clothing, and be ravening wolves. If we find such among us, we must put them away. Let there be none among us like Judas.[59]

Religious consciousness also contributed to black resistance the basis for moral judgment against white Jamaica, a judgment that was particularly irking to the whites in that it could be supported from a Christian tradition that was fully European. The *Royal Gazette*, an island newspaper that faithfully expressed the planter viewpoint, complained in an article in 1835 that the apprentices were made to see the proprietor as the enemy of Christ. "This sentiment is not only preached but is pretty well understood and acted upon by the apprentices." The apprentices misunderstood the "theologic sublety" of the doctrine of equality. "They take it in the literal sense, and act upon it accordingly."[60]

The radical nature of religious experience and conviction found in all-black religious groups was not due always or entirely to adoption of egalitarian tendencies in Christianity but also to the type of Christianity that black Jamaicans were building, which, because of its difference from missionary-taught religion, made them less susceptible to social control in the way that Trew had defined it. The foundation of this distinctly Afro-creole Christianity goes back, again, to the origins of the Native Baptists in the time of Liele and Baker. Making due allowance for his being a hostile witness, Hope Waddell gives an apt description of the theology and discipline of Native Baptist religion:

> The grand doctrine of these people was the Spirit's teaching. It gave life. The written word was a dead letter. If they could not read the Bible they could do without it, which was as good. The Spirit was sought in dreams and visions of the night, which thus became the source of their spiritual life. Without them inquirers could not be born again either by water or the Spirit. The leaders expounded these dreams to their kneeling followers in weekly

class meetings; which, when judged to be of a right kind, were called "the work", that is, of the Spirit, and supplied the place of knowledge, faith, and repentance. As Christ was led of the Spirit into the wilderness, his disciples must follow him into the wilderness to seek the Spirit. To the bush, the pastures, or the cane fields, those people resorted at night, when preparing for baptism, and were ordered to lie down, each apart, without speaking, but keeping eye and ear open to observe what way the Spirit would come to them. Doubtless they would see and hear strange things in their excited imaginations, and the leaders could make what they liked of them. The result of such a system among such a people may be imagined.[61]

Later missionary testimony corroborates the continuation and development of this religion. The Rev. Hugh Brown of the London Missionary Society, writing in 1836 from Mandeville, complained of "leaders of the Baptist denomination" who taught that baptism by immersion not only washed away sin but conveyed an inner wisdom and knowledge that made it unnecessary to go and hear the white minister, "because dem know all him can tell them." This knowledge also made the Bible unnecessary. Brown cited one leader who called himself John the Baptist and who claimed that he and his followers did not need the Bible; Brown quoted him as saying, "Dem no go by the book, but by dem heart. Massa Jesus himself no go by de book!"[62]

This belief, that religious knowledge was direct and need not be mediated by the minister or the written word, subverted the traditional belief in the Bible as the one and only source of saving knowledge. It was similar to the various forms of gnosticism that have appeared in the history of the Christian church, and which have always been considered aberrations or heresies. In Jamaica, however, the phenomenon was not purely a recurrence of earlier forms of gnosticism in Christian history; it was uniquely a creole development that can be understood not solely in terms of European Christianity but also as rooted in African religious experience.

The adherence to a source of inspiration outside the fold of the established or nonconformist churches indicated the limits of control of those churches and subverted their influence over the black population. Indeed, it was an established pattern before the commencement of missionary work. Phillippo wrote of freed blacks during slavery who, as itinerant preachers often unable to read scripture, relied on dreams and visions as sources for their knowledge of salvation,[63] similar to the practices in Moses Baker's church in St. James.

The fact that most black members of nonconformist churches could not read made them dependent on preaching for interpretation of scripture. The difficulty of understanding the white missionary, whose inflection, pronunciation, vocabulary, and syntax hampered communication with the creole-speaking blacks, made them depend on the leader or daddy to explain the sermon afterwards. The daddy, of course, might have the same difficulty in understanding the white preacher. Consequently, his interpretation could be highly original, and may or may not have coincided with the sense of the sermon intended by the preacher. The missionary's reliance on the daddy helped to strengthen further the latter's leadership.[64]

Missionaries perhaps did not realize that the very ceremony of baptism itself could have fostered the continuance of "African superstition" among the blacks. Herskovits has pointed out the importance of rivers in traditional West African religions, mentioning especially that, for the Dahomey river cults, immersion was believed to create a "new born brother."[65] In March of 1842 there appeared in the *Evangelical Magazine* a letter, signed by "Vindex," on Baptist churches in Jamaica. The writer observed how the one who was being baptized would be greeted affectionately by friends as he came up out of the water with the words, "O my new-born brother, I am glad you have got through so well." The writer continued: "No one is ever so addressed till he is baptized, and generally the particular phrase, which is a household term, occurs at the precise period of baptism."[66]

The propensity of Jamaican blacks for baptism can also be connected with the Asante belief in the divine origin of water, the belief that every river or important body of water was related to the Supreme God as a son of God. Bodies of water were looked upon in Asante as containing the power of the spirit of the Creator; as a woman gives birth to a child, it was believed, so could water to a god or son of God.[67]

The phenomenon that most dramatically evidenced the Afro-creolization of Christian belief and practice was Myalism. It was a form of religion noticed in Jamaica previous to the Liele/Baker origins of native Christianity.[68] The Jesuit ethnologist Joseph John Williams, writing in the 1930s, offered an explanation of its origins that has remained substantially unchallenged. He traces it to the eighteenth-century preponderance of Akan slaves in Jamaica, and relies much on Rattray's interpretations of Asante religion.[69] According to Williams, during slavery the Ashanti *okomfo*, whose original role was as a priest who, through public ritual, influenced the spirits for the health and well-being of the community, was forced to disguise what remained of the old rites under cover of one of the dances that were permissible in local amusements, gradually appropriating these dances to his own purposes. This was a necessary response to repressive legislation against native religious assemblies. This dance in its adapted form became known to the whites as the Myal dance.[70]

The *obayifo*, as opposed to the *okomfo*, was the witch who invoked the power for evil. In Asante culture, the *okomfo* openly opposed the work of the *obayifo*. In Jamaica, however, legislation against religious assemblies, drums, and "other unlawful instruments of noise" (Act of Assembly, 21 December, 1781) hampered the *okomfo* in his sphere of influence, even his title being changed to Myal man, while the *obayifo*, or Obeah man, who had always worked in secret, flourished.

The *okomfo* had to adapt and modify his practice, and went underground. His religion had aimed primarily at the welfare of the community, whereas the object of the *obayifo* was the harm of the individual. Open intercession for communal success and prosperity gave way to secret conspiracies against slavery as the greatest evil in Jamaica, and it was thus Myal, not Obeah, claims Williams, that provided the religious base for the numerous slave rebellions in Jamaica. Accounts of rebel leaders administering the oath with mixtures of gunpowder, rum, blood, and grave dirt really refer to the Myal work, and not, as was mistakenly believed, to Obeah. For these reasons, the role of the Myalist *okomfo* was little understood: his work was ascribed by the whites to the agency of Obeah, and Myalism came to be regarded as an offshoot of Obeah, while the real work of Obeah went largely ignored.

After emancipation, Myalism tried to regain its "pristine ascendance" and made war on Obeah. But the original priestly *okomfo* class was long dead; for a generation none had come from Africa. Without leaders, Myalism would have died. However, the tradition remained, and its revival was possible because of its syncretism with native Christianity, which provided an abundance of leaders.[71]

Williams's explanation is plausible, suggesting (Williams does not state it outright) that the function of the Myal man in Jamaica was similar in its combination of the roles of spiritual and physical healing to that of the "priest of witchcraft," the *bayi 'komfo* in Asante, who utilized the skills of both the priest (*okomfo*) and the doctor or herbalist (*sumanni*).[72] The Myal leaders in Jamaica acquired their spiritual power in the tradition of the *okomfo* and gradually assimilated the skills of physical healing both through the traditional knowledge of herbs and their experience in medicine acquired through their work in estate hospitals.[73]

Contemporary missionary writers noted the existence of Myal, but usually with little or no understanding of its provenance and development. J. H. Buchner, the historian of the Moravians, was able to give a graphic though, of course, hostile description of the phenomenon.[74] Dramatic manifestations of Myal in the post-emancipation period were reported at first in 1841, and as late as 1862. But the major public occurrence, before its capture of the Great Revival in 1860–61, was in 1842. Hope Waddell's description of the Myal "outbreak" of that year, "one of the most startling events in the history of Jamaican missions," as he put it, is one of the best pieces of evidence of a Christian missionary's encounter with it. His description was somewhat less sensational than other contemporary missionary as well as newspaper reports, and his understanding was likewise more penetrating. For example, he was clear in recognizing that Myal was not Obeah but wholly opposed to it, that its object was to cure sickness and remove evil. For that very reason, however, it may have been considered more of a rival power to the salvation offered by "pure" Christianity, as is indicated in Waddell's accounts of his spiritual wrestling with the Myalists. Moreover, he makes a point that J. J. Williams, writing in the 1930s, would overlook—that the arrival of several thousand Africans after emancipation from captured slavers fed a revival of the old beliefs—even though that did not imply a return to purely Akan origins—and that, as creole blacks attributed particular spiritual skills to the old Africans among them, the *arrivants* were considered to have even greater power. There occurred, then, a re-Africanization of creole religion through the influence of African *emancipados* and immigrants.[75]

The "outbreak" of Myal in 1841–42 was concentrated around several estates near the St. James coast between Montego Bay and the Trelawny border. It began around Christmas of 1841 on Spring and Running Gut estates and recurred with greater power in July 1842 at Flower Hill and Blue Hole. By September it included sixteen estates from Iron Shore to Moor Park, including Palmyra near Waddell's mission station.

A composite picture of Waddell's encounter with the Myalists in the area not only gives us more information but reveals a spiritual struggle out of which came no conclusive victory. They were sent by God to purge and purify the world, they claimed, and they were Christians of a higher order than common. "Most or all of them" were members of one of the principal missionary churches. They set out to dig up Obeah, accompanied by singing, dancing, and other rites. Baptist members who had gone Myal attempted to take over the class house on Palmyra and the chapel at Salter's Hill. Forty Myalists arrested for disturbing the peace staged a demonstration in magistrate's court: wearing head ties and swaying to and fro, they chanted continually, "We no mad; who say we mad? It is the Lord Jesus Christ. We dig out all dem badness. Ush, ush, ush." On Content, the Myalists had held down an African Obeah man, baptized him with eight pails of water at once, danced and sung around him for an hour, and called on him to confess and call on the Lord. Sometimes the spirit or spirits entering the Myalists were not known and therefore could not be readily controlled; the people would then beat themselves, spin, convulse, stagger, moan, and run up and down "like a mad dog." Old Africans who at first did not participate were eventually ignited by the Myal enthusiasm; they then did all they could to get the spirit, went to the graves, and even opened some to release the spirits. Waddell was present at one ceremony on Blue Hole during which a ring was formed around "some females who performed a mystic dance, sailing round and round, and wheeling in the centre with outspread arms, and wild looks and gestures. . . . Others hummed, or whistled a low monotonous tune," to which all kept time with hands and feet and swaying bodies. A director seemed to stand to the side, quietly watching. Waddell tried to break the circle but was ignored; he then requested the director to silence the people, which he "did so in a moment, and most gently." The people did not disperse but said that he could stay and preach. They quickly lost attention, however, and resumed the ceremony. Waddell's second attempt to quiet the "mad women" was met with: "'They are not mad.' 'They have the spirit.' 'You must be mad yourself, and had best go away.' 'Let the women go on; we don't want you.' 'Who brought you here?' 'What do you want with us?'" He tried to preach again, only causing more confusion; he then pushed some of his congregation members who had come along with him into the circle. The dancing women as a result were baffled and frantic, and dashed from side to side, knocking over bystanders and tearing at themselves with rage. The director then (expertly) called them into a house to conclude gently with a hymn and prayers.[76]

That Myalism was not a perfect Afro-Christian syncretism, in spite of the Christian claims and terminology of the Myalists, but manifested elements that were almost purely of African traditional religion is indicated in the above synopsis of Waddell's account. Two related elements of Myalism especially indicate this. One was the implicit theology of the human soul that emerges from a consideration of Myal practice. The other was the importance of the silk cotton tree.

It was believed that the Myal man could catch the shadow of a deceased person, either at or soon after interment. He alone could see the shadow hovering. He could either seize it or charm it as it sought to evade him. When caught, it would be put into a tiny coffin to be buried in the same grave or kept in the Myal man's house. It was believed also that the shadow of a living person could wander, get lost, or be stolen. This could result either as a consequence of the individual's own malice or the effect on him of someone else's malice, usually through the instrumentality of Obeah. Waddell was particularly sensitive to these beliefs when composing his book because of his experience as a missionary at Calabar in Africa and saw the Jamaican and African correspondences.[77]

Myalist theology seems traceable to Akan beliefs regarding the human soul. A human being is a compound of *mogya*: blood, physical or biological being, matrilineally inherited; *sunsum*: individual spirit determining one's character and personality, patrilineally inherited; and *kra*: undying soul, divinely inherited. The *sunsum* can get hurt or become sick and likewise affect the body. The hatred of another, directed through witchcraft, can do this, or one's own hatred for another could make one's *sunsum* sick. Once a year in Asante there was a public confession and testimony of private hatreds and animosities in order to cool and quiet the *sunsum* of those so suffering.[78]

There is a malicious and revengeful element to the *sunsum*—in Ashanti, *sasa*, in Jamaica, shadow or duppy—which can be disassociated from the rest of the personality through the effects of witchcraft or Obeah. In Akan, the essence of interpersonal evil is summed up in the phrase *eku obi sunsum*: to kill the individual personality of a man.[79] It was a function of the Myal man in Jamaica to regain a lost or wandering shadow lest the person it belonged to waste away to death. This shadow is also very demanding at death and must be properly laid or it will remain to annoy the living.[80]

The massive silk cotton tree (ceiba) is important because of its association with shadow catching. It was believed that when Obeah caused the shadow to leave a person it was often held fast or "nailed" to the cotton tree.[81] The Myal ceremony for the release of shadows from the tree was detailed and meticulously carried out. It involved special vestments (the victim was dressed in a white robe and white headtie), sacrifice of fowls, singing and dancing, and the capture of the shadow, usually in a white basin of water. A typical Myal hymn at the release of the shadow went like this:

> Lord, have mercy, oh!
> Christ, have mercy, oh!
> Obeah pain hot, oh!
> Lord, we come fe pull he, oh!
> A no we put he, oh!
> A pirit tek he, oh!
> And we come fe pull he, oh!
> 'You fada want you, oh!
> Bwoy, you fada want you, oh!
> Bwoy, you mother want you, oh![82]

After the great Myalist revival that gathered force upon full emancipation, the catching of shadows became almost as important a Myal function as the digging up of Obeah. It is at this point that Myal ceases to appear purely African and incorporates a radical Christian eschatology. It was a repeated claim of Myalists after emancipation that Christ's return was imminent, and that they had to restore the earth to health and purity in preparation for Him by pulling all Obeahs and catching and returning all shadows that were spellbound at the cotton trees. To purify themselves, Myalists would practice an asceticism that included no smoking or drinking of alcohol, the exclusion of notoriously bad people, and the turning out of anyone known to be in malice.[83] What is noticeable about this asceticism and discipline is that it did not display the excesses that one associates with medieval penitential movements (not likely that ex-slaves would take up whips against themselves). Rather, the measures taken were calculated to preserve and increase both individual and communal health.

A striking feature of Myalism that is not often commented upon is that it was an alternative form not only of religious expression but of faith and religious knowledge. Brown's observation that certain Baptist leaders dispensed with the Bible as a necessary source of religious knowledge coincides with another missionary's description of the Myal man's belief that he was directly taught by the Spirit of God and needed no intermediary. The Rev. Benjamin Franklin of the L.M.S. wrote from Morant Bay in 1839 about his observations of Myalism in the St. David's Mountains and Blue Mountain Valley. Myal leaders professed direct inspiration by the Spirit and were able to discern wicked people at first sight. Franklin had a conversation with one of the leading "faith men" (also called "angel men")[84] in one district, identified by the name of Pennock:

> He told me that if he laid down to sleep, and put the prayerbook or Bible on his breast, the Spirit would not speak to him, but if these were not there, he would have dreams, visions, voices, etc., and that when he had the Spirit, if he opened either of the above books, the paper would appear perfectly white and clean—no print could be seen. Pennock acknowledged that the Bible would teach him many good things, but he was firm in his doctrine, "That God by his Spirit taught him many things which could not be found in the Bible."[85]

In this case, the Bible was not only not necessary for religious knowledge, it could also be a positive hindrance to communication with the Spirit.

The same Pennock seems to have been known by other missionaries. In 1840, the Methodist James Atkins described him as "a fine looking black man" who was destitute of any religious knowledge—had scarcely ever seen or attended a place of worship, but of some old African superstitious observances, he had formed what he considered "a Christian System," and raised up a number of followers under the designation of *"The Faith People,"* who professed to be capable of discerning spirits—and were required to extirpate the wicked from the earth.[86]

Other Myal leaders and their followers did not consider it necessary to be independent of the missionary churches and persisted in identifying themselves as Baptists or Wesleyans.[87]

In this light, it is possible to see Myalism as a creole synthesis of evangelical Christianity and African religious experience, in which communication with the spirit world did not rely on the mediation of minister or book. This synthesis was hastened by the system of black leaders that the Baptists and other missionaries utilized. In this sense, Barrett and other critics were correct in observing that the system helped to preserve African "superstitions."

Socially and culturally, Myalism was important as the expression of black identity and resistance in a so-called free society in which the European presence continued to be the sign and source of political, economic, and cultural oppression, interpreted by the Afro-creole Myalists as a type of sorcery that had to be countered. The more dramatic public manifestations of Myal occurred at times of particularly severe community hardship and stress, when the motivation to counter Obeah and sorcery would be the strongest. Also noteworthy was the propensity of Myalists to claim a righteous superiority to more orthodox Christians and to civil authorities, even to the extent of denouncing the queen, remarkable at a time when, no matter what was thought of all other whites, the queen was venerated as a figure of superhuman benevolence.[88]

It is possible to conclude that Myalism combined the best of

Christian hope with the this-world–directed power of African traditional religion. It prevented a despairing acceptance of the post-emancipation social order as predestined and unshakable. No matter how agnostic one might be with regard to the claimed power of the Myal man, he was nevertheless the *bayi 'komfo* whose purpose was to protect his people against personal and social danger.

The consolidation of the synthesis of evangelical Christianity and African religion in Myalism was most dramatically manifested in the Great Revival of 1861. It began in October of 1860 among the Moravian congregations in the southwest then spread to the Methodist and Baptist congregations throughout the western half of the island. It was greeted with great joy by the missionaries who thought that finally the Holy Spirit had blown away the hardheartedness of the unregenerated blacks to bring about the decisive triumph of Christianity. By January of 1861, however, it had obviously taken a form that led to the chagrin of all the white ministers. The enthusiasm that was at first welcomed was causing a form of physical convulsion that was a problem because the ministers did not have a method of controlling it. Initially, the phenomenon was explained away: physical prostration was not to be confused with the work of the Spirit or to be mistaken for that which is inward, spiritual, and vital in religion; the Spirit works in the heart, not in the body; physical manifestations were merely secondary or accidental.[89] As the physical manifestations increased, the benefit of the doubt was still given to the stricken blacks: "There is so much extravagant excitement among the people, much of which, we fear, is the work of the adversary, and yet we feel timid to judge anyone."[90] In attempting to discern what were the causes of this development, the Methodist William Tyson listened to the explanation of one of the revivalists. There were two spirits working among the people, he explained. One was the spirit of Jesus, a spirit of peace and joy. The other was a violent spirit that seized hold of the people, making them frantic and heedless of their actions. It is interesting that the informant, when prompted by Tyson, refused to call this second spirit a bad spirit or to give it the name of Satan or Anti-Christ.[91]

By February, missionary observers were at last forced to admit that the revival had gone Myal and that many participants were less interested in their own regeneration than in digging up Obeah. There was "pandemonium" in the chapels: "simultaneous singing, shouting, groaning, praying, thumping, stamping, tumbling, rolling, dancing round and round in wildest frenzy."[92] The revivalists believed they were receiving immediate revelations by the Spirit, and some took it upon themselves to baptize others. Some professed "to see visions and to dream dreams, and firmly believe these to be of Divine inspiration."[93]

Numerous observers remarked on the wanton sexuality of the revivalists and the uncontrolled, animal-like behavior, the thrashings and writhings on the ground.[94] Explained in terms of traditional African religion, this behavior testifies to the presence in the revivalists of particularly violent or energetic spirits, and the seeming lack of control was possibly due to a deficiency of specialists or priests on hand to oversee and direct, a function of supreme importance in African religion and in its Jamaican Myal form. If this is true, then it is also possible that at the outset the Great Revival might have been as much a surprise for Myalist leaders as it was for the Christian missionaries. In any event, the Myalists captured the revival. They formed a circle, as it were, into which the missionary was less and less able to penetrate. And then the descriptions of it vary little from Waddell's earlier descriptions of Myal in 1842.[95]

While the Myal aspect of the Great Revival was not island-wide—Phillippo did not witness it in his district and in fact thought the revival the end of Myal and Obeah[96]—it nevertheless gave renewed strength to all forms of native religion throughout Jamaica. What is significant about revivalism as it developed from the early 1860s was that it was increasingly open, independent, and self-confident in a way that Obeah could never be and that Myalism had only been previously during periodic "outbreaks." It broke the walls of the churches, as it were, and took to the road. In some instances, impromptu revivalist services served the same purpose as many political marches and street demonstrations today. One case occurred, according to a *Falmouth Post* report in 1864, in the yard of the Hampshire Court House in Trelawny, during and after the sitting of the court. Some persons (the number was not given) from a district called Sawyers had been charged with petty larcenies. When they were brought up for the hearing, they were accompanied by a group of from three to four hundred supporters. The *Post*'s description of their religious demonstration is worth quoting for its revelation of the "respectable" viewpoint on black revivalism:

> [The crowd], after the passing of the respective sentences by the Justices, commenced a noise which beggars description, associated with indecent contortions of their bodies, with the loud singing of "revival" hymns, and with wild and execrable vociferations in which, under the guise of prayer, the sacred name of the Creator was blasphemed.[97]

To appreciate the response of white ministers in general to the revival, it is sufficient here to indicate something of the impact of it on the Baptist and Methodist missionaries. The outcome dashed any lingering hopes that the Jamaican blacks could be reclaimed totally from "heathenism." Shortly before the revival, Dr. Underhill had visited Jamaica to give encouragement to the Baptist parsons who were undergoing a crisis of confidence in the value and results of their work.[98] Whatever good Underhill could have done for the brethren was undermined by the emergent revivalism, a religious form that was seen to be on the same level with "idleness and prostitution, robberies and vagabondism, and depravity of every description."[99] Two distinct movements among churches that called themselves Baptist developed out of the Great Revival. There was an increase in the number of independent native congregations on the one hand and a drawing together of Baptist Union congregations in disciplined associations under District Boards on the other. In effect, this meant a consolidation of the gulf between the Native Baptists and the Baptist Union.[100] It also indicated a further modification of the Baptist principle of congregational democracy in reaction to black assertion of independence, a tendency that was initiated in 1845 with the formation of the accreditation panel to approve or disapprove congregational choice of ministers.

The Great Revival was to be as much a shock to Methodists as to other white missionaries, if not more so. When the first indications of revival appeared in October 1860 among black Methodists, the missionaries hastened to welcome them as signs of hope that they would be able to reverse their weakened influence. "That this is a *genuine* revival, no spiritually enlightened mind can doubt," wrote John Mearns.[101]

Having thus embraced the revival, it was all the more staggering for them when, from about the spring of 1861, the Methodists had to recognize that it had turned into a manifestation of Myal. It must have been particularly disconcerting when there arose, at Guy's Hill in October 1861, a certain black "queen" who claimed revelation from heaven and a vision of hell "without a covering." In that hell, she saw the local Methodist missionary, and she pronounced a dread judgment against all the Methodists. The missionary at Guy's Hill confirmed that her influence over her followers was total.[102]

Black resistance both during slavery and after emancipation was most dramatically manifested in periodic rebellions. Waddell noted that there were twenty-seven partial or general insurrections between 1678 and 1831.[103] Of the two largest rebellions of the nineteenth century, one was the last and greatest of the slave rebellions; occurring in 1831-32 in the western parishes, it was known variously as the Christmas Rebellion, the Baptist War, and the Black Family War (blacks called the Baptists the Black Family).[104] The rebellion was organized through connections established in the nonconformist system of congregations, classes, and class leaders; the leading rebels, the most famous of whom is Sam Sharp (or "Sharpe"), were able to organize and inspire the rebellion out of the convictions that were theirs as religious leaders in the Baptist church.

White Jamaica firmly believed that sectarian missionaries, mainly Baptists, were the rebellion's promoters and directors. The missionaries, however, were adamant in their denial that they had encouraged and directed the rebellion, and, in fact, no hard evidence could be gathered against them. Their message from the pulpit to the slaves had consistently been one of nonresistance. The few planters who were sympathetic to the missionaries explained that it was not religion but the absence of it that allowed the rebellion to take place. Many white missionaries, urgent to defend the purity of the Gospel of peace, also argued that it was the lack of religion that caused the slaves to rebel. The slaves who were truly religious, went the missionary argument, were held back by conscience from joining the rebellion.[105]

The argument was an evasion because it did not admit that the resolve of the slaves was grounded in a spiritual strength, in the belief that the Christian doctrines of the freedom of the sons of

God and the equality of all men were meant specifically for them. Preachers who realized this, especially Anglicans, were careful to censor portions of the Bible in sermons to slaves. When asked if he thought that the Scriptures might be misunderstood by the slaves, Rev. Mr. Hall, curate in Manchester in 1832, replied:

> Yes, if I were to preach in the same manner to them as the whites, they may be misunderstood. I conceive that the greatest caution is necessary in preaching to the slaves. . . . On Christmas day, a thought occurred to me to introduce into my discourse the words from the Bible, "If the son hath made you free, then you are indeed free;" but I immediately discarded it from my mind, from an apprehension that such an expression might be misunderstood by the slaves.[106]

Baptist ministers, however, were less careful in deleting scriptural texts with egalitarian and liberationist themes, themes which were interpreted by the slaves in the context of their own experience of bondage. The contradiction between the Christian ideal and slave reality had to be resolved. The rebels firmly believed that they were doing the will of God.[107]

The Baptist missionary Cornford's reclamation of Sam Sharp in 1855, in an article entitled "The Christian Hero" in the *Freeman*, is unabashed hagiography, yet his appreciation of Sharp's religious motivation is perhaps less anachronistic than the tendency of twentieth-century historians to secularize the thinking of the slave rebel leaders. Curtin's characterization of Sam Sharp, for example, implies that he was more astute as a trade union leader than convincing as a religious prophet.[108] According to Cornford, on the other hand, Sharp led a "holy protest": "The passion burned only in the fire of holy principle. . . . You cannot sever them. They brighten and burn in equal brilliance and in immortal flames."[109]

An eyewitness to Sharp's execution, who was, according to

Cornford, "extremely curious about the effect of religion in reference to such a death," provided this testimony:

> With a clear voice he told them he was going to die because he had thought they had a right to be free. He protested his innocence of every outrage and wrong. He professed his firm faith in the atoning blood of Jesus, and his hope of eternal life; whilst his closing words about "the coming rain from heaven" were interpreted by many as prophetic of freedom soon to come—and so he doubtless meant them.[110]

The truth of Sam Sharp and the rebels' motivation is both other and more than what either secular or pious interpretations have given us. The slaves sealed their agreements in the tradition of the *okomfo*'s oath, this time by kissing the Book, the Bible, the white man's fetish, which now had a power that transcended race. In the end, it did not matter too much what the white ministers actually preached, but what the slaves heard, interpreted through the hermeneutic of freedom and incorporated into an Afro-Christian mythology that gave renewed sense and meaning to protest and resistance.

The brutal suppression of the 1831–32 uprising—hasty and retaliatory executions resulting in the deaths of about six hundred blacks—followed in 1833 with Parliament's Emancipation Act, eliminated neither the conditions nor the consciousness that led to rebellion. Sixteen years after the Baptist War, a series of reports from the western parishes led authorities to fear another outbreak. The governor ordered an inventory of special constables, the doubling of police numbers at western stations, the distribution of arms to militia regiments, the concentration of Her Majesty's forces near the troubled areas, and a warship to be present during the August emancipation holiday. As in 1831–32, the disaffected peasantry and estate laborers were accused of being inspired by Baptist missionaries. Reports from Westmoreland were of preparation for war in Baptist meetings, growing especially out of discontent with the perceived injustices perpetrated by lower-echelon management on sugar plantations; schemes of resistance were being proposed by black Baptist leaders, in a manner reminiscent of preparation for rebellion in 1831. The catalyst that brought events to the threshold of active rebellion was the rumor that slavery was to be reimposed in Jamaica, a rumor that grew naturally out of the existence of a planter movement toward annexation of Jamaica to the United States. Baptist missionaries were actively involved only to the extent that they kept their congregations informed of planter intentions.[111]

Although no general uprising occurred in 1848, the similarities of the circumstances of that year with those of 1831–32 are obvious, especially the linking, or the attempt to link, Baptist ministers with rebel planning. There is, however, a significant difference between the events of 1831–32 and 1848, on the one hand, and 1865 on the other. In 1831–32 and 1848, Baptist ministers had a connection, however interpreted, with the prospect or actuality of rebellion; but in 1865, in spite of efforts to connect them with events in St. Thomas-in-the-East, white Baptist leadership can be unambiguously disconnected from any inspiration for rebellion there.

CHAPTER 5

Morant Bay and After

Between 1848 and 1865 there were several disturbances or riots in various parts of the island, resulting from grievances among the blacks which were symptomatic of uncompleted emancipation in post-slave Jamaica. None of them, however, approached in scale what would come to be known as the Morant Bay Rebellion of 1865.

On Saturday, 7 October 1865, petty sessions court was being held in the courthouse in Morant Bay in the parish of St. Thomas-in-the-East. A spectator in the courthouse called out to an assault defendant that he should not pay the costs but only the fine, both of which had been imposed by the presiding justice. When the magistrate ordered the man's arrest, he was rescued by the other spectators, who turned on the police, it was reported, and beat them. On Monday, 9 October, court was resumed for a case of trespass. Surveyors had been sent to Amity Hall, Hordley, and Middleton estates in St. Thomas; these estates were to be subdivided and sold to pay off their encumbrances. The surveyors were met by angry peasants from the village of Stony Gut, which bordered Middleton. These small farmers had occupied and cultivated portions of abandoned estate lands for several years. One of the farmers, Lewis Miller, was arrested, and it was his case that was being heard on 9 October. Miller was ordered to pay a fine with costs. As on Saturday, spectators—most of whom were supporters of Lewis from the Stony Gut area—called out in protest. Miller was allowed to enter an appeal.

On 10 October, Tuesday, warrants for the arrest of Paul Bogle, a Native Baptist parson and small farmer of Stony Gut, and several of his companions were issued. They were to be charged for the courthouse disturbances of 7 and 9 October. A contingent of eight policemen and constables were sent to Stony Gut to carry out the warrants. The police, who were black, were prevented by the villagers from arresting Bogle. They were beaten and forced to swear to "cleave to the black" and to "join their colour." It was alleged that Bogle intended to lead an attack on a parish vestry meeting in Morant Bay scheduled for the following day. Warned of this on Tuesday evening, the parish custos, Baron von Ketelhodt, informed Governor Edward John Eyre and requested that troops be sent to Morant Bay.

On the same Tuesday evening, Bogle and nineteen members of his congregation signed a petition to the governor, in which they protested that the incident of 7 October had been precipitated by the overbearing manner of the police acting on the orders of the justice; they asked, as loyal subjects of Her Majesty, for the governor's protection, and added the challenge: "which protection if refused to [we] will be compelled to put our shoulders to the wheel, as we have been imposed upon for a period of 27 years with due obeisance to the laws of our Queen and country, and we can no longer endure the same. . . ."[1] Bogle's reference to the oppressions of the twenty-seven-year post-emancipation period, from the ending of apprenticeship in 1838, indicates the broad historical view that he held as a context for the particular grievances and events that were coming to a head that October week in 1865.

A warship containing a hundred troops did not leave Port Royal for Morant Bay until Thursday morning, 12 October, too late to intervene in the confrontation that took place on Wednesday. The custos, who, with a small assemblage of the local militia, had failed to prevent Bogle and his followers from entering the courthouse square, began to read the riot act from the courthouse steps. Before he was able to finish, stones were thrown from the crowd. Von Ketelhodt ordered the militia to fire, and several people in the square fell. Angered further, the crowd rushed the courthouse, where the militiamen and the custos joined the vestrymen under siege. The courthouse was set on fire. The men inside were attacked when they rushed out to avoid the flames. Several of them were killed in the attack, including the custos and the Anglican curate of Bath, Rev. Mr. Herschell. The militant small farmers occupied Morant Bay. On Thursday, they marched out to take the town of Bath and to attack plantations along the Plantain Garden River.

When the governor learned on Thursday of the events in St. Thomas, he immediately declared martial law in the eastern third of the island and quickly deployed increased military forces, with Maroon assistance, in the parish and parts of Portland. Under his authority, the retaliatory toll of floggings, executions, and destruction of peasant property exceeded that which had been exacted after the 1831–32 slave rebellion. Governor Eyre wrote on 2 November, "The retribution has been so prompt and so terrible that it is never likely to be forgotten."[2] Among the executed were Paul Bogle, captured by Maroons, and George William Gordon, colored landowner and assemblyman, who had been arrested in Kingston, where martial law was not in effect, and transported to Morant Bay to be sentenced to death by court-martial. Both Bogle and Gordon were considered by the authorities to have been the ringleaders of the uprising.

Unlike earlier struggles, the Morant Bay Rebellion could not be linked with the Baptist missionary system. The concentration of Baptist activity in the western parishes had not been duplicated

5. Paul Bogle. Courtesy of the National Library of Jamaica.

6. George William Gordon. Courtesy of the National Library of Jamaica.

in the east. The B.M.S had had hardly any connection with St. Tho-mas-in-the-East. Baptist missionary activity was not focused on the Morant Bay area until after the rebellion. At the urging of Sir Henry Storks, head of the Royal Commission to investigate the re-bellion, and other influential persons in the island, the Rev. Wil-liam Teall moved from the pastorate of three churches in Hanover to establish a Baptist mission at Morant Bay. According to the Royal Commission testimony of the secretary of the Jamaica Bap-tist Union, Benjamin Millard, at the time of the rebellion there was only one Baptist missionary in the parish, with three congrega-tions—at Manchioneal, Leith Hall, and Stokes Hall. It was gener-ally acknowledged by missionaries at the time that there were fewer European ministers and more Native Baptists in the east than in any other parts of the island.[3]

Much of the suspicion that the preaching and activities of Baptist missionaries were behind the rebellion had much to do with the fa-mous "Underhill letter," written by the secretary of the B.M.S. and sent to the Secretary of State for the Colonies, Edward Cardwell. The letter described and analyzed the dire conditions of the island, especially with regard to the peasant and laboring population. Underhill's letter found its way into the hands of Governor Eyre, who published it with a request for opinions from the white sec-tors (planters and Anglican clergymen) of the island. Noncon-formist missionaries and the blacks, however, were key partici-pants in a series of "Underhill meetings," public discussions on the contents of the letter which were organized throughout the is-land in the spring and summer of 1865.[4] Even before the Underhill meetings had commenced, the leading ministers of the Jamaica Baptist Union had composed a letter (on April 19–20) that supported in great detail the picture of poverty and distress that Underhill had depicted. The ministers were compelled to write, they claimed, because they were "concerned in whatever related to the temporal and eternal interests of those committed to their pastoral oversight, or to the social well-being of the country in which they live." Similar but briefer memorials, agreeing substantially with the Baptist report, were sent to Eyre by the Wesleyans, Presbyterians, and Moravians.[5]

When taken together, various public and private responses of Governor Eyre to the Baptist influence on attitudes and events leading up to the rebellion reveal ambivalent if not contradictory evaluations on the part of the governor. In his testimony before the Storks Commission, Eyre exonerated the majority of the Baptist ministers from having any part in the rebellion and praised them for their support for the authorities, their teaching of loyalty and industry to the people, and their endorsement of the "Queen's Advice," a royal dispatch—in response to a hardship petition from the people of St. Ann—that promised the people that their lot could only improve by self-help and hard and consistent work for wages. Eyre singled out only "the nefarious" influence of five Baptist ministers—Henderson, Reid, Dendy, Hewitt, and Maxwell.[6]

At most other times, however, Eyre's vituperations against the Baptist ministers were sweeping. In his correspondence and addresses to the Assembly he tried to implicate them in general in fomenting riot and sedition, in propagating untruthful statements and innuendos, and in promoting the "nefarious proceeding" which had issued in rebellion and murder. He claimed that the Underhill meetings had been organized mostly through the agency of Baptist ministers or others acting or professing to act in connection with them, who took a prominent part in "addressing the mob, and joining in resolutions, adopting entirely, and vouching for, the correctness of Dr. Underhill's allegations." Eyre envisioned a Jamaican Act for "the deportation of all persons who, leaving their proper sphere of action as ministers of religion, become political demagogues and dangerous agitators," under which he would have attempted to rid the island of the Baptists, a measure that had been a goal of the Colonial Church Union in 1832. Only his suspension as governor forestalled the introduction of such a bill.[7]

Besides the fact that Underhill had not written his letter for publication in Jamaica, and that it was Eyre himself who had broadcast it, other evidence put forward by the Baptists clearly shows that their role preceding the rebellion was much less than what Eyre wanted the world to believe. Baptist ministers actually had a relatively small share in the Underhill meetings. Of the thirty-six Baptist ministers recognized by the Baptist Union on the island, only seven Europeans and four coloreds participated. Of the other ministers who addressed the meetings, three belonged to the Church of England, two were Methodists, three were Presbyterians, and one was Methodist secessionist.[8] Moreover, observed Underhill, the leadership of the ministers was not as necessary as it might have been in the days of Knibb and Burchell, for the blacks had become more aware of their rights and more articulate in defending them:

> The oppressed and down-trodden people were not without able expounders of their rights, men risen from their own ranks, who had happily enjoyed, and learnt how to know the value of, the privileges which education, civilisation, and religion had brought to them at the cost, and by the instruction, of the Christian teachers in their midst. . . . Reading and writing were their familiar acquisition. The Bible had been their primer, and its Divine teachings familiarised them with the great law of righteousness—that law which exalteth a nation. Some of them had proved apt scholars.[9]

Eyre, of course, could claim such native outspokenness as a form of sedition ultimately traceable to Baptist teaching.

Phillippo offered his proof of the relatively minor role of Union Baptists in the rebellion in the form of a set of rather surprising comparative figures on the religious affiliation of "the most respectable individuals" arrested on suspicion of complicity in the rebellion: "B.M.S.," 3; "Native Bap.," 3; "Jews," 3; "Native Wesl.," 1; "United Methodist," 1; "Independent," 1; "Scotch Kirk," 1; "Ch. of Eng.," 26; "R.C.," "30 and upwards."[10] Whatever the validity of these figures, it cannot be denied that St. Thomas-in-the-East had been a parish neglected by the B.M.S. The reputation of the B.M.S. and the Baptist Union as playing a key role in Paul Bogle's insurrection, in sum, is not deserved, and is due almost entirely to Eyre's fulminations and their amplification by his supporters in England.

Nevertheless, by the year 1865, the eastern parishes were suffused with a higher degree of politicized religion than had ever been preached by Baptist missionaries in earlier years. Perhaps the most well known of the propagators of this religion was the Assemblyman George William Gordon, whose speeches were characterized by critics as combinations of "garrulous display and scriptural citations."[11] Gordon appropriated religion to politics in a more deliberate way than had ever been done before by a native Jamaican not of the peasantry or laboring class.

It is possible that the conflict between Governor Eyre and Gordon was not purely one of a British official being challenged by a populist native political leader. It was complicated and exacerbated by the fact that both Eyre and Gordon claimed a religious basis for their interest in the peasantry. Eyre's emphasis, however, was on bourgeois morality and notions of proper social habits which made sense to those who were secure in property and a certain amount of wealth. What he held out to the peasantry was a middle class morality that they should strive for as an ideal. "I believe," testified Eyre, "that civilization must go hand and hand with Christianity, and that until the peasantry of the country, can be induced to erect better dwellings, and thereby obtain the means of adopting social habits more in accordance with decency and propriety, there can be little hope that the teaching of the Minister or the Schoolmaster will be able to withstand the corrupting influence of evil example at home."[12] Gordon's religion, on the other hand, served as a basis of protest against the oppression which prevented the ex-slaves and their children from attaining a position of relative security in wealth and property. No prominent politician in Jamaica had ever taken such a radical stance, and this was a shock even to those with outlooks more liberal than that of Eyre. It led the *Falmouth Post* to remark on Gordon's "hypocritical pretence of religion and of friendship with the labouring population," on his "pretence of religious fervour and zeal," and to characterize him as an "oily demagogue."[13]

Gordon's progression from Presbyterian to Native Baptist seemed calculated to bring his influence closer to the working class. It was a religious journey that Paul Bogle himself noted, and to which he gave his blessing in writing: ". . . in the *religious* [world] we are asurd [*sic*] your progress is great; may God grant it so." Correspondence between Gordon and Bogle on religious matters had been conducted from at least December of 1861. Before then, Gordon had participated in Congregationalist meetings; in 1857 he was a member of W. J. Gardner's church in Kingston. He was baptized by Phillippo on Christmas Day, 1861. A note from him to Phillippo later that day included these words: "May His grace keep and defend me in running the race which is now before me!"[14]

Gordon did not join a Baptist Union congregation, however, but commenced organizing meetings on his own. In March of 1863 he was elected to the Assembly for St. Thomas-in-the-East. The religious significance of that election, which he expressed personally to Phillippo, is that he had given much attention to the Native Baptists in that parish and attributed his election to their support. His claim is supported by Paul Bogle having conducted his own voter registration drive on behalf of Gordon; his work for Gordon was in progress from at least eight months before the March election. He wrote to Gordon in July of 1862 of his plans to increase the electorate by the registration of "independent freeholders," and of his need to borrow funds to pay the required taxes and registration fees.[15] Phillippo later remarked that he recommended all along that Gordon "originate an independent cause under his own superintendence." Gordon's known support of Underhill's analysis of the Jamaican situation and his criticism of the "Queen's Advice" were factors in Eyre's extending of his hatred of Gordon to the Baptists in general. For his shifts in religious affiliation, Gordon's old friend Gardner considered him deranged, and the *Post* called him a "psuedo-enthusiastic religionist." While the missionaries in general acknowledged that the blacks had serious grievances, they did not share Gordon's approach to them. They began to think him obsessed and his zeal too akin to that of the revivalists that had stung Europeans during the Great Revival.[16]

There were, nevertheless, a few exceptions to the general missionary disdain for Gordon. The L.M.S. missionary Duncan Fletcher was one of these. Fletcher felt compelled to resign from his ministry because he was censured by his fellow ministers after attending a meeting chaired by Gordon.[17] Gordon maintained an affectionate relationship with Phillippo and sought his counsel continually. His character was also defended by two Methodist ministers who had known him, the Revs. H. B. Britten and Edwin Blake. Neither Britten nor Blake, however, was resident in Jamaica at the time of the rebellion; they did not fear reprisals for their opinions. In Jamaica, the harshness of suppression would have intimidated into reticence anyone who held favorable views of Gordon, Paul Bogle, or native preachers as a whole. Methodist ministers in Jamaica would have been particularly intimidated by the vociferous dislike of District Chairman Edmondson for Gordon.[18]

The vehemence of the rebels against the Anglican clerics was not accidental. Some of the expressions in Gordon's letters referred to by the Storks Commission consisted of attacks on the clergy of the established church. "They will soon all find their level, and go like chaff against the wind," he wrote.[19] The indifference of the clergy to the problems of the laboring class was felt by the blacks and propagandized by individuals such as Gordon as well as by the revived *Jamaica Watchman and People's Free Press*. In June of 1865, the *Watchman* reminded its readers that "The Ministers of the Established Church are drones in the Bee Hive, good for nothing, but to feed on the labours of other men. . . . May the day soon come, when they will feel like other men, the pinchings of hunger." The edition of 21 August railed against the deceptions of the "crafty and jesuitical Priesthood" of the Anglican church, naming specifically Island Curate Herschell and Rector Cooke both of St. Thomas-in-the-East.[20] Herschell and three sons of Cooke were killed in the rebellion.

Not all the Anglican clergy deserved the criticisms of the *Watchman* and Gordon. Two of them who were not in agreement with Eyre and not totally sympathetic to the plantocracy were found worthy of note by Underhill. Both Rev. J. Garrett, the rector in Vere, and Rev. H. Clarke, curate of Westmoreland, suppressed the publication of the "Queen's Advice" in their districts. Clarke accused Eyre and his advisers of sharing in the guilt of inciting rebellion and of ignoring the universal distress; by publishing the "Queen's Advice," "they mocked the cry of the poor, and showed themselves the mere partisans of the class opposed to the negroes," and engaged in an act of sheer recklessness.[21] Both Garrett and Clarke, however, are noteworthy because they stand in sharp relief against the majority of their brethren.

The *Watchman* was the only local newspaper at the time to publicize consistently and sympathetically the protests of the peasants and black workers. In one of the paper's reports, a kind of "theology of liberation" was expressed by a native pastor, the Rev. James H. Crole, at an Underhill meeting in St. Ann's Bay on 29 July 1865. The resolution that Crole moved was:

> That this meeting desires to give expressions of gratitude and thankfulness to Almighty God for his unspeakable goodness, and mercy vouchsafed to the lately emancipated people of this Island, and would implore the divine interposition at this juncture in connection with the oppressed, distressed, wretched and deplorable condition in which the larger proportion of the population is placed by drought, and other causes, but especially by the unusual indigested [sic] and oppressive system of Government which is pursued, and feel that investigation and remedy are now loudly called for.[22]

The meeting was chaired by G. W. Gordon. Crole was pastor of the Tabernacle in Kingston, a native congregation that Gordon helped to found (he was called acting secretary of the Tabernacle), and at which he regularly attended meetings and services. Bogle was ordained deacon in the Tabernacle in March of 1865 by Cole's assistant, Richard Warren.[23]

The inability or unwillingness of those who maintained an anti-Baptist prejudice to make distinctions or to temper their criticisms with some appreciation of present realities led them also to extend unqualified suspicion toward all nonwhite parsons at the time of the rebellion, regardless of whether they were independent or affiliated with one of the missionary churches. Thus treated with the same suspicion and harshness in the aftermath of the rebellion were Rev. Edwin Palmer, a black Jamaican parson in the Baptist Union, minister of the Hanover St. Baptist church in Kingston; Rev. James Service, another black minister of the Baptist Union; Rev. Roach, an independent pastor, originally from Barbados and formerly a Methodist preacher; and Rev. Crole, already mentioned, associate of Gordon, Native Baptist, and pastor of the Kingston Tabernacle. These "dangerous" men, arrested for sedition, imprisoned without trial, maltreated, and later released for lack of evidence implicating them in the rebellion, barely escaped the fate of Gordon and Bogle. More reprehensible was the execution of a Mr. Cowell, who had formerly officiated at the chapel at Stony Gut, but who in 1865 was old and emaciated, powerless to participate actively in any rebellion.[24]

In spite of metropolitan protests by missionary societies against Governor Eyre, it was the almost unanimous opinion of nonnative Christian ministers in the island that he acted correctly in his suppression of the rebellion, lest the outbreak engulf the entire island.[25] W. J. Gardner affirmed that no religious group connected with European missionaries could be blamed for the rebellion. It was entirely the work of purely native congregations. To support his point, he observed that only a few months before the outbreak there had been a serious altercation among the leaders of a Native Baptist chapel near Morant Bay because two English ministers had been permitted to conduct a service there. The slogan "colour for colour" that was used in the rebellion had a basis in the emphasis of native pastors in St. Thomas-in-the-East on preventing any contact or allegiance with white pastors.[26]

Missionary correspondence is valuable for its observations on the influence of native pastors in 1865, as well as for revealing the loathing of European ministers toward them. The following from the Methodist District Chairman Edmondson is typical:

> In almost every Parish a number of uneducated, and I fear unprincipled men, have risen up as native Preachers, chiefly of the Bap-

tist persuasion. They have formed churches and become their ministers. Most of them are utterly incapable of instructing the people in the great principles of Gospel Truth; and it is highly probable that they have dwelt much on the claims of *classes*, and have represented the Black as an oppressed race, who ought to defend themselves. I have heard of language like the following as used by a black preacher—"You are black and I am black, and you ought to support your own colour." "The blacks are seven to one of the others, and they ought to have the Island."[27]

And this:

The parties principally complained of are the upstarts who have neither intelligence nor principle nor character for the Ministry. They form little churches of their own and are joined by many who would despise them, if not influenced by the idea that black must support black. This is one of the reasons why other churches cannot prosper.[28]

The B.M.S. and the Baptist Union, in their defense against Eyre's accusations, tried to disassociate themselves entirely from the Native Baptists. This led to some inaccurate if not dishonest claims. Underhill, for example, was true to history in acknowledging the independent origin of the Native Baptists in the 1780s in the preaching of freed slaves from the United States but seemed to distort the cooperation between the native group and the original B.M.S. missionaries, especially Burchell, by claiming there had never been any union with them, a claim that was true only in a formal or institutional sense. Underhill also iterated a theme that many missionaries used in their defense after the 1831 rebellion— that it was not religion but the absence of it that caused rebellion; thus he could claim that four-fifths of the people of St. Thomas-in-the-East were without religious instruction, giving no credence whatsoever to the strong Native Baptist communities there as a form of Christianity. Phillippo, who seems, strangely enough, to have had more appreciation of the Native Baptists by the 1860s than either Underhill or he himself in earlier years had had, supported the lack-of-religion theme by denying that even Native Baptists had anything to do with the rebellion (who, then, was Paul Bogle?): "The greater number of rebels by far consisted of men connected with no religious society, Africans as ignorant and debased as in their native wilds." Here is an echo of the voice of the earlier Phillippo of *Jamaica Past and Present*. In fact, as Schuler has shown, the participation of African immigrants in the insurrection was minimal. It was essentially a creole uprising.[29]

At the time, the publicity given to Gordon because of his prominent position in Jamaican society and politics caused him to overshadow vastly the figure of Paul Bogle in the public mind. Consistent with the stereotype of the native religious leader as ignorant and easily deceived, Bogle was seen as a mere factotum of Gordon.[30] On the relationship of Gordon and Bogle, the royal commissioners had this to say:

> If a man like Paul Bogle was in the habit of hearing such expressions as those contained in Gordon's letters, as that the reign of their oppressors would be short, and that the Lord was about to destroy them, it would not take much to convince him that he might be the appointed instrument in the Lord's hand for effecting that end; and it is clear that this was Bogle's belief, as we find that after the part he had taken in the massacre at Morant Bay, he, in his chapel at Stony Gut, returned thanks to God that "he had gone to do that work, and that God had prospered him in his work."[31]

In the type of history that it has been possible to write from documentary sources alone, less is known about Paul Bogle than about Sam Sharp. Bogle remains virtually submerged, of no notice to those who wrote and preserved the documents except for the brief episode in 1865 when he intrudes onto the stage of European Jamaica and is quickly dispatched. Even Sharp is the subject of much confusion and conflicting interpretations, and he is only more visible than Bogle ever was because he happened to be connected with those loquacious and avidly literate Baptist missionaries. But Bogle has never found his way into any missionary martyrology.

By 1865, even Sam Sharp was mostly forgotten, although there is indication that Sharp and the other slave martyrs of 1831–32 were remembered with the greatest affection by the likes of Bogle and his brethren. Storks Commission evidence reveals that a source of inspiration for the peasants in St. Thomas-in-the-East was a Baptist "book of martyrs" which allegedly extolled the example of Baptist slave rebels who died during the rebellion of 1831–32. This is given in the testimony of the Anglican clergyman E. B. Key on 3 March 1866. Phillippo, who questioned Curate Key during the Royal Commission hearings, suggested but did not verify that the book might have been the *Voice of Jubilee*, the published chronicle of the Baptist mission in Jamaica in honor of the fiftieth anniversary of its commencement in 1814.[32] It is reasonable to accept that some such book was at issue, as it was common in missionary writings, not only Baptist, to venerate the memory of slaves who had died, in and out of rebellion, in the cause of religion. The Baptist missionary Cornford's reclamation of Sharp as a Christian hero would have found its way into any subsequent Baptist "book of martyrs." Such a book would have carried forward Sharp's spirit and helped his preservation within an oral tradition that was augmented by, first of all, the Bible, and then by lesser writings like missionary memorials and reminiscences. Bogle did not have that advantage. By disassociating themselves so adamantly from the Native Baptists in 1865, the Baptists and other missionaries closed their books on him. Yet his memory remained strongest where his spirit dwells, among the black peasantry of St. Thomas who proclaim, as recorded by J. G. Moore in his study of Kumina, "Paul Bogle will return again."[33]

Even though Baptists and others were able to analyze the causes of distress in Jamaica with great acuity, there was a limit to their defense of the black population, a cultural and racial barrier that seemed even stronger in 1865 than it had been in 1832, and which corresponded to the increasing distance between native religion and the metropolitan-bound churches. A letter of the Baptist ministers dated April 19–20 to Governor Eyre is a case in point. Their portrayal of distress and poverty in the island was detailed and convincing. Yet their views on the social results of that distress reveal an attitude toward the black population that was part of prevailing racial assumptions with regard to barbarism and civilization: "The masses of the people have not yet advanced far in civilization. Their artificial wants are very few, whilst the climate is such as to induce habits of indolence." The descendants of the slaves had been getting used to certain comforts acquired without extraordinary labor, but now that they cannot be obtained "without an amount of energy and labour foreign to their habits," they are becoming despondent and careless. "There is no denying that had the people more persevering energy of character, they would, notwithstanding these discouragements, have accomplished more. But it must be considered that they are yet only in the incipient stages of civilization."[34]

Missionary thinking was influenced by the rudimentary social sciences in the metropole at the time, which had not yet broken away fully from being a branch of "moral philosophy," for which *savagery* and *barbarism* as well as *civilization* were technical terms of social theory, not just loosely used epithets. The West African, for example, was not generally seen as savage, but barbarous—a stage of development not yet civilized. This was linked to the prevailing view, from the late eighteenth century, that labor for wages was a basis of civilization. Tropical man, notably Africans, surrounded by an exuberant and bounteous nature, had little need of such labor, causing an inherent laziness.[35] Missionaries as well as planters in Jamaica ever feared the blacks' tendency to "revert to barbarism," i.e., to a kind of easy provision and subsistence agriculture that kept them lazy and subverted the wage-labor base necessary for civilization.

It was with these assumptions that the Baptist missionary Samuel Oughton proposed his theory of artificial wants in the 1860s. The theory was not original with him; it had first been enunciated among French and Scottish Enlightenment thinkers, and specifically by Adam Smith, over a hundred years previously, and had been emphasized from the turn of the century as a means of civilizing Africa.[36] Oughton is notable for applying it to the Jamaican situation. The idea was that Jamaica could achieve civilization only as a result of the desire of laborers for material goods; the black's laziness could only be overcome if he wanted more luxuries. These artificial wants were necessary for progress, for they created a need for useful crafts and skills. The more man wants beyond subsistence, the more skills of production are required, and the goal of civilization becomes closer. Moreover, the demand for luxuries leads to a raising of the standard of living of the working class in that the workers share in the general prosperity of a society that thrives on artificial wants.[37] The theory may be commended or criticized from several angles. But the point here is that it was linked to an idea of development that was supported by the sociological and pseudo-scientific racism of the nineteenth century, through its acceptance of the validity of the categories of *savagery*, *barbarism*, and *civilization*.

While the missionaries did not succumb to white nightmares of black rebels celebrating their slaughters with drunken orgies and pagan rites, their racial assumptions were more tenacious because more subtle and apparently more rational. Thus Underhill, so important in Jamaican history as a spokesman for the oppressed, could write matter-of-factly that the evidence showed no attempt at organization prior to the rebellion: "Negroes are incapable of it. They are excitable and impulsive enough, they may easily be provoked, perhaps, to the extent of a riot; but to combine for general and considered action they display little thought or skill."[38] Governor Eyre himself agreed that there had been no organized or combined action behind the rebellion. Yet he authorized by martial law the execution of 430 blacks and coloreds, the scourgings of 600 more, and the destruction of one thousand houses of the poor.[39]

Underhill himself, however, offers striking evidence of the ability of the black peasantry to combine and organize. It has already been mentioned that an important method of resistance under an oppressive judicial system was the organization in religious congregations of an alternative system of justice. This activity had reached a high level of sophistication by 1865. The peasantry in St. Thomas-in-the-East had, in fact, ceased to bring grievances before regular magistrates, settling disputes before secret tribunals of their own. There were numerous local efforts among the blacks to set up their own jurisdictions with the aim of never having to encounter that of the other Jamaica. Mr. W. C. Miller, a magistrate in St. Thomas-in-the-East, reported that the people "hold courts of their own in the interior districts of Manchioneal, and punish offences by money fines; and the same procedure had been carried on in the Blue Mountain Valley, at a village called Huntley, up to the time of the rebellion." Miller had in his possession a written summons, "taken from one of my Africans, since the rebellion, and signed John Lamont, J.P." Lamont was a field laborer on Serge Island Estate. The summons was dated 28 February 1865 and was issued in the name of "our Sovereign Lady the Queen," the offense being charged as "against her crown and dignity." Bogle himself had been a leader in the establishment of an alternative judiciary in the area of Stony Gut, a system that contained variously designated court officers as well as a ranked police force.[40]

The Great Revival of 1860–61 and the Morant Bay Rebellion of 1865 shocked most missionaries into a reaction of increased fear and condemnation of black effort at religious and political self-determination. In his introduction to *A Narrative of the Baptist Mission in Jamaica*, published to celebrate the fiftieth anniversary of the commencement of B.M.S. work in Jamaica, the Rev. David East deplored African superstition being "even yet in the ascendant" in the 1860s. The cause of this, according to East, was native revivalism, in which "animal excitement" was substituted for religion. East confirmed that, as Curtin observes, the earlier alliance of the blacks and missionaries against white hegemony finally broke when the Great Revival turned more African than Christian.[41] While planter distrust of nonconformist missionaries abated throughout the 1850s and 1860s, the old enmity toward non-Anglican churches came to be directed more toward native congregations as they asserted their independence and as the missionary churches became more respectable in white and colored society. It was clearly a reversal of earlier Baptist positions when many of their ministers joined with representatives of other religious bodies to address Governor Eyre expressing their gratitude for his prompt suppression of the rebellion. The B.M.S. in England criticized this Baptist action in Jamaica, which could be interpreted as justification of the government's unnecessary brutality.[42]

Revival and rebellion brought about a conservative reaction, a failure of nerve, on the part of groups that historically were seen as allies of the slave or freed black people. In this reaction there was cooperation among the missionary and "respectable" churches. When Presbyterian, Methodist, and Baptist ministers in Kingston cooperated to draw up a Bill for Regulating Places of Worship in the wake of the rebellion, in order to put down native preachers,[43] those who in earlier years had been the victims of persecuting legislation were now attempting to become perpetrators of it.

Toward the end of 1865, the Rev. Mr. East published his sermon to his Rio Bueno Baptist congregation on "Civil Government: What the Bible says about it: A Word for the Times." The sermon had been delivered in reaction to Morant Bay. The published version was prefaced by J. M. Phillippo. The theme was that the Christian religion should make its adherents lovers of law, order, and government. East gave thanks to God that the wicked ringleaders of the Morant Bay Rebellion had been put to death.[44]

For constitutional and institutional reform, the year 1865 appears at first glance to be a turning point. The old representative system was abolished and replaced by crown rule. Within ten years, a series of changes were effected that have often been pointed to as signs of progress during the administration of Governor John Peter Grant. There was an attempt to increase the efficiency if not destroy the bias of the judicial system by setting up district courts to hasten the hearing of cases. A unified police force was created. A government savings bank was instituted especially to serve smallholders. An island-wide medical service was organized and a new mental hospital built. Roads were improved under the administration of the new Public Works Department. Beneficial irrigation schemes were implemented. The Anglican church was disestablished, and the money saved was used to support a new grant-in-aid system of elementary education. There was no resolution, however, of the issues of religion and race which came to a head in the Morant Bay Rebellion.[45]

The churches seemed less in conflict over political and economic issues than they had been earlier. There was more cooperation, for example, on such socially beneficial projects as schemes to provide housing for the poor. In the second half of the century, the increasing problems of city overcrowding and the shortage of housing began to stir the consciences of many religious leaders. The post-1865 period saw the continuation of efforts to alleviate these problems, efforts which had actually begun at the beginning of the decade. The Scottish missionaries, through the Moral and Social Improvement Association, addressed themselves to the housing problem, although their main concern was not so much social as moralistic— that overcrowding caused "immoral and illicit intimacies."[46] A similar viewpoint was shown also by the Baptist minister, D. J. East, in his 1864 pamphlet on the problem, in which he made the point that the main evil of housing shortages and overcrowding was a negative influence on "Family Religion."[47] But it was the Congregationalist missionary and historian W. J. Gardner who made perhaps the most important contribution towards alleviating the problem of housing. His Benefit Building Society is a notable event in the history of religious involvement in social problems in Jamaica. The society offered small loans for building new homes or repairing old ones. On the occasion of the laying of the memorial stone for the first block of model cottages financed by the society in 1864, the *Morning Journal* published the comment:

> The movement, whilst doing great good to the humbler classes of Society, will do much towards the improvement of the city, and to aid the Government, by increasing the taxable property. No one who has not made it a point to visit the suburbs and back lanes of Kingston can form any idea of the squalor and misery presented

by the dwellings of a large portion of the population, betokening a far greater amount of poverty than actually does exist.[48]

The *Journal* seemed to view urban poverty as more of a blemish on an otherwise healthy society than as a serious problem in itself; moreover, the paper seemed more interested in new housing for bringing an increase in taxable property than for the housing of poor people. Indeed, the *Journal*'s comments reflect a basic class paternalism about the venture. While efforts like Gardner's were not isolated, they could not do a great deal to prevent the development of housing problems for the urban or rural poor in a continuingly poor society; in the end, only the better-paid laborers and craftsmen could afford the houses.[49]

While the effort of building societies was directed toward a real need, other types of charitable and philanthropic work that flourished in the metropole were limited in Jamaica because of minimal support from wealthy Christians. Those who had money to give in Jamaica generally retired to England to spend it. Yet whatever social and charitable work the various churches were able to perform was necessary because post-slave society continued to toss up human refuse for whom, both before and after 1865, the churches alone provided a net of charity, however feebly woven.

Concerning the causes of the problems that made charity and philanthropy necessary, however, missionaries refrained from fundamental analysis and action to affect the socioeconomic structures of the island. No matter how poor their people might be, they steadfastly maintained that they could only be saved by individual honesty, thrift, and hard work. Appeals for charity, helpful as they were, indicate a moderate and conservative trend within all the churches. Whereas in the earlier years there were always missionaries, usually Baptists, intimately involved with the workers in struggles over wages, labor, and land, in the later years this militancy was generally dissipated in a philanthropy that distanced rather than brought together benefactors and beneficiaries.

By 1875, there was no group of sectarian ministers identifiable as playing the role of advocates of an oppressed peasantry against the influence of the ruling class. In the Jamaican class/color system, white ministers were well on the way to achieving the full respectability that had been denied them in the earlier post-emancipation years; they came to stand in the same position with respect to the peasantry as that of the planters, merchants, clergymen of the Anglican and Presbyterian churches, and the majority of the white and brown political elite. In the crown colony period, the successors of earlier outspoken defenders of the black peasantry became polite dispensers of benevolence to an ex-slave class whose conditions of life showed little change from those existing in the immediate post-emancipation period. Missionaries became less and less *with* the working class, more and more *for* them, in a paternalistic sense.

The attitude is seen not only in benevolence projects, mounted especially at major holidays, such as Christmas, but in ventures such as the inter-church *Queen's Newsman*, a newspaper directed toward the peasantry, begun in July of 1870. The paper announced itself as an unsectarian, cooperative effort of "a Council of Missionaries, Merchants, Catholics, Presbyterians, Anglicans, and Baptists," a combination which in earlier years would have been extraordinary for whatever purpose. Their purpose in 1870 was the education of the peasantry and estate laborers in proper attitudes of industry. In no way was it a worker organ to express the needs and desires of peasants and workers. On the contrary, its tone was indoctrinating and condescending:

> Sir John Peter Grant, our good Governor, has gone away in the
> packet to England for a trip, and is coming back to Jamaica in six

months' time. He is to see the Queen when he goes to London, and when she asks him how the people in Jamaica are getting on, oh how pleased the Governor will be to tell the Queen, that owing to the good conduct of the people, Jamaica is doing well—the peasantry are becoming rich and respectable—their children are being educated, and although the taxes have been a little heavy for them to pay, they have paid them all with regularity and good heart, and relieved the island of a very heavy debt, which was driving it to destruction.[50]

The final item in that passage, the tax burden, was indeed a source of irritation that prevented the small farmer, peasant, and laborer from enthusiastic acceptance of the new constitution and administration. The Jamaica of J. P. Grant brought a higher tax burden that was explained as due partly to debts inherited from the former government, including the cost of suppressing the 1865 rebellion, and partly to the new reforms, especially the formation of new courts of justice to give "ready and cheap redress to the laboring classes,"[51] and the new system of elementary education. Not only did the Baptists join with other denominations, through organs like the *Queen's Newsman*, to convince the people of the need for the tax burden, they were also enlisted personally by J. P. Grant to reconcile the people to increased taxation, in a way that was reminiscent of Metcalfe's earlier enlistment of the Methodists to reconcile the population to his policies.[52]

In the 1870s another newspaper, the *Jamaica Instructor*, was also initiated, with a similar purpose of inculcating a spirit of subordination among the black peasantry, and of teaching the peasantry their religious and civic duties and devotion to government:

Eschewing politics or party animosities, we stand neutral in discussion tending to rouse strife or discord. If we have to notice the action of the government it is purely in the necessity existing to convey to the working orders, who have no medium . . . by which they can learn such matters as concern their interest, and the mutual relations that should be fostered between them and the masses of society at large above their level. . . . we know no distinction of creed, our labours directed broadly over the surface of a wide and expansive field of Christianity.[53]

The Baptists showed that they could still be pugnacious on certain issues. That of a native ministry was one of them, and the Baptists were critical of other denominations for not being serious about it.[54] On this score, however, the Baptists themselves were not yet successful; there either was no pool of sufficient size of black aspirants to the ministry in the Jamaica Union to tap at the attrition of white ministers, or if there was, there was not the will or the policy to do so.

This is suggested in the minor crisis over the successor to the Spanish Town pastorate. J. M. Phillippo, who died in 1879, had retired in 1872, although as pastor emeritus and by virtue of his extraordinarily long tenure from 1824 to 1872 he continued to have great influence over the affairs of the Baptist church in Spanish Town. The Rev. Thomas Lea became pastor after Phillippo. However, his defection to the Anglican church in 1877 left open the leadership of the church in Spanish Town—leadership which Phillippo might still influence but no longer fill. The search for a successor took place not in Jamaica but in England, where the Rev. J. H. Holyoak was recruited to take up the position. Poor Holyoak, however, lasted only six days in Jamaica before fleeing back to England. A more solid commitment to the vacant pastorate was found in 1878 in the person of the Rev. Carey B. Berry of Yorkshire. The point is that the Spanish Town vacancies were not seized upon as opportunities to "nativize" the pastorate; England, not Jamaica, was looked to as the source for a new minister. Phillippo, who could have looked among creole Baptist ministers for a protégé to take over Spanish Town, was prevented from doing so by a lingering suspicion that the black man carried within him the taint of the unregenerated African.[55]

The 1865 rebellion, as well as the fact that the Baptist Calabar College had yet to become a reliable and consistent source for a native ministry, caused fresh doubt among white Baptist ministers in the viability of their independence from the B.M.S. The society found it necessary to remind these ministers that pastors were servants of the churches, not agents of the B.M.S., when requests began to arrive from Jamaica for the society to resume the appointment and settlement of ministers. The society refused to resume direct management of the Jamaican Baptist church, other than the dispersal of grants from funds contributed by English Christians.[56]

The last great Baptist show of strength in the period was their part in the campaign to disestablish the Anglican church. Phillippo gave an account of that agitation in a letter to a friend on 8 October 1868:

> We Baptists have been inundating the Council Chamber with petitions against the renewal of the Clergy Act, soon to expire, and for the entire separation of Church and State. We possibly have gone too far in creating such a clamour so long before the matter is likely to come before the Council, but it will show our friends at home that we are alive to our condition and rights. We are emphatically the fighting sect. Some others cheer us on, but seem afraid of sharing the obloquy and labour of the first onset against us. Our Presbyterian brethren have shown their sympathy with us in combination, but our Independent brethren are slow in taking the field. From the Wesleyans we have no hope of aid at present.[57]

Phillippo and others who campaigned for the separation of church and state achieved their goal; the Clergy Act, which had been reenacted every eleven years since its original enactment in 1825, was not renewed in 1869, and instead was made null by the enactment of disestablishment at the end of that year. While this event had some social benefit in that funds from ecclesiastical expenditure could be channeled into more widely useful programs such as elementary education, it nevertheless did not initiate a rapid or even noticeable creolization of the Anglican church, let alone an opening to black aspirants for leadership in the way that Robert Gordon had called for.

Indeed, creole participation in the ministry and leadership of the Anglican church did not subside as an issue at disestablishment and seems even to have been exacerbated by that event. While there were a number of creole ordinations reported in the press during the fifteen-year period after 1865, the number of such ordinations was not sufficient to satisfy many Jamaicans who perceived a "ban on creolism," as the *Falmouth Post* (later the *Falmouth Gazette*) put it, in the Anglican church as well as in government after the institution of crown colony status for the island.[58] The church was still reluctant after the 1860s to build up a native ministry, while British priests continued to arrive, continued to be paid more than creoles, and continued as well to be culturally peripheral; if they had families, they preferred their children to remain in Britain rather than in Jamaica, lest they become, as one put it, "white niggers."[59]

The only concession made to "creolism" on the part of the church was restricted to the encouragement of ministerial candidates from among the ruling class. It seemed to be the thinking of the church leadership that, after severance of the official link with the state, it was all the more imperative that the church maintain its prestige and social purity through whatever means possible.

Under Bishop Courtenay's aegis in the 1870s, the church clung tightly to its image as an upper-class institution. In 1875, the bishop called for a training college for candidates for the clergy, not for the purpose of opening the offices of the church to black aspirants but specifically for "the sons and daughters of the upper class to take the places of the present State-paid Clergy"—and to make sure that other classes, under this renewed clerical elite, would be given the proper attitudes of social order and place.[60]

Bishop Courtenay, not only because of his position at the top of the Anglican hierarchy but because his actions as a church authority seemed unduly influenced by personal attitudes and prejudices, was the main object of the *Post*'s criticism. The paper seemed to make it a special campaign to point out the "high-handed and arbitrary acts" of Courtenay towards his clergy. It was the feeling of many members of the church that the bishop did not judge his priests by good behavior or good pastorship but only by how much money the priest could collect from his congregation and remit to Kingston; a priest's tenure depended on this. Moreover, Robert Gordon's criticism of the church was iterated by the *Post*, and the refusal to give Gordon a curacy in Jamaica was cited as only one example of Courtenay's racial prejudice.[61]

The problem of race continued to be critical not only in the Anglican church but in Jamaican society as a whole. Issues of rebellion and black racial assertion, raised by the 1865 rebellion, reverberated for years to come, both in Jamaica and abroad.[62] Within the churches, it produced a wave of commentary, the main point of which was summed up by the Anglican historian Ellis in his remark that, if the church had been more assiduous in her evangelizing of the blacks, the rebellion would have been impossible.[63] Others attributed the rebellion not so much to the failure of "true religion" as to the influence of "false religion," of fanaticism and heathenism. Bishop Spencer, writing in retirement in 1867, expressed the outlook of many when he contrasted this "fanaticism" with true Christianity. Those who had absorbed true religion, he claimed, could hardly be rebels; indeed, they were anti-rebels, manifesting their "fidelity" in support of the government in the suppression of the revolt.[64] Anglican appeals in England for funds for Jamaica had to explain the rebellion in terms that would make English people see the need for increased mission work in Jamaica:

> . . . it has been felt to be necessary to make special efforts on behalf of Jamaica, in order to prevent, if it be possible, that increase of lawlessness and ungodliness amongst our people with which we are now threatened, and avert that gradual decay and ruin of all our institutions, which their prevalence would inevitably occasion. The heathenism and barbarism still existing among the negroes, has in one district suddenly and unexpectedly exhibited a ferocity almost African, and whatever uncertainty there may be respecting the actual extent of disaffection, we can never be assured that it will not exhibit itself in forms yet more terrible, unless it be subdued by the influence of the Gospel of Christ.[65]

The disturbances of the post-emancipation period, of which 1865 was the greatest, are proof enough that all the efforts of religionists to tranquilize the blacks were not entirely successful. At the time of the Underhill meetings in 1865, the calls for more religious instruction for the blacks were repeated, as if the efforts of the 1830s and 1840s had never been made. The correspondent of the *Falmouth Post* who called for more education and religious instruction for the blacks in 1865 must have lapsed in his recall of the previous thirty years, for he claimed that, if his suggestion were to be carried out, "in the course of a few years, the cost of maintaining prisons would be lessened, and we should have thousands of the human family growing up in morality, influenced by religious motives and sentiments, and pursuing habits of industry."[66] His sanguinity was thirty years too late. Similarly, in the wake of the rebellion, the *Post* came up with the facile suggestion that the parish of St. Thomas-in-the-East be flooded with religious tracts in order to eradicate the sources of "rebellion, arson, and murder."[67]

Ten years after the Morant Bay Rebellion, there were reports of the likelihood of another "outbreak of the Peasantry" in St. Thomas-in-the-East. There was an increase in revivalist activity, and Native Baptist leaders were challenging the ministers of the white-led denominations as impostors. There was also an upsurge of protest that black people could not obtain justice in the District Courts. And there was discontent because East Indian indentured laborers were offered better medical attention than native workers and peasants.[68]

The constabulary in the parish was reinforced, and the gunboat *Bullfinch* was stationed in the harbor of Port Morant. Ministers of religion were urged to quell the rebelliousness of the people. The St. Thomas correspondent for the *Post* wrote:

> Those who have the opportunity—the Ministers of the Gospel for instance—should teach the People, that if they have grievances, real or imaginary, there is a constitutional mode of seeking redress, namely by petition to the Governor, or, if necessary, to the Queen. Unfortunately, however, the People prefer to seek the counsel of a set of Firebrands—men of their own class—who having acquired that dangerous thing, "a little learning," set themselves up as counsellors for their ignorant dupes. This class will ever be a dangerous element in this parish, and to them must be added those "blind leaders of the blind" who aspire to instruct the ignorant Peasantry in Spiritual matters.[69]

The correspondent seemed to have forgotten the effects of the "Queen's Advice" in response to the peasant petitioners of St. Ann in 1865, as well as the futility of Paul Bogle's petition to the governor for redress of grievances. Those frustrating responses were, however, not so easily forgotten by the peasantry.

If fears of social insubordination continued, so too did related fears of black racial assertion. All available documentation reveals race as an issue in the rebellion of 1865. A *Falmouth Post* editorial of 24 October 1865 mentioned the "demagogues" who inspired the rebellion with the wish that Jamaica should be entirely at the disposal and under the control of the black population. Regardless of the accuracy of the *Post*'s information, the paper saw fit to condemn such a goal for Jamaica.[70] And whether or not such reporting accurately revealed the degree of racial consciousness among the rebellious peasantry, it does show that race was an issue in this sense: that white and Euro-creole fear of black rebellion and the prospect of black dominance—never really dormant since the Haitian revolution—became outright hysteria when faced with aggression and force from the black population.[71]

In the wake of the rebellion, anti-white sentiments were considered not only inflammatory but seditious. The *Post* reported the case of two black men of Falmouth who went to trial because they were heard to make anti-white remarks. One of them, Alexander Campbell, had gone to the shop of Messrs. D'Souza and Lazarus, made a purchase, and after leaving the shop allegedly said:

> When a white man gives you a shilling, he takes it back in the shape of charges, and what the poor people are to sell to make a living, the rich people are doing. . . . If I had ten more like myself, I would walk into the Stores and Shops when they are opened on Monday morning, and take off every damned white man's head: but the place is gone to pieces, and the people of Falmouth are too damned deceitful.[72]

Campbell's counsel pleaded that he only be prosecuted for disorderly conduct instead of being sent to a higher court to answer the charge of sedition since his offense was not committed against public justice, the government, or any particular individual. The justice disagreed, and the depositions were forwarded to the attorney general.

The other man, Richard Brissett, was reported to have threatened that "every white rascal that passes I will shoot, especially that fellow at Nightingale Grove [Mr. Clement] and Mr. Purchas; they would be the first I would kill, because they are too fast and mannish, they do nothing but catch up all the people's jackasses and hogs." Both Campbell and Brissett were sentenced on 29 November 1865 to twelve months in the Falmouth District Prison.[73] The two cases illustrate the current of anti-white, anti-merchant, and anti-planter feeling that at various times since emancipation had galvanized sections of the Jamaican black peasantry and working class into actions of protest, whether designated as strikes, riots, or rebellions.

The whites of Jamaica kept watch nervously on the tenth anniversary of the Morant Bay Rebellion. In 1875, in St. Thomas-in-the-East, there were, as already mentioned, once again stirrings of rebellion, reported as arising out of a combination of race consciousness and religious revivalism. The event that could have sparked another rebellion was the case of one Fagin, which became something of a cause célèbre among the black peasantry. In the District Court at Bath, Fagin was convicted for assault on a white Cuban. His heavy sentence further strengthened black opinion that, when a white man was pitted against a black, the latter was surely to go to the wall.[74]

The native practice of settling disputes through a system of village justice continued, as did the use of that system as a kind of rehearsal for the inevitable engagement with the official system, an inevitability that could only have been confirmed for the blacks by cases such as those of Campbell, Brissett, and Fagin. In 1875 the *Falmouth Post* reported news from St. Thomas-in-the-East of the peasantry playing a game identified as "Mets," in which they played at courts of law, "at which presided their Judges, Attorney-General, Clerks of Court, and other legal Functionaries. It is said that at one of the Mock Courts held recently, the solemn mockery of sentencing one of the accused to death was gone through." The report observed that the practice was not a new one in 1875, and that these mock courts were a resumption of those which had proliferated in St. Thomas immediately prior to the "troubles" of 1865. "They are intended, these people say, to practice and familiarize themselves in judicial proceedings, so that when they get into the real Courts, they may be able to defend themselves!" The *Post* saw significance in the resumption of this mock judicial activity being simultaneous with a sudden increase in Native Baptist baptisms in St. Thomas-in-the-East. At least one of the prominent native pastors active in organizing the baptisms was known to have been ordained by the late George William Gordon.[75]

The increased communality of action and policy that is obvious among the white-led denominations after 1865 resulted greatly from the challenge they all faced from native congregations, whose African-revivalist identity had been consolidated in the Great Revival of 1860–61, and whose political potential had been dramatically demonstrated in the 1865 rebellion. The distinction between the European and Afro-creole paths need not be blurred by the acceptance of black pastors in the white-led denominations. Native pastors in the Baptist Union, as well as in other Protestant churches, accepted the hegemony of white ministers and came to cherish their British ties as fondly as did the whites. At the same time, native pastors tended to be treated as second class, and in 1875 the *Falmouth Post* took up their cause by complaining on their behalf that they continued to be paid less than European ministers.[76]

Cases of native pastors who accepted both the direction of white ministers yet practised a more revivalist form of religion in isolated country districts could no doubt be shown to have occurred. These cases would merely give testimony to the continuing propensity of Jamaican blacks to give formal allegiance to one type of religious worship while reserving affective attachment to another—or to a creative Afro-creole syncretism viewed from the European viewpoint as demeaning to true religion. The point remains that the two roads more clearly than ever diverged as black folk Christianity became more open and self-confident from the 1860s, notwithstanding the increasing black membership in Baptist Union churches after 1868. From that time, earlier criticisms of the Baptists were occasionally revived as they appeared indiscriminately to baptize large numbers, thus encouraging the "ignorance of the masses."[77] However characterized, the adherence of these "masses" to Baptist Union congregations was tenuous and depended on physical and economic health; drought and disease in 1874, for example, caused many to turn to "the spirit of fanaticism which took possession of those who stayed away, substituting the disorder, excitement, and animalism of a pagan orgy for united prayer and the study of God's word," as one Baptist writer put it.[78]

The failure of white religious leadership both to penetrate and to be fully accepted in the Afro-creole world ensured that black religious culture would develop according to its own values, mores, and customs. The irritation and challenge of revivalism persisted, and more staid religionists continued to be horrified by the "fanatics":

> Just now [April 1872], some parts of the island are greatly plagued by such mistaken people. They get into convulsions—become

dumb—then they shout and dance. This is called "trooping." They profess to see angels and talk a gibberish and say, it is "the unknown tongue." All persons who dare to question their nonsense, are denounced as "unbelievers". . . . Unfortunately, the system, as it is working in some parts of the country, is producing much immorality, as these converts evidently are spreading a Christianity without morality.[79]

Such manifestations provided testimony to the persistence of the African strain in creole religion. It became clear in the period of crown colony that black Christianity continued to develop as a vigorous alternative and as a source of Afro-creole identity and resistance at a time when European political and cultural hegemony was being reasserted.

CHAPTER 6

An Assessment

In 1866, Charles Savile Roundell, fellow of Merton College, Oxford, published in London his *England and Her Subject Races, with special reference to Jamaica*. Roundell had been secretary to the Jamaica Royal Commission to investigate the Morant Bay Rebellion. As such, he was well placed to observe the racial attitudes that had boiled to the surface of a society heated by that disturbance. The spirit of reprisal, the "anarchy of Jamaica Martial Law," exhibited in the official reaction to Paul Bogle and George William Gordon's protest, Roundell asserted, was "rooted in an utter absence of reverence for inferiors which exists . . . in the dominant class of every community in which there are sharply defined contrasts of race."

His ideas represented the most humanistic strain of nineteenth-century British social and imperial thought. In that view, racial and cultural differences were not seen as inherent but as socially determined; they should be attacked not as problems of nature but of human society. The unfinished task in Jamaica, as he saw it, was the reorganization of slave society upon the basis of free labor.

Roundell connected his observations with the Christian churches in Jamaica by noting that it had been primarily through the agency of dissenting ministers, "and a very few of the Established clergy," that post-slavery Jamaica had been introduced to the instincts of humanitarian and civilized life. But the achievement of civilization in Jamaica remained unfinished business because the Jamaican oligarchy had not seriously attempted to build the infrastructure of an emancipated society: a system of land tenure that would encourage the prosperity of the black peasantry, the abrogation of absentee estate ownership, systematic registration of births and deaths, a well-organized hospital and medical care system, road construction, and compulsory, nonsectarian education.

His concluding warning, and the key observation in his analysis, was that whatever the wisdom of various programs for the development of Jamaica, none of them could hope to succeed in a society in which there was one law for the European and another for the African, and in which public opinion did not accept blacks as civilized equals.[1]

It was not the oligarchy alone that hampered dissenting missionaries and the few sympathetic Anglican clergymen in their preferential work for the ex-slaves. There were numerous barriers that prevented white ministers of religion from being completely *with* the blacks, from reincarnating themselves, as it were, in black culture in a way that was analogous to God's emptying of himself to take on human flesh and feelings in Jesus, as Pauline theology explains it (Philippians 2: 5–7). The paradigm of the perfect missionary is one who empties himself or herself of past cultural prejudices in order to identify with the people of the mission, as, the Christian believes, God became one with humankind in Christ. For psychological and cultural reasons, no European missionary was ever perfect when measured against this ideal. Moreover, as in many Pauline concepts, there was an ambiguity that dulled the force of the ideal: Christ's becoming human entailed his obedience to the powers-that-be. Thus missionary obedience to the structure of authority and subordination of colonial society acted to prevent a closer identification with the interests of black Jamaicans.

Race and class together constituted a further barrier. Socio-racial divisions within Jamaican society affected the work of the churches and missions in spite of contrary claims. Some of the missionaries were more conscious of these realities than others and admitted that choices had to be made on class and color bases in order for them to be at all effective among certain sectors of society. Very few missionaries confronted racism either as a problem in itself or within themselves. As in many things, the Baptist William Knibb was exceptional in addressing himself to the problem. Thomas Pennock, the Wesleyan, and Thomas Dowson, the Baptist, confronted it in their own ways and found themselves compelled to break with their brethren over it. Robert Gordon, the black Anglican, as a victim of it, ended up in metropolitan exile.

Racism in Jamaica was related to the pseudoscientific theories of race in European intellectual currents that grew from the late eighteenth century and increased throughout the nineteenth. Jamaica's theoretical contribution had been the planter Edward Long's 1774 *History of Jamaica*. The credibility of the movement was enhanced by Charles Darwin's theories, which, while not overtly racist, were used by others to support racist conclusions. The extremes of biological and anthropological racism were reached by Robert Knox and James Hunt in Great Britain, and on the continent by the Count de Gobineau, all of whom began publishing in the 1850s.[2] Herbert Spencer lent the support of the new sociology in 1875 with *Descriptive Sociology: African Races*. The themes of the scientific racists were adopted by essayists and historians such as Thomas Carlyle ("Occasional Discourse on the Nigger Question," 1849), Anthony Trollope (*The West Indies and the Spanish Main*, 1860), and James Froude (*The English in the West Indies*, 1888).

The list should be balanced by one that includes those who spoke and wrote to counter the growing racism from within and outside the West Indies. It would include John Beecham (*Ashantee and the Gold Coast*, 1841), one of the secretaries of the Methodist Missionary Society, and one of the few missionary leaders to recognize that Africans had a culture and a genuine religion; John Stuart Mill, who sought to counter Carlyle's negative "Quashee" image of Jamaican blacks; John Bigelow (*Jamaica in 1850*, 1851), the U.S. observer who wrote a critique of the plantocracy and a celebration of the possibilities of a free black population in creating their own Jamaica; William Sewell (*The Ordeal of Free Labor*, 1861), another U.S. observer who defended the emancipated population against their planter detractors; Goldwin Smith, who spoke out in the 1860s against Froude's mendacity; Robert Gordon (*The Jamaica Church— Why It Has Failed*, circa 1872), who focused on the anti-black policies of the Church of England in Jamaica; J. J. Thomas (*Froudacity*, 1889), the Trinidadian schoolmaster whose purpose in writing is obvious in the title of his book; and Roundell himself, who wrote to counter the rampant racism of the defenders of Governor Eyre.

Where do the white missionaries and ministers of Christianity fit in the climate of racist opinion at the time? There is no easy answer, but some generalizations can be made. John Wesley manifested an ambivalence toward Africa and Africans that is indicative of similar confusion among most missionaries. On the one hand, as an opponent of slavery, he showed a humanitarian inclination to believe that civilization was possible in Africa. On the other hand, he expressed a view of African culture as degenerate—evidence of the effects of original sin on unredeemed man.[3] This dual outlook—friendly to individual Africans but inimical toward the collective African or Negro—pervaded much missionary writing and is palpable in J. M. Phillippo.

In Jamaica, Christian ministers were drawn into the racism of that society by the compromises that were seen to be necessary to allow them to do their work. The Anglican message to the blacks, accommodation to the interests of their former masters, was what the planters wanted conveyed, and they increasingly encouraged the preaching of the other churches insofar as it resembled that message. The successful experiments by certain planters during slavery with Christian instruction as a means of social control encouraged others after emancipation to patronize religious ministers they had formerly shunned or harassed as suspected agents of abolitionism. The effort was not unanimous, because some planters and overseers retained the fear that religious instruction might fail to replace pagan boldness with Christian humility.

Nevertheless, the acceptance by many white ministers of planter patronage compromised the "purity" of Christian teaching—a charge, ironically, that planters had always leveled against missionaries who spoke out against the evils of slavery—and made white/ black relations in religion more complicated than they might have been had missionaries resisted entirely the overtures of the traditional ruling class. The plantocracy, then, was an aspect of social reality with which the churches had to contend; the outcome of the encounter was a compromise that would be increasingly characteristic of the European churches in creole society.

A further barrier was the conception of Britain as home. Nonconformists as well as Anglicans shared this attachment and held to the goal of assimilating Jamaica into the Christian civilization represented by Victorian England. That all persons, black and white, were equal meant that they could all be assumed into the civilization which the missionaries represented. Members of nonwhite races, insofar as they become Christianized—or churched—were blessed to share in the wisdom and goodness of Western civilization. White ministers were therefore dismayed by the cultural alternative that the blacks lived, an alternative which, because it was different from British culture, was therefore seen as inferior. The most liberal of the missionaries, and British humanitarians in general, did not hold for the idea of black self-sufficiency, or self-determination, or cultural autonomy.

Afro-creole religious forms in the nineteenth century were neither relics of African civilization nor distorted images of European Christianity. They both preserved certain features of African traditional religion (the stubborn persistence of heathenism, as the missionaries saw it) and were open to new influences. There was change and development, but according to an internal rhythm that was always there even when the drum was outlawed. What persisted and endured was an African matrix that, womb-like, held and yielded, held and yielded, ensuring that the plantocracy and white missionary leadership would never be totally successful in attempting to acculturate the ex-slave population. Within this African matrix, Christian forms of worship, symbol, and vocabulary were appropriated to a different grammar, syntax, and rhythm.

Through religion, social forms and activities were created that linked the blacks to each other, that welcomed new African arrivals, and that regulated encounters between Afro-Jamaica and Euro-Jamaica. In the context of the missionary churches, the principal channel of encounter was the system of delegation and command, a replication of the system necessarily used on the slave plantation where the whites were a minority—an implicit recognition that the blacks could only be commanded when they had a share in the system of command and authority.[4] What was not anticipated was black initiative, the creation of black religion in its various but not contradictory forms and consequently the effecting of a black reality, an Afro-creole world. Thus religion served as a basis of identity and resistance. Dependence worked two ways, and the black leaders, deacons, or helpers in the churches realized the extent of white dependence on them. When the white ministers tried to deny that interdependence, then the road of independent action was consistently chosen by black leaders—no longer helpers but daddies and rulers in their own right.

The input of various African peoples in Jamaican history—first Akan, then Ibo, Yoruba, Bakongo, and others—is not as confusing as it might at first seem in understanding Afro-creole religion. As Sidney Mintz and Richard Price have observed, "in religion as in many other West African cultural subsystems, an apparent diversity of form fits with certain widely shared basic principles," such as the ability of divination to reveal specific causes, the active role of the dead in the lives of the living, the responses of the deities to human actions, and the close relationship between social conflict and illness or misfortune.[5] Once a pattern of African religion was established in Jamaica, the later arrival of new Africans from other cultural and ethnic areas led to secondary elaborations but nothing fundamentally new. Relatedly, the openness of most West African religions to experimentation helps to explain the openness to missionary Christianity, an openness initially misinterpreted by white missionaries as an eagerness for the pure Gospel truth and a rejection of heathenism. In Afro-Jamaican religion, the absorption of external (European) influences acted as a catalyst for the evolution of internal (African) factors. Comparable to more recent African Christian movements, such as that of Simon Kimbangu in the Congo, the Harrist churches of the Ivory Coast and Ghana, and the Church of the Messiah in Ghana, black Jamaicans embraced certain elements of missionary Christianity, rejected others, and remolded others to create new and unique syntheses, new modes of conceptualization of reality, in order to cope with contemporary social concerns and dislocations.

The blacks grounded their religion in Jamaica. Part of the struggle over land tenure and ownership, such as that which contributed to the 1865 rebellion, was more than for security of farming and pride of ownership in the European sense, but included a religious respect for the earth, for a piece of ground where the living could settle, the unborn enter, the dead could be buried, the deities could descend, and the ancestors could be venerated locally. The free villages that the Baptist and other missionaries sponsored so thoroughly—even though the goal was the institutionalization in Jamaica of Victorian ideals of ownership, self-help, and the nuclear family—provided loci for the realization of these concrete African desires and a partial basis for the development of the Afro-creole world.

In Jamaica today, there has developed, in the tradition of Myal, a spectrum of African or Africanized religion—from Kumina and Pukkumina to Zion, Revival, Tabernacle, and Baptist. Each apparently approaches closer to the European pole. However, the gravity is always toward the almost purely African base of Kumina, and not towards the complete Europeanization (or North Americanization) of religion. In Kumina, which Schuler grounds in Central African immigration into Jamaica in the nineteenth century, participants call themselves African by virtue of their membership; to be a member ordinarily indicates that one's family, one's ancestors, trace back to Africa, and are therefore linked forever to the African gods.[6] Religious forms in black Jamaica, however they could be placed on a scale from pure African to more European, should not be seen as oases in a desert of European domination but as persistent and increasingly vigorous searchings for paths to a world as real as the African world had once been.

Finally, there was the development of what might be called creole nationalism in religion, as exemplified and seen most dramatically in the protest of Robert Gordon. Whereas the other and more well-known Gordon, George William, came out of the plantocracy and gravitated toward Afro-creole religion, Robert's journey was almost the opposite: native and of pure African blood (his own identification), he was nevertheless "instinctively inclined" to the religious institution that most symbolized and preserved the colonial connection of Jamaica, the Anglican church. In his view, that church could have become a beneficial social and political force if it had been open to being transformed (creolized) as a black church. His criticism of the native dissenter tradition was based on the view that it could not erase the contempt for blackness in Jamaican society that would continue as long as institutions of undeniable power such as the Anglican church continued to be white in structures of authority and command. If the church was so much a part of the problem, he might have reasoned, then it had to be turned around into a solution. Gordon's goals and career were thwarted in Jamaica: proof enough, in his mind, that forty years after emancipation the church was not yet ready, as he had summoned it to be, to pay a moral debt for the crimes of slavery.

Notes

ABBREVIATIONS

B.M.S.   Baptist Missionary Society
C.M.S.   Church Missionary Society
C.O.   Colonial Office
corr.   correspondence
J.R.C.   Jamaica Royal Commission
L.M.S.   London Missionary Society
M.M.S.   Methodist Missionary Society
S.P.C.K. Society for the Propagation of Christian Knowledge
S.P.G.   or S.P.G.F.P., Society for the Propagation of the Gospel in Foreign Parts

Chapter 1

1. Edward Brathwaite, *The Development of Creole Society in Jamaica, 1770–1820* (Oxford: Clarendon Press, 1971), 23–24.

2. J. B. Ellis, *The Diocese of Jamaica* (London, 1913), 57 and 61–65.

3. Ibid., 61–65.

4. C.O. (Colonial Office), 137/270: Goderich to Lipscomb, 21 Sept. 1831.

5. Ellis, *The Diocese of Jamaica*, 65, 80–81, 88, 92, 117, and 123–24.

6. Ibid., 114–20.

7. Revs. Henry Otis Dwight, H. Allen Tupper, Jr., and Edwin Munsell Bliss, eds., *The Encyclopedia of Missions*, 2d ed. (New York: Funk and Wagnalls, 1904), 163–64.

8. C.O. 137/270: Goderich to Lipscomb ("Canceld"), July 1832. See also C.M.S. corr. CW/02a/1/9a: Dallas to Lipscomb, 16 May 1832, and Lipscomb to Dallas, 17 May 1832.

9. C.M.S. corr. CW/02a/1/24d: memorandum of Rev. Mr. Panton, July 1840. Eugene Stock, *The History of the Church Missionary Society* (London, 1899), vol. 1: 237.

10. William Law Mathieson, *British Slavery and Its Abolition, 1823–1838* (London, 1926), 148.

11. C.M.S. corr. CW/02a/1/18: Lipscomb, 14 Dec. 1836. Mary Turner, *Slaves and Missionaries: The Disintegration of Jamaican Slave Society, 1787–1834* (Urbana: Univ. of Illinois Press, 1982), 15–30, describes the shifting requirements, procedures, and prejudices involved in the licensing system for missionaries in Jamaica.

12. Turner, *Slaves and Missionaries*, 25–26.

13. See Dorothy Ann Ryall, "The organization of the missionary societies, the recruitment of the missionaries in Britain and the role of the missionaries in the diffusion of British Culture in Jamaica during the period 1834–1865," Ph.D. diss., Univ. of London, 1959, 143–44.

14. John Dillenberger and Claude Welch, *Protestant Christianity: Interpreted through Its Development* (New York: Charles Scribner's Sons, 1954), 134–35. Philip Wright in *Knibb 'the Notorious': Slaves' Missionary, 1803–1845* (London: Sidgwick and Jackson, 1973), 203, claims that it was Wesleyan policy never to use slaves as leaders; he does not document this. Henry Bleby, however, a Methodist missionary and a contemporary source, asserts in *Death Struggles of Slavery* (London: Hamilton, Adams, and Co., 1853), 100, that by 1832 there were 446 Wesleyan slave leaders. Bleby's authority is preponderant here.

15. Dwight, Tupper, and Bliss, *Encyclopedia of Missions*, 67.

16. Gordon A. Catherall, "The Baptist Missionary Society and Jamaican Emancipation, 1814–1845," M.A. thesis, Liverpool Univ., 1966, 140; John Clarke, *Memorials of the Baptist Missionaries in Jamaica* (London, 1869), 156.

17. Ryall, "The organization of the missionary societies," 137, has 1854 as the date for this. The current Jamaican authority on the Baptist church, the Rev. Dr. Horace Russell, however, affirmed in conversation with me (Apr. 1983) that trust deeds for the entire Baptist properties were drawn up in 1847 preparatory to the amalgamation of the two unions, which was effected in 1849.

18. Wright, *Knibb*, 203.

19. Cf. Timothy L. Smith, *Revivalism and Social Reform: American Protestantism on the Eve of the Civil War* (1957; Baltimore: Johns Hopkins Univ. Press, 1980), 190–91.

20. Dwight, Tupper, and Bliss, *Encyclopedia of Missions*, 403.

21. Hope Masterton Waddell, *Twenty-Nine Years in the West Indies and Central Africa, 1829–1858* (London: T. Nelson and Sons, 1863), 110–11.

22. Ibid., 111–13.

23. Following is a list of the main churches, denominations, and missionary societies in Jamaica during all or part of the nineteenth century, with approximate dates of commencement of work: Moravians, 1754; Black Baptists, 1783; Wesleyan-Methodist Missionary Society, 1789; Baptist Missionary Society, 1814; Established Church of Scotland, 1819; Scottish Missionary Society, 1823; Anglican Diocese of Jamaica, 1825; Church Missionary Society, 1825; Society for the Propagation of the Gospel in Foreign Parts, 1834; London Missionary Society (Congregational), 1834; American Congregational, 1837; United Christian Missionary Society (U.S.), 1856.
    The Roman Catholic church during most of the period did not have a local bishop but was under the ordinary jurisdiction of the vicar apostolic of the Antilles who resided in Trinidad. Most of the R.C. clergy from the 1830s to the 1890s were Jesuits under the direction of the English Province of the Society of Jesus.

24. Elsa Goveia, *Slave Society in the British Leeward Islands at the End of the Eighteenth Century* (New Haven, Conn.: Yale Univ. Press, 1965), 269–70, and 278; Clement Gayle, *George Liele: Pioneer Missionary to Jamaica* (Kingston: Jamaica Baptist Union, 1982), 29–30 and 39; Horace O. Russell, "The Church in the Past—a Study on Jamaican Baptists in the 18th and 19th Centuries," *Jamaican Historical Society Bulletin* 8 (1983): 207 and 231; C. S. Reid, "Early Baptist Beginnings," *Jamaica Journal* 16, no. 2 (1983): 5–6.

25. Goveia, *Slave Society*, 302. Goveia has here perhaps not filtered critically enough the missionary stereotype of the Christian black; see Horace O. Russell, "The Emergence of the Christian Black: The Making of a Stereotype," *Jamaica Journal* 16, no. 1 (Feb. 1983): 51–58.

26. Clarke, *Memorials*, 17.

27. *Parliamentary Papers*, House of Commons, 1831–32, vol. 47, no. 285, "Despatches relative to the recent rebellion among the slaves": Goderich to Belmore, 1 Mar. 1832.

28. Thomas Burchell, "Testimony of Faith," MS notebook, begun in England and completed in Jamaica, 1823, Eastern Baptist Theological College, Philadelphia, 20.

29. Edward Bean Underhill, *Life of James Mursell Phillippo, Missionary in Jamaica* (London: Yates and Alexander, 1881), 37.

30. *Missionary Register*, Aug. 1832, 328.

31. M.M.S. instructions for missionaries, 1834, Article 5, cited in Ryall, "The organization of the missionary societies," 451. M.M.S. corr. W.I. 1833–34, Jan. to May: Whitehorne to Beecham, Kingston North, 17 Mar. 1834.

32. Ernest A. Payne, *Freedom in Jamaica* (London: Carey Press, 1933), 21 and 36.

33. Goveia, *Slave Society*, 300. See David Brion Davis, *The Problem of Slavery in Western Culture* (Ithaca, N.Y.: Cornell Univ. Press, 1966), 388, where he observes that Thomas Coke moderated Wesley's anti-slavery principles in his American mission for fear of his life. Mathieson, *British Slavery and Its Abolition*, 112.

34. Turner, *Slaves and Missionaries*, 26–27 and 28.

35. See Roger Anstey, "Pattern of British Abolitionism in the Eighteenth and Nineteenth Centuries," and James Walvin, "The Rise of British Popular Sentiment for Abolition, 1787–1832," 152 and 155–56, both in *Anti-Slavery, Religion and Reform*, ed. Christine Bolt and Seymour Drescher (Hamden, Conn.: Archon, 1980), 26.

36. M.M.S. corr. W.I. 1833–34, Jan.–May: Crookes to Beecham, Parade Chapel, Kingston, 19 Apr. 1833.

37. John Howard Hinton, *Memoir of William Knibb, Missionary in Jamaica* (Lon-

don, 1849), 49. See also *History and Proceedings of the Baptist Missionary Stations, Salter's Hill, Maldon, Bethtephil, and Bethsalem* (London, 1841), 43.

38. See Goveia, *Slave Society*, 251.

39. W. G. Barrett, *Baptist Mission in Jamaica: an exposition of the system pursued by the Baptist Missionaries in Jamaica, by Missionaries and Catechists of the London Missionary Society in that Island* (London: John Snow, 1842), 30; see "Remonstrance of Jamaica Presbytery with Baptist missionaries," app. 1 in Waddell, *Twenty-Nine Years*, 661–63.

40. *Baptist Herald*, 1 Mar. 1843.

41. William F. Burchell, *Memoir of Thomas Burchell* (London, 1849), 175.

42. MS autobiography of J. M. Phillippo (B.M.S. folder WI/1, undated), 177–79; Phillippo's ideas here were expressed in his discussion of his being summoned to appear before the House of Assembly's Committee on Apprenticeship in Nov. 1834. Dendy to Underhill, Salter's Hill, 4 May 1852, quoted in Philip Curtin, *Two Jamaicas: The Role of Ideas in a Tropical Colony, 1830–1865* (1965; New York: Atheneum, 1970), 115. Leonard Tucker, *Glorious Liberty, the Story of a Hundred Years' Work of the Jamaica Baptist Mission* (London, 1914), 159.

43. The impetus behind this activity and the determined and organized political involvement of the Baptists in the 1840s is discussed in great detail by Swithin Wilmot in "Political Developments in Jamaica in the Post-Emancipation Period, 1838–1854," Ph.D. diss., Oxford Univ., 1977.

44. Wilmot, "Political Developments," ii, 276–79, 287–96, 306, 313–14, and 353; *Baptist Herald*, 14 Dec. 1842; Hinton, *Memoir of William Knibb*, 472–73.

45. The special magistracy was created by the Abolition Act of 1833. Special magistrates were to be chosen from outside the plantocracy, were to be "free from local passions," in the words of Colonial Secretary Edward Stanley, and were to provide fair and protective adjudication for the ex-slave apprentices in disputes with their masters. See W. L. Burn, *Emancipation and Apprenticeship in the British West Indies* (London: Jonathan Cape, 1937), chap. 5, and William A. Green, *British Slave Emancipation: The Sugar Colonies and the Great Experiment, 1830–1865* (Oxford: Clarendon Press, 1976), 136–44.

46. Wilmot, "Political Developments," 168. These figures represented solely registered freeholds, not lands settled by squatting or "capture."

47. Clarke, *Memorials*, 98; James M. Phillippo, *Jamaica, Its Past and Present State* (London: Paternoster Row, 1843), 431.

48. *Morning Journal*, 12 Feb. 1839.

49. Jesuit archives, London, MR/5: Cotham to Jenkins, 22 Sept. 1838.

50. Wilmot, "Political Developments," 114 and 123. This erosion is one of the themes throughout Philip Curtin, *The Image of Africa: British Ideas and Action, 1780–1850* (Madison: Univ. of Wisconsin Press, 1964). See also Christine Bolt, *Victorian Attitudes to Race* (Toronto: Univ. of Toronto Press, 1971), xi, 22, 82, 85, 88, 91, 94–95, and 97.

51. Edward Bean Underhill, *The Tragedy of Morant Bay* (London: Alexander and Shepheard, 1895), 43; Wilmot, "Political Developments," 167.

52. Wilmot, "Political Developments," 353; Underhill, *The Tragedy of Morant Bay*, 43.

53. Edward Bean Underhill, *A Letter addressed to the Rt. Honourable E. Cardwell with Illustrative documents on the condition of Jamaica and an explanatory statement* (London: Arthur Miall, 1865).

54. Underhill to East, extracts of 31 Aug., quoted in Ryall, "The organization of the missionary societies," 282.

55. Ryall, "The organization of the missionary societies," 236–37.

56. Rev. D. J. East, *Civil Government: What the Bible says about it: A Word for the Times* (Jamaica, 1865).

57. *Missionary Register*, July 1837, 334.

58. M.M.S. corr. Ja. 1833–39: Williams to Beecham, St. Ann's Bay, 30 Nov. 1837.

59. M.M.S. corr. Ja. 1833–39: Harding, Beechamville, St. Ann's, 19 Oct. 1838.

60. M.M.S. corr. Ja. 1833–39: Hornby to Beecham, Stewart's Town, 10 Feb. 1838.

61. M.M.S. corr. W.I. 1833–34, Jan.–May: Pennock to Beecham, Kingston, 5 Aug. 1833.

62. M.M.S. corr. Ja. 1833–39: Bleby, Kingston, 31 May 1838.

63. Peter Samuel, *The Wesleyan-Methodist Mission, in Jamaica and Honduras, Delineated* (London, 1850), 79–80, 186, and 290. M.M.S. corr. Ja. 1833–39: Edmondson to Beecham, Kingston, 31 Oct. 1837; Edmondson, Kingston, 5 Nov. 1839; Kerr, 26 Nov. 1839; M.M.S. Ja. 1840–42: Bleby, St. Ann's, 3 May 1842.

64. M.M.S. corr. Ja. 1833–39: Edmondson to Beecham, Kingston, 31 Oct. 1837.

65. Samuel, *The Wesleyan-Methodist Mission*, 187. M.M.S. corr. Ja. 1833–39: Harding, Beechamville, St. Ann's, 19 Oct. 1838.

66. M.M.S. corr. Ja. 1843–47: Edmondson, Black River, 3 Nov. 1845.

67. M.M.S. corr. Ja. 1833–39: Hornby to Beecham, Stewart's Town, 10 Feb. 1838.

68. M.M.S. corr. Ja. 1833–39: Edmondson, Kingston, 11 May 1837.

69. M.M.S. corr. Ja. 1833–39: Hornby, Port Antonio, 3 May 1839; Hornby, 14 Aug. 1839.

70. M.M.S. corr. Ja. 1858–65: Tyson, Brown's Town, Mar. 1858.

71. Ibid.

72. Graeme, S. Mount, "Maritime Methodists in Bermuda: Their Attitudes Towards Black Bermudians from 1799 to the Methodist Schism of 1870," paper presented at Fifteenth Conference of Caribbean Historians, Mona, Jamaica, April 1983, 5.

73. Thomas Carlyle, "Occasional Discourse on the Nigger Question," *Fraser's Magazine* 40 (Dec. 1849): 670–79.

74. M.M.S. corr. Ja. 1858–65: Fraser to the Sec. of the Anti-Slavery Society, Mar. 1858.

75. Ibid.

76. Cf. Roger Bastide, *The African Religions of Brazil*, trans. Helen Sebba (1960; Baltimore: Johns Hopkins Univ. Press, 1978), xvii and 403.

77. Samuel, *The Wesleyan-Methodist Mission*, 71.

78. Elsa Goveia, *A Study on the Historiography of the British West Indies* (Mexico: Instituto Panamericano de Geografia e Historia, 1956), 102–7.

79. S.P.G. corr. C/W.1, Ja. IB: Burton, return from the Parish of St. Thomas-in-the-Vale, Dec. 1834; Campbell to Bishop, Devon Pen, 6 July 1834.

80. Trew was later secretary of the African Civilization Society, archdeacon of the Bahamas, and agent in Jamaica for the Mico Trust. Waddell, *Twenty-Nine Years*, 23, wrote that, during his time, Trew had been the most assiduous of Anglican clergymen in Jamaica in attempting the instruction of slaves.

81. J. M. Trew, *An Appeal to the Christian Philanthropy of the People of Great Britain and Ireland, in behalf of the Religious Instruction and Conversion of Three Hundred Thousand Negro Slaves* (London, 1826), 10, 22, and 30. See also Trew, *Report of the St. Thomas-in-the-East Branch of the Incorporated Society for the Conversion and Religious Instruction and Education of the Negro Slaves* (London, 1826).

82. Christopher Lipscomb, *An Address delivered On Laying the First Stone of a New Chapel at Lincoln Estate in Westmoreland, Jamaica, by Christopher, Lord Bishop of Jamaica* (Kingston, 1837), 1.

83. S.P.G. C/W.1 Ja. 2B: Lipscomb, 16 Aug. 1839. L.M.S. 1/3/B: Woolbridge to Ellis, Kingston, 27 Nov. 1835.

84. *Church Societies a Blessing to the Colonies: A Sermon Preached at the Parish Church of St. Michael-Le-Berry, York, by Christopher, Lord Bishop of Jamaica, on Thursday, 29 October* (London, 1840), 12–13.

85. *Church Missionary Record*, Mar. 1838, 55.

86. *An Address delivered by the Rev. Henry Browne, on the occasion of the laying of the Foundation Stone of St. Paul's Church, Annandale, St. Ann's, Jamaica* (Kingston: Shamon and Lunan, 1838), 10 and 12.

87. C.O. 137/272: *A Form of Prayer to be used in the Island of Jamaica, 1 Aug., 1838, the Termination of Apprenticeship* (Kingston: J. R. Cordova, 1838).

88. *Church Missionary Record*, Aug. 1832, 185–86. Robert Gordon, *Education, A Lecture delivered . . . by Robert Gordon* (Kingston, 1856), 20.

89. L.M.S. corr. 1/2/C: Woolbridge to Ellis, Kingston, 27 Nov. 1835; L.M.S. 1/3/B: Woolbridge to Ellis, Kingston, 26 Feb. 1839.

90. *Church Missionary Record*, Aug. 1832, 185–86; Gordon, *Education*, 20; *Church Missionary Record*, Dec. 1834, 280.

91. Turner, *Slaves and Missionaries*, 23 and 109; William Law Mathieson, *British Slave Emancipation, 1838–1849* (London, 1932), 11; Davis, *Problem of Slavery in Western Culture*, 203.

92. *Missionary Register*, May 1847, 225, and Mar. 1835, 156. See also Clarke, *Memorials*, 111.

93. C.O. 137/181: printed copy of the dispatch from Viscount Goderich to the Earl of Belmore, Downing St., 1 Mar. 1832, 44–45. *Missionary Register*, Mar. 1834, 129; Oct. 1834, 554; May 1835, 235. See also Ellis, *The Diocese of Jamaica*, 73. Ellis, p. 71, reports that, at emancipation, the C.M.S. increased the number of its agents and stations, the Incorporated Society for the Conversion of the Negro renewed its efforts, the S.P.G. began its connection with the diocese of Jamaica, the Religious Tract Society provided aid, and the S.P.C.K. came to the fore with liberal grants.

94. *Missionary Register*, June 1834, 254, and Mar. 1835, 156. M.M.S. corr. W.I. Jan.–May 1832: Edney to James, Grateful Hill, 13/1/32; M.M.S. Ja. 1848–57: Ritchie, Falmouth, 3 Sept. 1848.

95. *Jamaica Courant*, 13 Mar. 1833.

96. M.M.S. corr. Ja. 1840–42: Simmons, Kingston, 20 Apr. 1841; Green to Beecham, Bath, St. Thomas-in-the-East, 20 June 1842; Fraser, 3 May 1841. M.M.S. Ja. 1848–57: Young, Beechamville and Watsonville Circuit, Moneague P.O., 5 Sept. 1848; Ja. 1833–39: Lofthouse, Mt. Ward, 17 Aug. 1838.

97. James M. Phillippo, *Jamaica*, 431. This is similar to Waddell's viewpoint in *Twenty-Nine Years*, 152. Swithin Wilmot, "Sugar and the Gospel: Baptist Perspectives on the Plantation in the Early Period of Freedom," *Jamaican Historical Society Bulletin* 8 (1983): 215.

98. Phillippo, *Jamaica*, 431.

99. Phillippo to Dyer, 7 July 1838, in Underhill, *Life of James Mursell Phillippo*, 162 and 169.

100. Samuel, *The Wesleyan-Methodist Mission*, 79.

101. W. J. Gardner, *A History of Jamaica from its Discovery by Christopher Columbus to the year 1872* (London, 1873), 366.

102. M.M.S. corr. Ja. 1833–39: Harding to Beecham, St. Thomas-in-the-Vale, 20 Oct. 1837.

103. L.M.S. corr. 1/1/B: Taylor to Ellis, Spanish Town, 6 Feb. 1835; L.M.S. 1/2/ A: Barrett to Ellis, Four Paths, Clarendon, 23 June 1835.

104. Waddell, *Twenty-Nine Years*, 37.

105. "On the Education of the People," in *Postscript to the Royal Gazette*, 21–28 Nov. 1835.

106. Samuel, *The Wesleyan-Methodist Mission*, 150.

107. Letter signed "Kelokron" in *Postscript to the Royal Gazette*, 28 Nov.–5 Dec. 1835.

108. Underhill, *Life of James Mursell Phillippo*, 305.

109. M.M.S. corr. Ja. 1848–57: Sinclair, Ocho Rios, 1 Sept. 1848.

110. Underhill, *Life of James Mursell Phillippo*, 170–73 and 198–202; B.M.S. letterbook: Phillippo, Spanish Town, 22 Oct. 1844; M.M.S. Ja. 1848–57: Sinclair, 1 Sept. 1848; *Missionary Register*, May 1842, 247.

111. Wilmot, "Political Developments," 158–60.

112. *Parliamentary Papers* 1847, 39 (325), 124–26.

113. M.M.S. corr. Ja. 1848–57: Sinclair, 1 Sept. 1848; S.P.G. C/W.1 Ja. 3: Spencer, 30 June 1848; Wilmot, "Political Developments," 151–66, passim.

114. Wilmot, "Political Developments," 261–62.

115. *Jamaica Standard and Royal Gazette*, 24 Aug. 1842.

Chapter 2

1. Phillippo, *Jamaica*, 426; Clarke, *Memorials*, 98.

2. Address to Lionel Smith from the Baptist Congregations at Rio Bueno and Stewart Town, and address from the Baptist Missionaries assembled at a meeting in Montego Bay, in *Morning Journal*, 12 Feb. 1839.

3. L.M.S. corr. 2/3/A: Vine to Ellis, First hill, Rio Bueno P.O., 4 Sept. 1838.

4. L.M.S. corr. 1/1/B: Taylor to Ellis, Spanish Town, 6 Feb. 1835.

5. L.M.S. corr. 1/2/A: Barrett to Ellis, Four Paths, Clarendon, 23 June 1835; *Missionary Register*, Aug. 1837, 369–70.

6. Ryall, "The organization of the missionary societies," 101–2.

7. M.M.S. corr., Curtis, 23 Nov. 1840, quoted in Ryall, "The organization of the missionary societies," 379.

8. *Church Missionary Record*, Nov. 1838, 282.

9. Tucker, *Glorious Liberty*, 47.

10. *Church Missionary Record*, Nov. 1838, 284–85. The missionary account mysteriously does not take into consideration the possibility of any previous experiences of eclipses that the slaves may have had.

11. *Missionary Register*, July 1845, 331.

12. Phillippo, *Jamaica*, 445; *Church Missionary Record*, Sept. 1841, 215.

13. M.M.S. corr. Ja. 1840–42: Sinclair, St. Ann's Bay, 21 July 1842.

14. R. C. Dallas, *The History of the Maroons* (London, 1803), 2: 449–50; Carl Campbell, "Missionaries and Maroons: Conflict and Resistance in Accompong, Charles Town and Moore Town (Jamaica), 1837–1838," *Jamaican Historical Review* 14 (1984): 42–58.

15. Campbell, "Missionaries and Maroons," 44 and 51–53. Barbara K. Kopytoff, "Religious Change Among the Jamaican Maroons: The Ascendance of the Christian God Within a Traditional Cosmology," *Journal of Social History* 20, no. 3 (1987): 468–69. C.M.S. CW/01a/16: minutes of the Jamaica Corresponding Committee, 4–6 July 1838.

16. C.M.S. CW/01a/19: minutes of Ja. Corr. Comm., 5–6 Dec. 1838.

17. Ibid., Jan. 1839 and 3–8 Apr. 1839.

18. Journal of H. L. Dixon, Siloah, 31 Dec. 1841, in *Missionary Register*, July 1843,

390; see also *Missionary Register* 1841: 421. Kopytoff, "Religious Change Among the Jamaican Maroons," 472–73.

19. Campbell, "Missionaries and Maroons," 45–48 and 51.

20. Ibid., 52; Kopytoff, "Religious Change Among the Jamaican Maroons," 465–67 and 472.

21. Campbell, "Missionaries and Maroons," 53–54; Ryall, "The organization of the missionary societies," 127.

22. Kopytoff, "Religious Change Among the Jamaican Maroons," 470; C.M.S. corr. W/M4, 1837–40: Gillies, report of Mar. 1838.

23. Jesuit archives, London, MR/4: Woollett, Retreat, Brown's Town, 4 Dec. 1873.

24. Jesuit MR/4: Woollett, Reading, Montego Bay, 12 Feb. 1874.

25. Ibid.

26. Jesuit MR/4: Hathaway, 26 North St., Kingston, 24 Nov. 1873.

27. Jesuit MR/6: Jaeckel, Kingston, 10 Mar. 1874. The college was eventually founded as St. George's on North St. in Kingston.

28. Jesuit MR/6: Woollett, Retreat, 12 Nov. 1874.

29. Jesuit MR/4: petition from the Catholics of Kingston, 1873.

30. English Jesuit Province Register, MS, Jacobus T. Splaine, 330. James J. Phillips, "Land Tenure at Silver Hill," unpub. MS, Kingston, 1971, 5–7. Diary of James Splaine, S.J., MS, Jamaica 1872 (English Jesuit archives): entry for 5 Feb. 1872; subsequent references will be to "Splaine Dairy," followed by date of entry.

31. Phillips, "Land Tenure," 7–8.

32. Ibid., 6, 10, 11, 13–16. Splaine Diary, 18 Feb. 1872.

33. Splaine Dairy, 29 Feb. 1872.

34. Ibid., 15 Apr. 1872.

35. Ibid., 29 Feb. 1872.

36. Ibid., 13 Apr. 1872.

37. Ibid., 13 June 1872.

38. For discussions of West and Central African beliefs in ghosts and the dual soul see John S. Pobee, *Toward an African Theology* (Nashville, Tenn.: Abingdon, 1979), 49, 92; and Monica Schuler, *"Alas, Alas Kongo": A Social History of Indentured African Immigration into Jamaica, 1841–1865* (Baltimore: Johns Hopkins Univ. Press, 1980), 41–42, 70–73, 139n, and 152n. See also Joseph Graessle Moore, "Religion of Jamaican Negroes: A Study of Afro-Jamaican Acculturation," Ph.D. diss., Northwestern Univ., 1953, 27, 33–34; and Joseph John Williams, *Psychic Phenomena of Jamaica* (New York: Dial Press, 1934), 164–66, for discussions of these beliefs in Jamaica.

39. Splaine Dairy, 1 Feb. 1872. This sense of failure was not confined to Splaine; it is also strikingly evident in the letters of other Jesuits in Jamaica, e.g., Dupeyron, Kingston, 24 Aug. 1863; Hathaway, Kingston, 30 June–3 July 1870 and 6 May 1871 (Jesuit archives file MR/6). A survey of Protestant and Anglican evangelical missionary correspondence shows that from the mid-1840s there was a similar perception of failure. The Congregationalist missionary W. J. Gardner, in *A History of Jamaica*, 340–91, noted this and warned his brethren against any facile optimism, admitting, in his own way, that insofar as blacks had their own African-derived religion, this area of their lives would be the last to give way under Christian teaching.

40. Splaine Dairy, 27 Feb. and 16 Apr. 1872.

41. Ibid., 16 Apr. 1872.

42. Ibid., 5 Aug. 1872.

43. M.M.S. corr. Ja. 1833–39: Hornby to Beecham, Stewart's Town, 5 May 1838. Ryall, "The organization of the missionary societies," 388–89. For a summary of Protestant ideas of sin and justification, see Dillenberger and Welch, *Protestant Christianity*, 28–31.

44. Splaine Dairy, 2 Apr. 1872.

45. See Pobee, *Toward an African Theology*, 103–4 and 107–10; and Schuler, "*Alas, Alas Kongo*," 36.

46. Splaine Dairy, 20 June 1872.

Chapter 3

1. A. Caldecott, *The Church in the West Indies* (London: S.P.C.K., 1898), 96.

2. Ibid., 192–93.

3. Ibid., 192–93.

4. Ibid., 192–93.

5. Ibid., 194.

6. Thomas Harvey and William Brewin, *Jamaica in 1866* (London: A. W. Bennett, 1866), 73.

7. *Jamaica Despatch and Kingston Chronicle*, 13 and 14 Feb. 1839.

8. *Morning Journal*, 12 Feb. 1839.

9. Ibid.

10. M.M.S. corr. Ja. 1840–42: Kerr, Montego Bay, 26 Nov. 1839.

11. M.M.S. Ja. 1833–39: Inglis, Parade Chapel, Kingston, 3 Mar. 1838. See also M.M.S. Ja. 1840–42: Simmons, Kingston, 20 Apr. 1841: "I am delighted to see how readily and cheerfully many highly respectable and influential members of our Community are giving their sanction and support to our ministerial exertions."

12. M.M.S. Ja. 1833–39: Randerson, Spanish Town, 10 Oct. 1838.

13. L.M.S. corr. 1/1/B: Taylor to Ellis, Spanish Town, 6 Feb. 1835.

14. L.M.S. 1/2/A: Barrett to Ellis, Four Paths, Clarendon, 23 June 1835.

15. L.M.S. 1/2/C: Barrett to Ellis, Four Paths, Clarendon, 28 Nov. 1835.

16. L.M.S. 1/3/B: Barrett to Ellis, Four Paths, 30 Mar. 1836.

17. L.M.S. 1/4/C: Brown to Ellis, Mandeville, 3 Oct. 1836.

18. Ryall, "The organization of the missionary societies," 303.

19. Mahlon Day, "Journal of a Trip to the West Indies, 1839–1840" (MS copy, New York Historical Society), entry for 29 Mar. 1840.

20. Curtin, *Two Jamaicas*, 166.

21. M.M.S. corr. W.I. 1833–34, Jan.–May: Whitehouse to Beecham, Kingston North, 17 Mar. 1834.

22. Pennock to Beecham, Morant Bay, 20 Feb. 1834.

23. Ibid.

24. Ibid.

25. Ibid.; Murray to Beecham, Stony Hill, 4 Mar. 1834.

26. Whitehouse to Beecham, Kingston, 8 Feb. 1834.

27. Pennock to M.M.S. Committee, Morant Bay, 20 Feb. 1834.

28. Wilcox to Beecham, Kingston, 27 Mar. 1834.

29. Murray to Beecham, Stony Hill, 4 Mar. 1834.

30. Pennock to M.M.S. Committee, Morant Bay, 20 Feb. 1834.

31. Pennock to Beecham, Morant Bay, 21 Mar. 1834.

32. M.M.S. corr. Ja. 1833–39: undated anonymous letter to Beecham, received 28 July 1834.

33. Edmondson and Crookes to Beecham, Wesley Chapel, Kingston, 27 May 1837.

34. Edmondson to Beecham, Kingston, 13 June 1837.

35. Bleby to Beecham, 20 June 1837.

36. Randerson to Adler, 12 Oct. 1837.

37. Ibid.

38. M.M.S. corr. W.I. 1833–34, Jan.–May: Ward to Beecham, Falmouth, 4 Mar. 1834; Wedlock to Beecham, 5 Mar. 1834.

39. M.M.S. Ja. 1833–39: Pennock to Hooke, 23 June 1837; Edmondson to Beecham, Kingston, 26 June 1837.

40. Pennock to Hooke, 23 June 1837; Edmondson to Beecham, Kingston, 26 June 1837; Wedlock to Beecham, Spanish Town, 12 July 1837.

41. Edmondson to M.M.S. Committee, Kingston, 20 July 1837.

42. Ibid.

43. Edmondson, Kingston, 12 Aug. 1837; Simmons to Beecham, Stony Hill, 6 Sept. 1837; M.M.S Ja. 1840–42: Edmondson, Kingston, Jan. 1840.

44. Seccombe to Adler, Oracabessa, 13 Oct. 1837; Simmons to Bunting, 21 Nov. 1837.

45. See, e.g., Gardner, *A History of Jamaica*, 367; Clarke, *Memorials*, 67; and Samuel, *The Wesleyan-Methodist Mission*, 81–82.

46. M.M.S. corr. W.I. 1833–34: Pennock, Morant Bay, 20 Feb. 1834.

47. M.M.S. Ja. 1843–47: Millson, Kingston Circuit, 23 Dec. 1845.

48. Quotation from the *Sentinel* in *Falmouth Post*, 12 May 1864.

49. Curtin, *Two Jamaicas*, 166.

50. Clarke, *Memorials*, 192. Also Underhill, *Life of James Mursell Phillippo*, 174; Underhill discusses the Dowson controversy on 226–37. William Green, in *British Slave Emancipation*, 342, mentions Dowson but is in error in identifying him as Phillippo's "black assistant."

51. B.M.S. corr. WI/1: copy of letter from Dowson to Phillippo, 25 Sept. 1842.

52. *Morning Journal*, 13 Dec. 1850.

53. Ibid.

54. Ibid. *Full Report of the Proceedings in Chancery in the Important Case of the Baptist Chapel, Spanish Town, Oct., 1845* (Kingston: Guardian and Patriot Office, 1845), 4, 21, and 26. B.M.S. WI/5: Evans to Angus, Vale Lionel, 20 Apr. 1845.

55. B.M.S. WI/5: Abbott to Angus, Spanish Town, 22 Apr. 1845; Evans to Angus, Vale Lionel, 20 Apr. 1845; Hands to Angus, Yallahs, 19 Apr. 1845; Wood to Angus, Kingston, 22 Apr. 1845; Phillippo, Spanish Town, 23 Jan. 1845; WI/1: Phillippo, Spanish Town, 22 Feb. 1845. See also *Morning Journal*, 13 Dec. 1850.

56. B.M.S. WI/5: Evans to Angus, Vale Lionel, 20 Apr. 1845; Evans to Angus, Yallahs, 19 Apr. 1845.

57. B.M.S. WI/1: Phillippo to Angus, Spanish Town, 20 Dec. 1844; Phillippo, Spanish Town, 23 Jan. 1845; Phillippo to Angus, 7 June 1845 and 5 Jan. 1846; WI/2: Phillippo to Green, Spanish Town, 7 Apr. 1845; WI/5: Phillippo, Spanish Town, 20 Sept. 1846.

58. B.M.S. WI/1: Phillippo to Angus, 5 Jan. 1846; WI/2: Phillippo to Green, Spanish Town, 21 Nov. 1845.

59. B.M.S. WI/1: Phillippo, Spanish Town, 20 Sept. 1846; Harvey, 6 Mar. 1845; Phillippo, "Brief Historical Sketch of occurrences at Spanish Town from the arrival of Mr. Dowson to the Present Time," 22 Apr. 1845.

60. B.M.S. WI/1: Phillippo to Angus, 7 May 1845. James Carnegie, in his review article on Phillippo's book in *Jamaica Journal* 5 (Mar. 1971): 11–15, gives no indication of what contemporary critics might have seen as outright racism or color prejudice in the book, beyond what is obviously Phillippo's lack of understanding and appreciation of slave folk culture.

61. B.M.S. WI/1: Phillippo, Jericho, 22 Feb. 1845.

62. B.M.S. WI/1: Phillippo to Angus, 22 May 1845; WI/2: Phillippo to Hinton, 21 Apr. 1846; *Morning Journal*, 13 Dec. 1850; Clarke, *Memorials*, 192.

63. B.M.S. WI/1: Phillippo to Angus, 7 July 1845.

64. *Morning Journal*, 13 Dec. 1850; Clarke, *Memorials*, 192; Underhill, *Life of James Mursell Phillippo*, 229–30.

65. See chapter 1.

66. B.M.S. WI/1: MS autobiography of Phillippo, 177–79. Cf. Howard Temperley, "Anti-Slavery as a Form of Cultural Imperialism," in *Anti-Slavery, Religion and Reform*, ed. Bolt and Drescher, 335–50.

67. Underhill, *Life of James Mursell Phillippo*, 230.

68. Ibid., 231.

69. Phillippo, *Jamaica*, 386–87.

70. Ibid., 154–55, 241–44, 247, 269, and 418.

71. Ibid., 253, 260, 263, and 283.

72. Russell, "The Emergence of the Christian Black," 51–58.

73. B.M.S. WI/1: enclosure, Phillippo to Angus, Spanish Town, 6 Sept. 1845.

74. Clarke, *Memorials*, 172–73; Ryall, "The organization of the missionary societies," 406. A correspondent from St. James writing in the *Jamaica Standard and Royal Gazette* of 21 Aug. 1841 alleged that in his town (possibly Montego Bay, although it is not named) a faction of Baptist members had determined to shut out all white preachers, claiming "that the *Chapels* are *theirs*, as they paid for them, and that they should do as they please."

75. B.M.S. WI/5: Speech of Wm Knibb before the B.M.S. in Exeter Hall, 28 Apr. 1842, 35; Burchell, *Memoir of Thomas Burchell*, 325; Underhill, *Life of James Mursell Phillippo*, 96; *The Freeman* (London), 12 Nov. 1860.

76. M.M.S. Ja. 1843–47: Armstrong to Beecham, Kingston, 28 Apr. 1843.

77. Armstrong to Beecham, Kingston, 24 Sept. 1842.

78. L.M.S. corr. 1/2/A: Barrett to Ellis, Four Paths, Clarendon, 23 June 1835.

79. C.M.S. CW/01a/10-11-12: Minutes of the Jamaica Corresponding Committee, 1827–40.

80. C.O. 137/272: Bishop to Lord John Russell, Seven Oaks, 19 Nov. 1840.

81. Caldecott, *The Church in the West Indies*, 194.

82. S.P.G. letterbook D40/2, W.I. 1868–74: Gordon to Bullock, 31 Jan. 1868.

83. Ibid.

84. Ibid.

85. Cf. the case of the Methodist Mr. Ward, described earlier in this chapter, and the case of the Anglican John Duport of St. Kitts, in Noel Titus, *Missionary Under Pressure: The Experiences of the Rev. John Duport in West Africa* (Barbados: Caribbean Group for Social and Religious Studies, 1983).

86. S.P.G. D28, Ja.: printed circular "To the Clergy of the Island of Jamaica," from Reginald Kingston, 6 Dec. 1861.

87. Ibid.

88. Ibid.

89. Ibid.

90. Ibid.

91. Ibid.

92. Ibid.

93. Ibid.

94. Ibid.

95. S.P.G. letterbook D40/2, W.I. 1868–74: Gordon to Bullock, 31 Jan. 1868.

96. Ibid.

97. Ibid.

98. Ibid. S.P.G. D40/2: testimonial for Gordon from the Bishop of Oxford, 29 Jan. 1868.

99. S.P.G. D40/2: Reginald Kingston to Bullock, 22 Feb. 1868.

100. *Jamaica Instructor*, 22 Apr. 1872.

101. Rev. Robert Gordon, curate of parish church of St. John of Wapping, *The Jamaica Church, Why It Has Failed* (London, undated, probably 1872 or 1873, vol. 14928 in S.P.G. pamphlet collection), 6–8.

102. Ibid., 15–16.

103. Ibid., 17 and 22. See Gad J. Heuman, "Coloreds and Blacks in the Jamaican Assembly: A Biographical Profile," *Jamaican Historical Society Bulletin* 8 (Dec. 1982): 177–83.

104. Gordon, *Education*, 17–18.

105. Ibid., 26. See Brathwaite, "The 'Folk' Culture of the Slaves," chap. 15 in *The Development of Creole Society*.

106. S.P.G. letterbox C/W.1, Ja. 2B, Bishop Lipscomb, 1836–43: 14 Nov. 1837, 12 June 1841, 27 July 1841, and 15 Sept. 1841.

107. S.P.G. letterbook D28, Ja. 1860–67: Courtenay to Grant, 15 Nov. 1866.

108. S.P.G. D28: Courtenay, 24 Nov. 1866.

109. *The Standing Committee of the S.P.G.F.P. and the Jamaica Clergy* (Kingston: M. DeCordova, McDougell & Co., 1867), 5.

110. *Letter of the Rev. Henry Venn, Honorary Secretary of the Church Missionary Society, to the Lord Bishop of Kingston (Jamaica), on the state of the Negroes of Jamaica* (London: Church Missionary House, Jan. 1867).

111. Ibid., 5.

112. Ibid., 6.

113. *Centenary Pamphlet of the Jamaica Church Missionary Society* (Kingston, 1961), 7.

114. Splaine Dairy, 13 Jan. 1872.

115. *Falmouth Post and Jamaica General Advertizer*, 30 June 1876.

116. *Letter of the Rev. Henry Venn . . .* , 10.

Chapter 4

1. The full and official name of the African Civilization Society was "the Society for the Suppression of the Slave Trade and the Civilization of Africa"; it was founded about 1839 by Thomas Fowell Buxton. More information on the society is in Curtin, *The Image of Africa*, 302–3, 333, and 339.

2. *Report of the Committee of the African Civilization Society at Public Meeting, Exeter Hall, Tuesday, 21 June, 1842* (London, 1842), cix–cx: appendix MM, "Concerning tour of J. M. Trew, Secretary of the Society."

3. Ibid., cx.

4. Holt, Rock Spring, Hanover, June 1836 in *Missionary Register*, Aug. 1837, 368–69.

5. M.M.S. corr.: Sergeant, Russell Penn, St. Thomas-in-the-Vale, 26 June 1840. T. B. Freeman, son of a British mother and an African father, was famous not only as one of the most effective Wesleyan missionaries on the Gold Coast but as an inland explorer. Curtin observes that he, with Samuel Crowther of the C.M.S., were less culture-bound than most Western explorers and depicted real people rather than cardboard savages; Freeman's reports were a major source of John Beecham's *Ashantee and the Gold Coast* (London, 1841). However, both Freeman and Crowther had become acculturated to European values to a high degree. Freeman's acceptance of these values was no doubt one reason why missionaries in Jamaica readily promoted his journal. Freeman appears later to have become critical of the implementation of the African Civilization Society's philosophy of commerce as the basis of civilization in Africa; he perceived that it caused more false hopes, corruption, and dishonesty than legitimate progress. See Curtin, *The Image of Africa*, 321, 335, and 430.

6. Catherall, "The Baptist Missionary Society and Jamaican Emancipation," 129; John Young, "The Missionaries' Father, or The Blessings of Truth and the Evil of Infidelity," biography of William Knibb, B.M.S. MSS booklet WI/3; *History and Proceedings of the Baptist Missionary Stations*, 44; *Freedom in Jamaica, or, The First of August, 1838* (London, 1 Nov. 1838), 12.

7. Payne, *Freedom in Jamaica*, 74.

8. Rev. W. N. Ashby, Rural Hill, quarterly report ending 31 Mar. 1841, in *Church Missionary Record*, Sept. 1841, 199–200. *History and Proceedings of the*

Baptist Missionary Stations, 35, 58, and 61. *Missionary Register*, June 1839, 310, and Oct. 1841, 441. M.M.S. corr. Ja. 1840–42: Sergeant, Port Royal Mts., 20 May 1842, and Samuel, Manchester, 28 July 1840. Payne, *Freedom in Jamaica*, 72. Jamaican Baptist missionaries began going to Africa in 1842, first to Fernando Po, later to the Cameroons. In December 1843, forty-two Jamaicans, including children, sailed for Fernando Po. The Jamaica Presbyterian Mission went to old Calabar in 1845. The Moravians sent six couples from Jamaica to Africa under two missionaries from the Basle Missionary Society in 1842. The West Indian Anglican mission to the Rio Pongas area was organized from Barbados. The missionary who went with the first Jamaican Baptist mission, John Clarke, made a collection of African words used by his congregation members in Jamaica. In England in 1848 he completed and published *Fernandian Grammar and Specimens of African Tongues*. He also translated and published a portion of the Gospel of Matthew in Fernandian. Examples of expressions of a missionary spirit among both creoles and African immigrants to Jamaica are many. For example, Schuler in *"Alas, Alas, Kongo,"* 21 and 81, notes that some of the original Yoruba immigrants in the early 1840s expressed interest in returning to Yorubaland to assist the C.M.S. mission there, a mission, along with the M.M.S., which they were familiar with before their departure from Africa.

9. *History and Proceedings of the Baptist Missionary Stations*, 54; Schuler, *"Alas, Alas, Kongo,"* 57.

10. Rev. C. W. Winckler, quarterly report ending 30 June 1843, in *Church Missionary Record*, Jan. 1844, 21.

11. M.M.S. corr. Ja. 1843–47: Thompson, Bath, 18 Dec. 1845.

12. M.M.S. corr. Ja. 1858–65: Tyson, Brown's Town P.O., 8 Dec. 1858.

13. M.M.S. corr. Ja. 1848–57: Hodgson, Beechamville, St. Ann's, 9 Apr. 1853.

14. Samuel, *The Wesleyan-Methodist Mission*, 112. Samuel's reference to the apprenticing of the Africans is perhaps clarified by Dr. K. O. Laurence's observation in *Immigration into the West Indies in the 19th Century* (Barbados: Caribbean Universities Press, 1971), 15: "The value of the African immigrants was . . . much diminished by a general tendency to forsake the estates on which they were located, to wander off either in search of other work or into the villages. After 1842, liberated Africans were therefore indentured for the first year, after 1850 for two years and eventually for

three. These indentures were justified on the plea that these Africans were primitive and helpless and in need of special protection."

15. Jesuit corr. MR/5: Cotham to Provincial, 28 June 1838.

16. M.M.S. corr. W.I. 1833–34, Jan.–May: Bleby to Beecham, Stony Hill, 13 May 1833. Bleby did not indicate into which denomination they were received. It was from this group of rescued Africans that Governor Mulgrave's wife adopted two young sisters—said to be the daughters of an African chief—a gesture, we can imagine, that was well received by the black population.

17. M.M.S. corr. Ja. 1840–42: Sergeant, Port Royal Mts., 20 May 1842.

18. Journal of Sessing at Birnam Wood, St. George, entry for 17 Sept. 1837 in *Missionary Register*, Aug. 1838, 379.

19. Ibid. Schuler, *"Alas, Alas, Kongo,"* 20–21.

20. Waddell, *Twenty-Nine Years*, 172.

21. Splaine Dairy, 24 June 1872.

22. Schuler, *"Alas, Alas, Kongo,"* 81. B.M.S. corr. WI/5: Teall to Baynes, Annotto Bay, 13 June 1889.

23. Laurence, *Immigration into the West Indies*, 14–15.

24. Testimony of John Baillie, Esq., *Evidence Upon Oath touching the Condition and Treatment of the Negro Population of the British West Indies colonies: Part I—Island of Jamaica. Taken before a Select Committee of the House of Lords Session 1832* (London, 1833), 29. Splaine Dairy, 21 May 1872. See also Schuler, *"Alas, Alas, Kongo,"* 65 and 67.

25. Brathwaite, *The Development of Creole Society*, 218. See the discussion of African conceptions of time and afterlife in Kwesi A. Dickson and Paul Ellingworth, *Biblical Revelation and African Beliefs* (Maryknoll, N.Y.: Orbis Books, 1969), 159–70.

26. M. G. Lewis, *Journal of a West India Proprietor, 1815–1817* (London, 1834), 89–90 and 287.

27. *Scottish Missionary and Philanthropic Register*, 1834: 252.

28. *Church Missionary Record*, Jan. 1833, 11. The younger slaves, however, expected the same result even though willing to accept a new ceremony; like the older slaves, they wished basically to placate the spirit of the deceased.

29. Gardner, *A History of Jamaica*, 386.

30. Phillippo, *Jamaica*, 388; Gardner, *A History of Jamaica*, 175–76.

31. Schuler, *"Alas, Alas, Kongo,"* 65, 68, 72–83, 93–96, and 108–9.

32. *Falmouth Post*, 16 June 1865. Schuler, *"Alas, Alas, Kongo,"* 105, uses this placard as evidence of the emergence of a politico-revolutionary aspect of the religious tradition represented by Myal and the Great Revival of 1860–61. There is an even earlier manifestation of a proto-Rastafarian consciousness in Jamaica in a movement identified as the Sons of Chus; see *Journals of the Assembly of Jamaica*, vol. 3, 18 May 1748, 122–23.

33. G. M. Foster, "Peasant Society and the Image of the Limited Good," *American Anthropologist* 67: 293–315, cited in Sidney Mintz and Richard Price, *An Anthropological Approach to the Afro-American Past: A Caribbean Perspective* (Philadelphia: Institute for the Study of Human Issues, 1976), 5; see also 6. A similar typology of orientations is presented in Edward Brathwaite's *Contradictory Omens: Cultural Diversity and Integration in the Caribbean* (Kingston: Savacou, 1974), 34, 40, and 41.

34. Schuler, *"Alas, Alas, Kongo,"* 65. Cf. the idea of "religious matrix" with Brathwaite's concept of "nam," which is pervasive in that author's recent work, e.g., in "Kumina—The Spirit of African Survival," *Jamaica Journal* 42 (Sept. 1978): 45–63; "Gods of the Middle Passage: A Tennament" in *Caribbean Review* 11 (Fall 1982): 18–19, 42–44; and most fully in *Afternoon of the status crow*, Savacou Workingpaper, no. 1 (Mona, Kingston, 1982). Brathwaite's "nam" is also discussed in Gordon Rohlehr, "The Problem of the Problem of Form: The Idea of an Aesthetic Continuum and Aesthetic Codeswitching in West Indian Literature," unpub. paper, Interdepartmental Conference, Univ. of the West Indies, St. Augustine, Trinidad, May 18–20, 1983.

35. *Missionary Register*, Mar. 1831, 127. Bleby, *Death Struggles*, 100.

36. Clarke, *Memorials*, 178.

37. L.M.S. corr. 1/1/C: Alloway to Ellis, 19 May 1835.

38. Ryall, "The organization of the missionary societies," 399.

39. Gardner, *A History of Jamaica*, 461. See also Barrett, *Baptist Mission in Jamaica*, 5, 7, 12, 13, 23, and passim. This attack was answered by *Remarks on An Exposition of the System Pursued by the Baptist Missionaries of Jamaica, etc.* (London: Baptist Missionary Society, 1843).

40. Waddell, *Twenty-Nine Years*, 111–14.

41. L.M.S. corr. 3/1/A: Milne to Ellis, Jan. 1840.

42. Ryall, "The organization of the missionary societies," 156.

43. Barrett, *Baptist Mission in Jamaica*, 8.

44. Ibid., 17 and 24; *Evangelical Magazine and Missionary Chronicle*, Mar. 1842, 115.

45. Ryall, "The organization of the missionary societies," 408.

46. Payne, *Freedom in Jamaica*, 19; Beverly Brown, "George Liele: Black Baptist and Pan-Africanist 1750–1826," *Savacou* 11–12 (Sept. 1975): 65.

47. Barry Chevannes, "Revival and Black Struggle," *Savacou* 5 (June 1971): 30. Barrett, *Baptist Mission in Jamaica*, 30. Important contemporary sources for Black Baptist origins and experience are Clarke, *Memorials*, esp. 10–17, 19–28, and 30; *Baptist Annual Register 1798–1801*; and Waddell, *Twenty-Nine Years*, 25–27 and 35–36. Useful secondary sources are "Letters Showing the Rise and Progress of Early Negro Churches of Georgia and the West Indies," *Journal of Negro History* 1 (Jan. 1916): 69–92; Horace Russell, "The missionary outreach of the West Indian Church to West Africa in the nineteenth century," Ph.D. diss., Oxford Univ., 1972; Russell, "The Church in the Past"; Chevannes, "Jamaican Lower Class Religion," M.Sc. diss., Univ. of the West Indies, 1971; Chevannes, "Revival and Black Struggle"; Brown, "George Liele"; C. S. Reid, "Early Baptist Beginnings"; Clement Gayle, *George Liele*; Gayle, "George Liele, Jamaica's First Black Preacher," *Jamaica Historical Society Bulletin* 8 (1983): 199–204; and Albert J. Raboteau, *Slave Rebellion: The "Invisible Institution" in the Antebellum South* (New York: Oxford Univ. Press, 1978), 28, 140–41, and 267–68.

48. Waddell, *Twenty-Nine Years*, 26 and 27; Barrett, *Baptist Mission in Jamaica*, 16.

49. Waddell, *Twenty-Nine Years*, 134.

50. M.M.S. corr. Ja. 1833–39: D. Barr, 30 Oct. 1834.

51. M.M.S. corr. Ja. 1833–39: Edmondson, Kingston, 3 Apr. 1838; Randerson, Spanish Town, 25 May 1839; Samuel, Lime Savanna, Clarendon, 29 Aug. 1839; Ja. 1840–42: Williams, Stony Hill, 25 Jan. 1840.

52. The quotation is from Mary Turner's dissertation, written as Mary Reckord, "Missionary Activity in Jamaica Before Emancipation," Univ. of London, 1964, 114, which was the basis of her *Slaves and Missionaries*.

53. Brathwaite, *The Development of Creole Society*, 219.

54. *History and Proceedings of the Baptist Missionary Stations*, 6. See also "The Covenant of the Anabaptist Church began in America in 1777 and in Jamaica in 1783," articles 9 and 11, in Brown, "George Liele," 61–63, and in Gayle, *George Liele*, 44–45.

55. Gardner, *A History of Jamaica*, 388.

56. Wilmot, "Political Developments," 34 and 127–28; Noelle Chutkan, "The Administration of Justice in Jamaica as a Contributing Factor in the Morant Bay Rebellion of 1865," *Savacou* 11–12 (Sept. 1975): 79, 85, and passim; Tucker, *Glorious Liberty*, 78; *Falmouth Post*, 12 Jan. 1875. See Claude McKay's description, in *My Green Hills of Jamaica* (London: Heinemann, 1979), 60–61, of the authority of his father in the latter quarter of the nineteenth century as a village leader and Baptist deacon in Clarendon, Jamaica. Instead of going to court, villagers would bring their disputes over land boundaries, straying animals, and crop destruction to him for settlement. "Generally, he was always obeyed."

57. *History and Proceedings of the Baptist Missionary Stations*, 39.

58. Ibid., 58.

59. Ibid., 63. It is not clear whether this is the same Scott who spoke at the 1841 Salter's Hill meeting.

60. *Postscript to the Royal Gazette*, 15–22 Aug. 1835. Timothy L. Smith, "Slavery and Theology: The Emergence of Black Christian Consciousness in Nineteenth Century America," *Church History* 41 (Dec. 1972): 500–501 and 507.

61. Waddell, *Twenty-Nine Years*, 26–27. Cf. Stephen D. Glazier's description of belief, ritual, and leadership among the Spiritual Baptists of Trinidad in his *Marchin' the Pilgrims Home: Leadership and Decision-Making in an Afro-Caribbean Faith* (Westport, Conn.: Greenwood, 1983), esp. chaps. 2 and 3.

62. L.M.S. corr. 1/4/C: Brown to Ellis, Mandeville, 3 Oct. 1836.

63. Phillippo, *Jamaica*, 270–73.

64. L.M.S. corr. 3/1/A: Milne to Ellis, Jan. 1840.

65. Melville J. Herskovits, *The Myth of the Negro Past* (1941; Boston: Beacon Press, 1958), 232.

66. *Evangelical Magazine and Missionary Chronicle*, Mar. 1842, 116. See the Baptist missionary Joshua Tinson's admonition against the black conception of conversion as being "bowed down and brought through" in his essay *On Conversion, being The First Circular Letter of the Baptist Missionaries to the Churches in Jamaica, forming the Baptist Association, Assembled at East Queen Street, Kingston, March 9th, 10th, and 11th—1836* (Kingston, 1836), 9. Cf. Brathwaite's discussion of "lemba/limbo" and of water and spirit symbolism in "Kumina," 57–59; also his poem "Chad" in *Masks* (London: Oxford Univ. Press, 1968), 18.

67. Williams, *Psychic Phenomena*, 173.

68. Edward Long, *The History of Jamaica* (London, 1774), vol. 1: 146; vol. 2: 416–17.

69. See especially correspondence to J. J. Williams from R. S. Rattray, Mampon, Ashanti, 5 May, 5 June, and 5 Oct., 1925, in the Williams files in the Rare Book and Jesuitana section of the Dinand Library at the College of the Holy Cross, Worcester, Mass.

70. Williams (*Psychic Phenomena*, 72) did not claim to know the origin of the word, ruling out any Akan origin because of the absence of the letter *l* in the Ashanti alphabet. Leonard Barrett in *Soul-Force, African Heritage in Afro-American Religion* (Garden City, N.Y.: Anchor Doubleday, 1974), 68, however, probably using T. G. Christaller's *Dictionary of the Asante and Fante Language*, 2d ed. (Basel, 1933), ventures the explanation that the word derives from the Twi *mia*, "to squeeze," or "to press," referring to the method of juicing the weeds used in curing illness. That interpretation remains speculative, however, and the origin of the word is still a mystery. The word is current in twentieth-century Revival and Kumina in Jamaica, especially in St. Thomas, where it refers primarily to the dance ceremony in preparation for the descent and incarnation of spirits and deities in the bodies of the participants; see esp. Moore, "Religion of Jamaican Negroes," 101, 143–44, 160–63, 164–66, 168–71, and 173; see also Schuler, *"Alas, Alas, Kongo,"* 78.

71. Williams, *Psychic Phenomena*, 66–68, 72–75, 90–91, 98–99, 166–68, 195–96, 215, and 247–48.

72. T. C. McCaskie, "Innovational Eclecticism: the Asante Empire and Europe in the Nineteenth Century," *Comparative Studies in Society and History* 14 (Jan. 1972): 38.

73. Phillippo, *Jamaica*, 263.

74. J. H. Buchner, *The Moravians in Jamaica* (London, 1853), 139–40.

75. Waddell, *Twenty-Nine Years*, 137 and 187–95.

76. Ibid., 187–94.

77. Ibid., 137–39.

78. Pobee, *Toward an African Theology*, 49. Cf. Moore, "Religion of Jamaican Negroes," 27. Williams, *Psychic Phenomena*, 164. Schuler, "*Alas, Alas, Kongo*," 36, indicates that public confession was likewise demanded by Myalists in Jamaica.

79. Pobee, *Toward an African Theology*, 92.

80. Williams, *Psychic Phenomena*, 165–66; Schuler, "*Alas, Alas, Kongo*," 70–73; Moore, "Religion of Jamaican Negroes," 27 and 33–34.

81. Buchner, *The Moravians in Jamaica*, 139–40. Rev. R. Thomas Banbury, *Jamaica Superstitions or The Obeah Book* (Kingston: DeSouza, 1894), 23. For the continuing importance of the cotton tree in twentieth-century Afro-Jamaican religion see Maureen Warner Lewis, "The Nkuyu: Spirit Messengers of the Kumina," *Savacou* 13 (1977): 61–66, and Brathwaite, "Kumina," 47 and 49.

82. Banbury, *Jamaica Superstitions*, 26; Williams, *Psychic Phenomena*, 168.

83. Banbury, *Jamaica Superstitions*, 24; Williams, *Psychic Phenomena*, 166–67.

84. Schuler, "*Alas, Alas, Kongo*," 41, observes that there were three grades of membership for Myalists: archangels, angels, and ministering angelics.

85. L.M.S. corr. 2/5/C: Franklin to Ellis, Morant Bay, 21 Oct. 1839.

86. M.M.S. corr. Ja. 1840–42: Atkins, Morant Bay, 21 Dec. 1840.

87. L.M.S. corr. 2/5/C: Franklin to Ellis, Morant Bay, 21 Oct. 1839.

88. Schuler, *"Alas, Alas, Kongo,"* 33, 36, 42, and note 8 on 136; Waddell, *Twenty-Nine Years*, 189.

89. *The Freeman*, 5, 19, and 26 Dec. 1860 and 2 Jan. 1861.

90. Ibid., 23 Jan. 1861.

91. M.M.S. corr. Ja. 1858–65: Tyson, Brown's Town P.O., 23 Apr. 1861.

92. *The Freeman*, 20 Feb. 1861.

93. Ibid.

94. Cf. Moore, "Religion of Jamaican Negroes," 171.

95. Waddell, *Twenty-Nine Years*, 187–95. Much of the violent activity observed during the Great Revival resembles what Moore ("Religion of Jamaican Negroes," 168–69) has described as the second phase of Myal possession, when the dancers must be attended constantly. It is also possible to explain the apparently disturbed behavior of the revivalists as a result of the lack of understanding on the part of the white ministers of the essential unity of spirit and body in African traditional religion and psychology, as seen in the claim that physical expression was merely secondary or accidental. Maureen Warner Lewis's discussion in "The Nkuyu," 76, is relevant here. See also Bastide, *The African Religions*, 377, and Brathwaite's interpretive comments on his *Mother Poem* in Rohlehr, "Problem of the Problem of Form," 26.

96. Underhill, *Life of James Mursell Phillippo*, 306–14.

97. *Falmouth Post*, 21 Oct. 1864.

98. Tucker, *Glorious Liberty*, 66.

99. *Falmouth Post*, 6 Jan. 1865.

100. Tucker, *Glorious Liberty*, 70.

101. M.M.S. corr. Ja. 1858–65: Mearns, Mt. Ward, 22 Nov. 1860.

102. Holdsworth, Guy's Hill, Pear Tree P.O., 23 Oct. 1861.

103. Orlando Patterson, "Slavery and Slave Revolts: A Socio-historical Analysis of the First Maroon War, 1665–1740," in *Maroon Societies: Rebel Slave Communities in the Americas*, ed. Richard Price (Baltimore: Johns Hopkins Univ. Press, 1979), 246. Waddell, *Twenty-Nine Years*, 19.

104. Bleby, *Death Struggles*, 25. For details of the 1831–32 rebellion, see Mary Turner's narrative in *Slaves and Missionaries*, 148–73, and Edward Brathwaite's meticulous accounts in "Caliban, Ariel and Unprospero in the Conflict of Creolization: A Study of the Slave Revolt in Jamaica in 1831–32," *Annals of the New York Academy of Sciences* 292 (1977): 41–62; "Rebellion: Anatomy of the Slave Revolt of 1831–32 in Jamaica," *Jamaica Historical Society Bulletin* 8 (Dec. 1981): 80–96; and "The Slave Rebellion in the Great River Valley of St. James—1831–32," *Jamaica Historical Review* 13 (1982): 11–30. The two best contemporary accounts, one giving the missionary viewpoint and the other totally biased toward the planters, are Henry Bleby's *Death Struggles of Slavery* and Bernard Martin Senior, *Jamaica as it was, as it is, and as it may be, etc.* (London: T. Hurst, 1835). Similar to Senior's account is that of Theodore Foulks, *Eighteen Months in Jamaica; with Recollections of the Late Rebellion* (London, 1833).

105. Thomas F. Abbott, *Narrative of certain events connected with the late disturbances in Jamaica and the charges preferred against the Baptist missionaries in that Island: being the substance of a letter to the Secretary of the Baptist Missionary Society, dated March 13, 1832* (London, 1832), 31–32; Waddell, *Twenty-Nine Years*, 48; Bleby, *Death Struggles*, 12 and 42–43.

106. C.O. 137/181: notes from the trial of Rev. Henry Gottlob Pfeifer, 16–19 Jan. 1832, 19–20.

107. M.M.S. C/70: Murray to Watson, Montego Bay, 10 Mar. 1832; C/59: Bleby to James, Kingston, 17 Feb. 1832. C.O. 137/181: Confession of Robert Gardiner. Senior, *Jamaica as it was*, 183 and 264.

108. Curtin, *Two Jamaicas*, 86. Mary Turner (Reckord), in her interpretation of the Baptist War in "Missionary Activity," assumed a separation of religious and political aspirations in the minds of the rebels, which she modifies greatly in the account in *Slaves and Missionaries*, in which she better appreciates the unity of thought and feeling, of politics and religion, in the Afro-creole perception of reality.

109. "The Christian Hero," *The Freeman*, 10 Oct. 1855.

110. Ibid. See also an account of Sharp's martyrdom in *Jamaica Advocate*, 29 Aug. 1896, reprinted in *Jamaica Historical Society Bulletin* 8 (Dec. 1981): 99.

111. C.O. 137–299: Evelyn to Grey, Savanna-la-Mar, 12 June 1848; "The Examinations or Statements upon Oath of William Hoss of the Parish of St. James, Planter, and others taken this 28th day of June, 1848"; Sworn testimony of Edward Hewitt, 3 July 1848; Grey to Grey, King's House, 22 July 1848; Memorial from the Baptist Western Union to the Governor, 21 July 1848.

Chapter 5

1. Jamaica Royal Commission Report, *Parliamentary Papers*, 1866, xxx [C.3683], 14, quoted in Curtin, *Two Jamaicas*, 197. See also Don Robotham, *"The Notorious Riot": The Socio-Economic and Political Bases of Paul Bogle's Revolt* (Jamaica: Univ. of the West Indies, Institute of Social and Economic Research, 1981), 26a, 27, 39, and 98; Robotham's analytical account constitutes a compelling argument against the traditional view of Morant Bay as a mere riot ignited by ignorant and unorganized peasants.

2. Douglas Hall, *Free Jamaica, 1838–1865: An Economic History* (1959; rpt. Barbados: Caribbean Universities Press, 1969), 248.

3. Teall to Baynes, Annotto Bay, 13 June 1889. Underhill, *The Jamaica Mission, in its Relations with the Baptist Missionary Society from 1838 to 1879* (London, 1879), 14; *Letter addressed to the Rt. Honourable E. Cardwell*, 8; *Life of James Mursell Phillippo*, 346–47; and *The Tragedy of Morant Bay*, 180–83. C.O. 137/418: Jamaica 1866, Minutes of Evidence, Testimony of Benjamin Millard, 8 Mar. 1866. L.M.S. corr.: Clark to Tidman, Four Paths, Clarendon, 23 Oct. 1865. Clarke, *Memorials*, 223–24.

4. Underhill's letter to Secretary of State Cardwell was dated 5 January 1865. Underhill was informed by Cardwell on 27 January that he had forwarded the letter to Gov. Eyre for his comment. Underhill learned in April that Eyre had made the dispatch public.

5. Underhill, *Letter addressed to the Rt. Honourable E. Cardwell*, 22–23, 24–48, and 49–57.

6. Ibid., 5, and Underhill, *The Tragedy of Morant Bay*, 158–59.

7. Underhill, *Letter addressed to the Rt. Honourable E. Cardwell*, 1, and *The Tragedy of Morant Bay*, 21, 168–70, and 173–74.

8. Underhill, *The Tragedy of Morant Bay*, 22–23.

9. Ibid., 23–24.

10. Underhill, *Life of James Mursell Phillippo*, 341.

11. *Falmouth Post*, 1 Mar. 1864.

12. Ibid., 23 Aug. 1864.

13. Ibid., 22 Sept. 1865.

14. J.R.C. evidence App. V, 1150: Bogle to Gordon, 25 July 1862; Gordon to Bogle, 11 Dec. 1861; Bogle et al. to Gordon, 25 July 1861. Underhill, *Life of James Mursell Phillippo*, 319. See also Robotham, "The Notorious Riot," 20.

15. Underhill, *Life of James Mursell Phillippo*, 320. J.R.C. evidence App. V, 1150: Bogle to Gordon, 25 July 1862.

16. Underhill, *Life of James Mursell Phillippo*, 319, 320, and 330, and *The Tragedy of Morant Bay*, 89. L.M.S. corr.: Gardner to Tidman, Kingston, 24 Oct. 1865. Rhodes House MSS W.Ind. S.27/556: Evidence in the case of Mr. Gordon; letter to *Morning Post* from A. E. Shannon. See also Robotham, "The Notorious Riot," 20. *Falmouth Post*, 31 Oct. 1865.

17. L.M.S. corr.: Fletcher to Tidman, 4 Feb. 1859. See Fletcher's encomium to Gordon entitled *Personal Recollections of the Honourable George W. Gordon, Late of Jamaica* (London: Elliot Stock, 1867).

18. M.M.S. corr. Ja. 1858–65: Tyson to Arthur, 3 Garden Terrace, Newcastle-on-Tyne, 4 Dec. 1865, and Demondson, Kingston, Nov. (no date), 1865.

19. Rhodes House MSS W.Ind. S.27/556: Evidence in the case of Mr. Gordon.

20. *Jamaica Watchman and People's Free Press*, 5 June 1865 and 21 Aug. 1865.

21. Underhill, *The Tragedy of Morant Bay*, 167–68.

22. *Jamaica Watchman*, 7 Aug. 1865.

23. Underhill, *The Tragedy of Morant Bay*, 112–23. J.R.C. evidence App. V. 1150: R. Warren, endorsed by G. W. Gordon, certification of Bogle's ordination, 5 Mar. 1865.

24. C.O. 137/413: Jamaica 1866, Testimony of Rev. Edwin Palmer, 13 Feb. 1866; *Falmouth Post*, 7 Nov. 1865; Underhill, *Life of James Mursell Phillippo*, 335–36, and *The Tragedy of Morant Bay*, 112–13, 115–17, and 175–77. More needs to be known about these men in order to give us a fuller understanding of the religious and racial dynamics of the time. As it stands now, however, they are mere blips on our historical radar, noticed only on the periphery of the focus of the documents pertaining to 1865.

25. Rhodes House MSS W.Ind. S.27/556: Short Summary of the Late Mr. Edward John Eyre's Services.

26. Gardner, *A History of Jamaica*, 487. See also Robotham, *"The Notorious Riot,"* 20.

27. M.M.S. corr. Ja. 1858–65: Edmondson, Kingston, 23 Oct. 1865.

28. M.M.S. Ja. 1858–65: Edmondson, Kingston, 9 Dec. 1865.

29. Underhill, *Letter addressed to the Rt. Honourable E. Cardwell*, 8, *The Tragedy of Morant Bay*, 180–81, and *Life of James Mursell Phillippo*, 340. Schuler, *"Alas, Alas, Kongo,"* 107–9.

30. *Falmouth Post*, 17 Oct. 1865.

31. Rhodes House MSS W.Ind. S.27/556: Comment on the Case of Mr. Gordon by the Royal Commissioners, 9 Apr. 1866.

32. C.O. 137/417: Ja. 1866, Testimony of Rev. E. B. Key, 3 Mar. 1866.

33. Moore, "Religion of Jamaican Negroes," 13, note 2; Moore observes that Bogle is well known at cult ceremonies where he comes as an ancestral zombie to take possession of the body of a dancing zombie for periods of the dance. See also Schuler, *"Alas, Alas, Kongo,"* 107–8 for the memory of Bogle sustained in Kumina.

34. Underhill, *Letter addressed to the Rt. Honourable E. Cardwell*, 35 and 37.

35. Curtin, *The Image of Africa*, 62, 64, 224, and 270.

36. Ibid., 272; also Temperley, "Anti-Slavery as Cultural Imperialism," in *Anti-Slavery, Religion and Reform*, ed. Bolt and Drescher, 345–46. The theory appeared around 1750 in France, among Scottish Enlightenment thinkers, and in Adam Smith's Edinburgh lectures of 1750–51.

37. Samuel Oughton, "The Influence of Artificial Wants on the Social, Moral, and Commercial Advancement of Jamaica," *West India Quarterly Magazine* (Kingston), vol. 1 (May 1862): 474–83; also Oughton's *Jamaica: Why it is Poor, and How it May Become Rich* (Kingston, 1866).

38. Underhill, *The Tragedy of Morant Bay*, 47, 135, and 136–37; quotation is from p. 135.

39. Ibid., 52–53. In the private opinion of certain British military officers, official death figures may have been greatly underestimated; see Robotham, "The Notorious Riot," 11–12.

40. Underhill, *The Tragedy of Morant Bay*, 56 and 149. Robotham, "The Notorious Riot," 90 and 94. Similarly contradictory observations were made by contemporary commentators on the 1831–32 rebellion, who opined on the inability of blacks to organize while offering evidence of their actually doing so; see, e.g., Foulks, *Eighteen Months in Jamaica*, 73, 75, 78, and 80.

41. *Falmouth Post*, 2 June 1865; Curtin, *Two Jamaicas*, 172; Gardner, *A History of Jamaica*, 465.

42. Ryall, "The organization of the missionary societies," 219.

43. *Falmouth Post*, 28 Nov. 1865.

44. Ibid., 8 Dec. 1865.

45. H. Hoetink, *Caribbean Race Relations: A Study of Two Variants* (London: Oxford Univ. Press, 1967), 70.

46. Ryall, "The organization of the missionary societies," 261.

47. *Falmouth Post*, 1 Mar. 1864.

48. *Morning Journal*, 2 Aug. 1864.

49. Ryall, "The organization of the missionary societies," 264. For more on Gardner's building society see *Falmouth Post*, 4 Mar., 22 Mar., and 29 Apr. 1864, and 3 Sept. 1875; *Morning Journal*, 27 Feb. 1864; and Gardner, *A History of Jamaica*, 470.

50. *Queen's Newsman*, 2 July 1870.

51. Underhill, *Life of James Mursell Phillippo*, 358.

52. Ibid., 358.

53. *Jamaica Instructor*, 22 Apr. 1878.

54. *Falmouth Post*, 14 July 1876.

55. Underhill, *Life of James Mursell Phillippo*, 410, 414, 416, and 421.

56. Underhill, *The Jamaica Mission*, 14–17.

57. Underhill, *Life of James Mursell Phillippo*, 364.

58. *Falmouth Post*, 23 Mar. and 3 Sept. 1875; *Falmouth Gazette*, 4 July, 29 July, and 8 Aug. 1879.

59. S.P.G. corr. D40/2: R. B. Lynch, Malvern P.O., 8 Jan. 1873. *Falmouth Post*, 27 Aug. 1875.

60. *Falmouth Post*, 31 Aug. 1875.

61. Ibid.,19 Feb. 1875 and 7 July 1876; see also 19 and 26 Feb., 11 and 15 June, and 9 July 1875, and 30 June 1876.

62. Christine Bolt, in *Victorian Attitudes to Race*, esp. xi and 76–97, discusses the importance of the 1865 rebellion as an element in metropolitan (including United States) debates on race and slavery in the latter part of the nineteenth century.

63. Ellis, *The Diocese of Jamaica*, 99.

64. S.P.G. corr. D.28, Ja. 1860–67: Spencer to Courtenay, 12 Jan. 1867.

65. *Appeal to England for Aid by the Committee of the Jamaica Church of England Home and Foreign Missionary Society* (Kingston, 1867), 11.

66. *Falmouth Post*, 11 Apr. 1865.

67. Ibid., 1 Dec. 1865.

68. Ibid., 2 Apr. 1875.

69. Ibid., 2 Apr. 1875.

70. Ibid., 24 Oct. 1865.

71. Rex Nettleford, "Aggression, Violence and Force: Containment and Eruption in the Jamaica History of Protest," in *Violence and Aggression in the History of Ideas*, ed. J. Fisher and P. P. Wiener (New Brunswick, N.J.: Rutgers Univ. Press, 1974), 143.

72. *Falmouth Post*, 21 Nov. 1865.

73. Ibid., 21 Nov. 1865 and 1 Dec. 1865.

74. Ibid., 2 Apr. 1875. The reporter did not say what Fagin's sentence was, except to observe that it was a heavy one.

75. Ibid., 12 Jan. 1875.

76. B.M.S. corr. WI/5: Teall to Baynes, Annotto Bay, 13 June 1889. *Falmouth Post*, 22 Jan. 1875.

77. *Falmouth Post*, 14 July 1876.

78. Tucker, *Glorious Liberty*, 86–91.

79. *Jamaica Instructor*, 22 Apr. 1872.

Chapter 6

1. Charles Savile Roundell, *England and Her Subject Races, with special reference to Jamaica, by Charles Savile Roundell, M.A., fellow of Merton College, Oxford, Secretary to the late Royal Commission in Jamaica* (London, 1866), 18, 20, 32, 36–39, 40–41, and 43.

2. Curtin, *The Image of Africa*, 13, 24, 29, 38, 43–45, 291, 293–94, 363–64, 372, and 387; Bolt, *Victorian Attitudes*, 1, 6, 10–11, and 18.

3. Curtin, *The Image of Africa*, 26 and 53.

4. Mintz and Price, *Anthropological Approach*, 13.

5. Ibid., 23.

6. Brathwaite, "Kumina," 60–61; Moore, "Religion of Jamaican Negroes," 65, 115, and 177–78; Schuler, *"Alas, Alas, Kongo,"* 71.

Bibliography

PRIMARY SOURCES

Manuscripts

Missionary and Church Archives
Archives of the English Province of the Society of Jesus
    Diary of James Splaine, S.J. MS. Jamaica 1872–73.
    "Jacobus T. Splaine." Province Register, MS. [1901?]: 330.
    General Missionary Correspondence MR/4, MR/5, MR/6, and MR/7.
Baptist Missionary Society Papers
    General Missionary Correspondence WI/1, WI/2, and WI/5.
    MS WI/1: Autobiography of J. M. Phillippo. N.d.
    Letterbook of copies of letters received from Jamaica, 1840–46.
    MS booklet WI/3: Young, Rev. John. "The Missionaries' Father, or The Bless-
    ings of Truth and the Evil of Infidelity." Biography of William Knibb. N.d.
Church Missionary Society Papers
    Minutes of the Jamaica Corresponding Committee
    CW/01a: 1827–40.
    CW/02a: 1. Lipscomb 1824–43.
            2. Spencer 1843–72.
London Missionary Society Papers
    General Missionary Correspondence 1/1/B, 1/2/A, 1/2/B, 1/2/C, 1/3/A,
    1/3/C, 1/4/C, 2/1/C, 2/2/A, 2/2/C, 2/3/A, 2/4/A, 2/4/B, 2/4/C, 2/5/
    A, 2/5/C, 8/3, 8/4, 9/1.
Wesleyan-Methodist Missionary Society Papers
    General Missionary Correspondence W.I. 1832, W.I. 1833–34, Ja. 1833–39, Ja.
    1840–42, Ja. 1843–47, Ja. 1848–57, Ja. 1858–65.
Society for the Propagation of the Gospel in Foreign Parts

General Correspondence
    C/W.1 Ja.1Ac. 1820–36.
    C/W.1 Ja.1B. Bishop Lipscomb 1826–35.
    C/W.1 Ja.2A. 1836–43.
    C/W.1 Ja.2B. Bishop Lipscomb 1836–43.
    C/W.1 Ja.3. 1843–55.
    D.16 Ja. 1850–59.
    D.28 Ja. 1860–67.
    D.40/2 W.I. 1868–74.
    D.42 Africa, Australasia, America. 1875.

Private Papers and Library Research Archives

New York. New York Historical Society. Day, Mahlon. "Journal of a Trip to the West Indies, 1839–1840." MS copy.
Oxford. Rhodes House. MSS W. Indies S.23, 40–48. Rev. T. W. P. Taylder. Extracts from journal and letter from Jamaica, 1843–44. Also MS W. Ind. r. 1. Frederick White. Magistrate's Diary. St. George, Jamaica, 1834. Also MSS W. Ind. s. 27/556. Correspondence regarding attacks upon Gov. Eyre in Olivier's book.
Philadelphia. Eastern Baptist Theological College. Private papers of Dr. Horace O. Russell. "Testimony of Faith." MS notebook of Thomas Burchell. Completed in Jamaica in 1823. Also "T. Burchell: The Missionary Enthusiast." Anon. MS. Also Russell, Horace. "Samuel Sharpe: A Case for an Award of National Hero." Unpub. MS. N.d.
Philadelphia. History Society of Pennsylvania. Edward Carey Gardiner Collection. Martha Powel Bowen Estate Papers. Also Papers of James Johnston, 1781–1837.
Worcester, Mass. Dinand Library of the College of the Holy Cross. Rare Book and Jesuitana Section. The J. J. Williams, S.J. files.
Public Record Office (U.K.), Colonial Office Records.
C.O. 137/178–82, 185, 270–72, 299, 411–12, 415–20: Jamaica 1831 Despatches; Public Offices and Miscellaneous. Jamaica 1832 Despatches; Abstracts of Trials by Court-Martial during the continuance of Martial Law in Jamaica. Jamaica Ecclesiastical 1831–41. Jamaica 1848, Vol. 5, Apprehended Outbreak in Western Parishes and St. Mary's. Jamaica 1866, Original of the Report of the Jamaica Royal Commission of 1866 and Minutes of Evidence 23 Jan. to 3 April.
C.O. 142/54–94: Jamaica Blue Book Returns 1840–80.

Printed Sources

Baptist Annual Register 1798–1801.
Church Missionary Record.
Evangelical Magazine and Missionary Chronicle.
Evidence Upon Oath touching the Condition and Treatment of the Negro Population of the British West Indies colonies: Part I—Island of Jamaica. Taken before a Select Committee of the House of Lords Session 1832. London, 1833.
"Father James Splaine." *Letters and Notices* [of the English Province of the Society of Jesus] 26 (1901–2): 352–58.
Jamaica Royal Commission 1866—Appendix V: Correspondence and Documents relative to the Case of George William Gordon.
Journals of the Assembly of Jamaica, 1663–1826, vol. 3.
Missionary Register.
Parliamentary Papers.
Scottish Missionary and Philanthropic Register.
"The Sligo Papers: Excerpts from the Letter Books of Howe Peter Browne, 2nd Marquis of Sligo, Governor of Jamaica April 1834–August 1836, from the Manuscript Collection of the National Library of Jamaica." *Jamaica Journal* 17, no. 3 (1984): 11–17.
United Presbyterian Missionary Register.
Votes of the Honourable House of Assembly of Jamaica. . . 27th of October, 1840. . . 22d of December, 1840. St. Jago de la Vega: William John Pearson, 1841.

Newspapers

British
The Freeman.
Jamaican
Baptist Herald.
Cornwall Courier and Jamaica General Intelligencer.
Emancipator.
Falmouth Gazette and Jamaica General Advertiser.
Falmouth Post and Jamaica General Advertiser.
Jamaica Courant.
Jamaica Creole.
Jamaica Despatch and Kingston Chronicle.
Jamaica Despatch and New Courant.
Jamaica Instructor.

Jamaica Standard and Royal Gazette.
Jamaica Watchman and People's Free Press.
Morning Journal.
Royal Gazette.
Queen's Newsman.
Watchman and Jamaica Free Press.

Selected Secondary Sources

Abbott, Thomas F. *Narrative of certain events connected with the late disturbances in Jamaica and the charges preferred against the Baptist missionaries in that Island: being the substance of a letter to the Secretary of the Baptist Missionary Society, dated March 13, 1832.* London, 1832.

Anderson, James S. M. *The History of the Church of England in the Colonies and Foreign Dependencies of the British Empire.* 3 vols. London, 1845–56.

Appeal to England for Aid by the Committee of the Jamaica Church of England Home and Foreign Missionary Society. Kingston, 1867.

Appeal to the English Public from the Bishop, Clergy, and Laity of the Church of England in Jamaica. Kingston, 1870.

Banbury, Rev. R. Thomas. *Jamaica Superstitions or The Obeah Book.* Kingston: DeSouza, 1894.

Barrett, Leonard. *Soul-Force, African Heritage in Afro-American Religion.* Garden City, N.Y.: Anchor Doubleday, 1974.

Barrett, W. G. *Baptist Mission in Jamaica: an exposition of the system pursued by the Baptist Missionaries in Jamaica, by Missionaries and Catechists of the London Missionary Society in that Island.* London: John Snow, 1842.

Bastide, Roger. *The African Religions of Brazil.* Trans. Helen Sabba. 1960. Baltimore: Johns Hopkins Univ. Press, 1978.

Beecham, John. *Ashantee and the Gold Coast.* London, 1841.

Bigelow, John. *Jamaica in 1850, or The Effects of Sixteen Years of Freedom on a Slave Colony.* 1851. Westport, Conn.: Negro Universities Press, 1970.

Bleby, Henry. *Death Struggles of Slavery, Being a Narrative of Facts and Incidents Which Occurred in a British Colony, During the Two Years Immediately Preceding Negro Emancipation.* London: Hamilton, Adams, and Co., 1853.

Bolt, Christine. *Victorian Attitudes to Race.* Toronto: Univ. of Toronto Press, 1971.

———, and Seymour Drescher, eds. *Anti-Slavery, Religion and Reform.* Hamden, Conn.: Archon, 1980.

Brathwaite, Edward Kamau. *Afternoon of the status crow.* Savacou Working paper, no. 1. Mona, Kingston, 1982. Rpt. in *Missile and Capsule,* ed. Jurgen Martini. Bremen, Germany, 1983: 11–54.

————. "Caliban, Ariel and Unprospero in the Conflict of Creolization: A Study of the Slave Revolt in Jamaica in 1831–32." *Annals of the New York Academy of Sciences* 292 (1977): 41–62.

————. *Contradictory Omens: Cultural Diversity and Integration in the Caribbean.* Kingston: Savacou, 1974.

————. *The Development of Creole Society in Jamaica, 1770–1820.* Oxford: Clarendon Press, 1971.

————. "Gods of the Middle Passage: A Tennament." *Caribbean Review* 11 (Fall 1982): 18–19, 42–44.

————. "Kumina—The Spirit of African Survival." *Jamaica Journal* 42 (Sept. 1978): 45–63.

————. *Masks.* London: Oxford Univ. Press, 1968.

————. "Rebellion: Anatomy of the Slave Revolt of 1831–32 in Jamaica." *Jamaica Historical Society Bulletin* 8 (Dec. 1981): 80–96.

————. "The Slave Rebellion in the Great River Valley of St. James—1831–32." *Jamaica Historical Review* 13 (1982): 11–30.

Bridges, G. W. *The Annals of Jamaica.* 2 vols. London, 1827.

Brown, Beverly. "George Liele: Black Baptist and Pan-Africanist, 1750–1826." *Savacou* 11–12 (Sept. 1975): 58–67, 110–11.

Browne, Rev. Henry. *An Address delivered by the Rev. Henry Browne, on the occasion of the laying of the Foundation Stone of St. Paul's Church, Annandale, St. Ann's, Jamaica.* Kingston, 1838.

Buchner, J. H. *The Moravians in Jamaica.* London, 1853.

Burchell, William F. *Memoir of Thomas Burchell.* London, 1849.

Burn, W. L. *Emancipation and Apprenticeship in the British West Indies.* London: Jonathan Cape, 1937.

Caldecott, A. *The Church in the West Indies.* London: S.P.C.K., 1898.

Campbell, Carl. "Missionaries and Maroons: Conflict and Resistance in Accompong, Charles Town and Moore Town (Jamaica), 1837–1838." *Jamaica Historical Review* 14 (1984): 42–58.

Carey, William. *An Enquiry into the Obligations of Christians to Use Means for the Conversion of the Heathens.* London, 1792.

Carlyle, Thomas. "Occasional Discourse on the Nigger Question." *Fraser's Magazine* 40 (Dec. 1849): 670–79.

Carnegie, James. "'Jamaica Past & Present' Book Review," *Jamaica Journal* 5 (Mar. 1971): 11–15.

Catherall, Gordon A. "The Baptist Missionary Society and Jamaican Emancipation, 1814–1845." M.A. thesis. Liverpool Univ., 1966.

Centenary Pamphlet of the Jamaica Church Missionary Society, formerly the Jamaica Home and Foreign Mission Society. Kingston, 1961.

Chevannes, A. Barry. "Jamaican Lower Class Religion." M.Sc. diss. Univ. of the West Indies, Mona, 1971.

————. "Revival and Black Struggle." *Savacou* 5 (June 1971): 27–39.

Christaller, T. G. *Dictionary of the Asante and Fante Language.* 2d. ed. Basel, 1933.

Chutkan, Noelle. "The Administration of Justice in Jamaica as a Contributing Factor in the Morant Bay Rebellion of 1865." *Savacou* 11–12 (Sept. 1975): 78–85, 112–13.

Clarke, John. *Fernandian Grammar and Specimens of African Tongues.* London, 1848.

————. *Memorials of the Baptist Missionaries in Jamaica.* London, 1869.

Curtin, Philip D. *The Image of Africa: British Ideas and Action, 1780–1850.* 2 vols. Madison: Univ. of Wisconsin Press, 1964.

————. *Two Jamaicas: The Role of Ideas in a Tropical Colony, 1830–1865.* 1965. New York: Atheneum, 1970.

Dallas, R. C. *The History of the Maroons.* 2 vols. London, 1803.

Davis, David Brion. *The Problem of Slavery in Western Culture.* Ithaca, N.Y.: Cornell Univ. Press, 1966.

Dickson, Kwesi A., and Paul Ellingworth. *Biblical Revelation and African Beliefs.* Maryknoll, N.Y.: Orbis, 1969.

Dillenberger, John, and Claude Welch. *Protestant Christianity: Interpreted through Its Development.* New York: Charles Scribner's Sons, 1954.

Duncan, Rev. Peter. *A Narrative of the Wesleyan Mission to Jamaica.* London, 1849.

Dwight, Henry Otis, LL.D.; H. Allen Tupper, Jr. D.D., and Edwin Munsell Bliss D.D., eds. *The Encyclopedia of Missions.* 2d ed. New York: Funk and Wagnalls, 1904.

East, Rev. D. J. *Civil Government: What the Bible Says About It: A Word for the Times.* Kingston, 1865.

Ellis, J. B. *The Diocese of Jamaica.* London, 1913.

First Annual Report of the St. George's Home and Reformatory for Boys. Established in Kingston, Jamaica, on the first day of July, 1858. Kingston, 1859.

The First Report of the Jamaica Church of England Home and Foreign Missionary Society. Kingston, 1862.

Fletcher, Duncan. *Personal Recollections of the Honourable George W. Gordon, Late of Jamaica.* London: Elliot Stock, 1867.

Foulks, Theodore. *Eighteen Months in Jamaica; with Recollections of the Late Rebellion.* London, 1833.

Freedom in Jamaica, or, The First of August, 1838. London, 1 Nov. 1838.

From Journal of the Third Synod of the Church of England in Jamaica, being the Second Annual Synod Under Law 30, 1870, from 3 August to 14 August, 1871. Kingston, 1871.

Froude, James Anthony. *The English in the West Indies.* London, 1888.

Full Report of the Proceedings in Chancery in the Important Case of the Baptist Chapel, Spanish Town, Oct., 1845. Kingston: Guardian and Patriot Office, 1845.

Gardner, W. J. *A History of Jamaica from its Discovery by Christopher Columbus to the Year 1872.* London, 1873.

Gayle, Clement. "George Liele, Jamaica's First Black Preacher." *Jamaica Historical Society Bulletin* 8 (1983): 199–204.

————. *George Liele: Pioneer Missionary to Jamaica*. Kingston: Jamaica Baptist Union, 1982.

General Results of Negro Apprenticeship as shown by Extracts from the Public Speeches and Despatches of the Governors of Various Colonies and of Lord Glenelg as Secretary of State for the Colonial Department. London, 1838.

Glazier, Stephen D. *Marchin' the Pilgrims Home: Leadership and Decision- Making in an Afro-Caribbean Faith*. Contributions to the Study of Religion, no. 10. Westport, Conn.: Greenwood, 1983.

Gordon, Robert. *Education, A Lecture delivered . . . by Robert Gordon*. Kingston, 1856.

————, Curate of parish church of St. John of Wapping. *The Jamaica Church. Why It Has Failed*. London, ca. 1872.

Goveia, Elsa V. *Slave Society in the British Leeward Islands at the End of the Eighteenth Century*. New Haven, Conn.: Yale Univ. Press, 1965.

————. *A Study on the Historiography of the British West Indies*. Mexico: Instituto Panamericano de Geografia e Historia, 1956.

Green, William A. *British Slave Emancipation: The Sugar Colonies and the Great Experiment, 1830–1865*. Oxford: The Clarendon Press, 1976.

Hall, Douglas. *Free Jamaica, 1838–1865: An Economic History*. 1959. Rpt. Barbados: Caribbean Universities Press, 1969

Harvey, Thomas, and William Brewin. *Jamaica in 1866*. London: A. W. Bennett, 1866.

Herskovits, Melville J. *The Myth of the Negro Past*. 1941. Boston: Beacon Press, 1958.

Heuman, Gad J. "Coloreds and Blacks in the Jamaican Assembly: A Biographical Profile." *Jamaican Historical Society Bulletin* 8 (Dec. 1982): 177–83.

Hinton, John Howard. *Memoir of William Knibb, Missionary in Jamaica*. London, 1849.

History and Proceedings of the Baptist Missionary Stations, Salter's Hill, Bethtephil, Maldon, and Bethsalem, in the Island of Jamaica. London, 1841.

Hoetink, H. *Caribbean Race Relations: A Study of Two Variants*. Trans. Eva M. Hooykaas. London: Oxford Univ. Press, 1967.

Kopytoff, Barbara K. "Religious Change Among the Jamaican Maroons: The Ascendance of the Christian God Within a Traditional Cosmology." *Journal of Social History* 20, no. 3 (1987): 465–84.

Laurence, K. O. *Immigration into the West Indies in the 19th Century*. Barbados: Caribbean Universities Press, 1971.

"Letters Showing the Rise and Progress of Early Negro Churches of Georgia and the West Indies," *Journal of Negro History* 1 (Jan. 1916): 69–92.

Lewis, Maureen Warner. "The Nkuyu: Spirit Messengers of the Kumina." *Savacou* 13 (1977): 57–78, 83–86.

Lewis, M. G. *Journal of a West India Proprietor, 1815–1817*. London, 1834.

Lipscomb, Christopher. *An Address delivered On Laying the First Stone of a New*

Chapel at Lincoln Estate in Westmoreland, Jamaica, by Christopher, Lord Bishop of Jamaica. Kingston, 1837.

———. *Church Societies a Blessing to the Colonies: A Sermon preached at the Parish Church of St. Michael-Le-Berry, York, by Christopher, Lord Bishop of Jamaica, on Thursday, 29 October, on Anniversary of the York Diocesan Committee of the SPCK*. London, 1840.

———. *A Sermon preached at the Parish Church of Spanish Town, on Wednesday, the First of August, 1838, by Christopher, Lord Bishop of Jamaica*. Kingston, 1838.

Long, Edward. *The History of Jamaica*. 3 vols. London, 1774.

Madden, R. R. *A Twelvemonths' Residence in the West Indies*. 2 vols. London, 1835.

Mathieson, William Law. *British Slavery and Its Abolition, 1823–1838*. London, 1926.

———. *British Slave Emancipation, 1838–1849*. London, 1932.

McCaskie, T. C. "Innovational Eclecticism: The Asante Empire and Europe in the Nineteenth Century." *Comparative Studies in Society and History* 14 (Jan. 1972): 30–45.

McKay, Claude. *My Green Hills of Jamaica*. Ed. Mervyn Morris. London: Heinemann, 1979.

Mintz, Sidney, and Richard Price. *An Anthropological Approach to the Afro-American Past: A Caribbean Perspective*. ISHI Occasional Papers in Social Change, no. 2. Philadelphia: Institute for the Study of Human Issues, 1976.

M'Mahon, Benjamin. *Jamaica Plantership*. London, 1839.

Moore, Joseph Graessle. "Religion of Jamaican Negroes: A Study of Afro-Jamaican Acculturation." Ph.D. diss. Northwestern Univ., 1953.

Morris, Rev. David R., Rector of St. James, Jamaica. *Letters of Self-Defence and for Christian Truth and Duty, to the Archbishop of Canterbury, in Rejoinder to Culpable Injustice, and to Sinful Disavowal of Holy Principle*. Kingston, 1872.

Mount, Graeme S. "Maritime Methodists in Bermuda: Their Attitudes Towards Black Bermudians from 1799 to the Methodist Schism of 1870." Paper presented at the Fifteenth Conference of Caribbean Historians, Univ. of the West Indies, Mona, Jamaica, April 15–20, 1983.

Nettleford, Rex. "Aggression, Violence and Force: Containment and Eruption in the Jamaica History of Protest." In *Violence and Aggression in the History of Ideas*, ed. J. Fisher and P. P. Weiner. New Brunswick, N.J.: Rutgers Univ. Press, 1974. 133–57.

Oughton, Samuel. "The Influence of Artificial Wants on the Social, Moral, and Commercial Advancement of Jamaica." *West India Quarterly Magazine* (Kingston), vol 1 (May 1862): 474–83.

———. *Jamaica: Why it is Poor, and How it May Become Rich*. Kingston, 1866.

Patterson, Orlando. "Slavery and Slave Revolts: A Sociological Analysis of the First Maroon War, 1665–1740." *Social and Economic Studies* 19 (1970): 289–25. Rpt. in *Maroon Societies*, ed. Price.

Payne, Ernest A. *Freedom in Jamaica: Some chapters in the story of the Baptist Missionary Society*. London: Carey Press, 1933.

Phillippo, James M. *Jamaica, Its Past and Present State*. London: Paternoster Row, 1843.

Phillips, James J. "Land Tenure at Silver Hill." Unpub. MS. Kingston, Jamaica, 1971.

Pobee, John S. *Toward an African Theology*. Nashville, Tenn.: Abingdon, 1979.

Price, George. *Jamaica and the Colonial Office—Who Caused the Crisis?* London, 1866.

Price, Richard, ed. *Maroon Societies: Rebel Slave Communities in the Americas*. Baltimore: Johns Hopkins Univ. Press, 1979.

Raboteau, Albert J. *Slave Religion: The "Invisible Institution" in the Antebellum South*. New York: Oxford Univ. Press, 1978.

Ramsay, James. *An Essay on the Treatment and Conversion of African Slaves in the British Sugar Colonies*. London, 1784.

Reckord, Mary. "Missionary Activity in Jamaica Before Emancipation." Ph.D. diss. Univ. of London, 1964.

Reid, C. S. "Early Baptist Beginnings." *Jamaica Journal* 16, no. 2 (1983): 2–8.

Remarks on An Exposition of the System Pursued by the Baptist Missionaries of Jamaica, etc. London: Baptist Missionary Society, 1843.

Report of the Committee of the African Civilization Society at Public Meeting, Exeter hall, Tuesday, 21 June, 1842. London, 1842.

Robotham, Don. *"The Notorious Riot": The Socio-Economic and Political Bases of Paul Bogle's Revolt*. Working paper 28. Jamaica: Univ. of the West Indies, Institute of Social and Economic Research, 1981.

Rohlehr, Gordon. "The Problem of the Problem of Form: The Idea of an Aesthetic Continuum and Aesthetic Codeswitching in West Indian Literature." Unpub. paper. Interdepartmental Conference, Univ. of the West Indies. St. Augustine, Trinidad, May 18–20, 1983.

Roundell, Charles Savile. *England and Her Subject Races, with special reference to Jamaica, by Charles Savile Roundell, M.A., fellow of Merton College, Oxford, Secretary to the late Royal Commission in Jamaica*. London, 1866.

Russell, Horace O. "The Church in the Past—a Study on Jamaican Baptists in the 18th and 19th Centuries." *Jamaican Historical Society Bulletin* 8 (1983): 204–11, 231–36, and 264–71.

————. "The Emergence of the Christian Black: The Making of a Stereotype." *Jamaica Journal* 16, no. 1 (Feb. 1983): 51–58.

————. "The missionary outreach of the West Indian Church to West Africa in the nineteenth century." Ph.D. diss. Oxford Univ., 1972.

Ryall, Dorothy Ann. "The organization of the missionary societies, the recruitment of the missionaries in Britain and the role of the missionaries in the diffusion of British Culture in Jamaica during the period 1834–1865." Ph.D. diss. Univ. of London, 1959.

Samuel, Rev. Peter. *The Wesleyan-Methodist Mission, in Jamaica and Honduras, Delineated*. London, 1850.

Schuler, Monica. *"Alas, Alas, Kongo": A Social History of Indentured African Immigration into Jamaica, 1841–1865*. Baltimore: Johns Hopkins Univ. Press, 1980.

The Second Report of the Jamaica Church of England Home and Foreign Missionary Society. Kingston, 1863.

Senior, Bernard Martin. *Jamaica, as it was, as it is, and as it may be, etc.* London: T. Hurst, 1835.

Sewell, William G. *The Ordeal of Free Labor in the British West Indies.* 1861. London: Frank Cass and Co., 1968.

Smith, Timothy L. *Revivalism and Social Reform: American Protestantism on the Eve of the Civil War.* 1957. Baltimore: Johns Hopkins Univ. Press, 1980.

———. "Slavery and Theology: The Emergence of Black Christian Consciousness in Nineteenth Century America," *Church History* 41 (Dec. 1972): 479–512.

Speech of the Rev. William Knibb before the B.M.S. in Exeter Hall, April 28, 1842 to which is prefixed a Letter to W. B. Gurney, Esqu., Treasurer of the Society. London, 1842.

Spencer, Aubrey George, Lord Bishop of Jamaica. *A Charge Delivered at the Primary Visitation of the Clergy of the Archdeaconry of Jamaica, in the Cathedral of St. Jago de la Vega, 12th December, 1844.* London, 1845.

The Standing Committee of the S.P.G.F.P. and the Jamaica Clergy. Kingston: M. DeCordova, McDougell & Co., 1867.

Stock, Eugene. *The History of the Church Missionary Society, Its Men and Its Work.* 4 vols. London, 1899–1916.

Sturge, Joseph, and Thomas Harvey. *The West Indies in 1837.* London, 1838.

Summary of the Proceedings of the First Synod of the Church of England in Jamaica, which commenced in Kingston on Thursday, the 13th January, and continued until Wednesday, the 19th January, 1870. Kingston: reprint from the Packet Summary of the *Jamaica Guardian*, Mon., Jan. 24th, 1870.

Thomas, J. J. *Froudacity.* Port of Spain, Trinidad, 1889.

Tinson, Joshua. *On Conversion, being The First Circular Letter of the Baptist Missionaries to the Churches in Jamaica, forming the Baptist Association, Assembled at East Queen Street, Kingston, March 9th, 10th, and 11th—1836.* Kingston, 1836.

Titus, Noel. *Missionary Under Pressure: The Experiences of the Rev. John Duport in West Africa.* Barbados: Caribbean Group for Social and Religious Studies, 1983.

Trew, Rev. J. M., Rector of St. Thomas-in-the-East. *An Appeal to the Christian Philanthropy of the People of Great Britain and Ireland, in behalf of the Religious Instruction and Conversion of Three Hundred Thousand Negro Slaves.* London, 1826.

———. *Report of the St. Thomas-in-the-East Branch of the Incorporated Society for the Conversion and Religious Instruction and Education of the Negro Slaves in the British West Indies.* London, 1826.

Trollope, Anthony. *The West Indies and the Spanish Main.* London, 1860.

Tucker, Leonard. *Glorious Liberty, the Story of a Hundred Years' Work of the Jamaica Baptist Mission.* London, 1914.

Turner, Mary. *Slaves and Missionaries: The Disintegration of Jamaican Slave Society, 1787–1834.* Urbana: Univ. of Illinois Press, 1982.

Underhill, Edward Bean. *The Jamaica Mission, in its Relations with the Baptist Missionary Society from 1838 to 1879.* London, 1879.

———. *A Letter addressed to the Rt. Honourable E. Cardwell with Illustrative documents on the condition of Jamaica and an explanatory statement.* London: Arthur Miall, 1865.

———. *Life of James Mursell Phillippo, Missionary in Jamaica.* London: Yates and Alexander, 1881.

———. *The Tragedy of Morant Bay.* London: Alexander and Shepheard, 1895.

Venn, Rev. Henry. *Letter of the Rev. Henry Venn, Honorary Secretary of the Church Missionary Society, to the Lord Bishop of Kingston (Jamaica), on the state of the Negroes of Jamaica.* London: Church Missionary House, Jan. 1867.

Waddell, Hope Masterton. *Twenty-Nine Years in the West Indies and Central Africa, 1829–1858.* London: T. Nelson and Sons, 1863.

Williams, Joseph John. *Psychic Phenomena of Jamaica.* New York: Dial Press, 1934.

Wilmot, Swithin. "Political Developments in Jamaica in the Post- Emancipation Period, 1838–1854." Ph.D. diss. Oxford Univ., 1977.

———. "Sugar and the Gospel: Baptist Perspectives on the Plantation in the Early Period of Freedom." *Jamaican Historical Society Bulletin* 8 (1983): 211–15.

Wright, Philip. *Knibb 'the Notorious': Slaves' Missionary, 1803–1845.* London: Sidgwick and Jackson, 1973.

Index

Abbot, Rev. Thomas (Baptist), 22, 85

Abeokuta (Westmoreland parish): and Africans in Baptist congregation in, 117

abolition of slavery, xv; and decline of planter prosperity, 70; and missionary policy, 13-16, 25, 44, 113

Accompong (St. Elizabeth parish), 50-54, 60

Africa: Jamaicans' identification with, 96, 105-6, 113-14, 116-17, 118-22, 197, 198; and memory of, 110-14, 116-17, 118-22, 220n; and missionary image of, xix, 111-17, 193; and missionary outreach, 5-6, 80, 111, 113, 117, 220n

African Civilization Society, 111, 219n

African religion, xix-xx, 227n; creolized, xvi, xviii, 50, 52-53, 59-64, 90-93, 105, 110, 115-17, 118-20, 122, 124-25, 128, 130-47, 173, 187-89, 195-97

Afro-Jamaican character and personality: and Anglican prejudice, 67-68, 104-5, 109; and Carlyle, 31; missionary defense of, 31, 44; and missionary prejudice, 88-93, 114-15, 173, 180; view of planter class, 30, 43

after-life: and Afro-creole belief, 119-20

Akan: and Afro-creole culture, 50, 136, 138, 141, 196

American Congregational church, 201n

Anglicans. *See* Church of England in Jamaica; organization: of Church of England in Jamaica

Anti-Church State Convention, 19

apprenticeship, xvi; and missionary policy, 25-28, 71-72

Asante, or Ashantee: 112, 136-37, 141, 193, 219n

Assembly of Jamaica (legislature), xv, 19-21, 23, 29-30, 31, 32, 41, 42-43, 69

Avocat: and Jesuit mission at, 59

Baker, Rev. Moses (Black Baptist), 127, 128, 131-36 passim

baptism: in Afro-creole belief, 134, 135-36, 225n

Baptist missionaries: and Morant Bay Rebellion, 158, 159, 161; and planter criticism of, 69; and popular influence of, 13, 44-45

Baptist Missionary Society, 7-9, 12, 127, 158, 173, 180, 201n; and abolition of slavery, 14; and Morant Bay Rebellion, 161, 167, 173; and the Phillippo and Dowson controversy, 87-88. *See also* organization: of Baptist mission

Baptist politics. *See* political activity: of Baptists

Baptist Union, 158, 160-67 passim, 179, 187, 188, 201n. *See also* native ministry: and the Baptist Union; organization: of Baptist mission

Baptist War (1831-32 slave rebellion), xxi, 33, 45, 149-51, 155, 167, 169